WORLD WIDE WEB MARKETING

2ND EDITION

Jim was explaining electronic customer relationship management back in 1994 before most companies had heard of the Web. He has the unique grasp of business trends and technical possibilities necessary to make the most of the Web. Jim has stayed on target and ahead of the game, and is able to articulate his perspective on cultivating loyal and satisfied customers in the most accessible style.

—Patricia Seybold, **author of** *Customers.com: How to Create a Profitable Business Strategy for the Internet and Beyond*

WORLD WIDE WEB MARKETING

2ND EDITION

Integrating the Web into Your Marketing Strategy

JIM STERNE

WILEY COMPUTER PUBLISHING

John Wiley & Sons, Inc.

NEW YORK • CHICHESTER • WEINHEIM • BRISBANE • SINGAPORE • TORONTO

Publisher: Robert Ipsen
Editor: Cary Sullivan
Managing Editor: Marnie Wielage
Text Design & Composition: North Market Street Graphics

Designations used by companies to distinguish their products are often claimed as trademarks. In all instances where John Wiley & Sons, Inc., is aware of a claim, the product names appear in initial capital or ALL CAPITAL LETTERS. Readers, however, should contact the appropriate companies for more complete information regarding trademarks and registration.

This book is printed on acid-free paper. ⊚

Published by John Wiley & Sons, Inc.
Published simultaneously in Canada.

This publication is designed to provide accurate and authoritative information in regard to the subject matter covered. It is sold with the understanding that the publisher is not engaged in professional services. If professional advice or other expert assistance is required, the services of a competent professional person should be sought.

Library of Congress Cataloging-in-Publication Data:

Sterne, Jim, 1955–
    World wide web marketing / Jim Sterne. — 2nd ed.
      p.   cm.
    Includes index.
    ISBN 0-471-31561-3 (pbk. : alk. paper)
    1. Internet marketing. 2. World Wide Web
(Information retrieval system) 3. Internet (Computer
network) I. Title.
HF5415.1265.S742   1998
658.8′4—dc21   98-30145
                                    CIP

Printed in the United States of America.
10 9 8 7 6 5 4 3 2

This book is dedicated to Colleen.

Contents

The Continuing Saga of the World Wide Web

If you count Web time in dog years, it's been nearly 28 years since this book first hit the street. A lot can happen in 28 years. A lot did. When I wrote the first edition of *World Wide Web Marketing*, Java had barely seen the light of day; the rash of Internet IPOs and their subsequent abatement had not yet been forecast; Amazon.com was not yet a household word; and only a rare few were putting URLs in print. Nobody put them on TV. Yes, it's truly time to revisit, review, and rethink what is happening on the Web and what you need to do about it.

When my friends at John Wiley & Sons suggested I write a second edition I thought about the subsequent books I have written. *Customer Service on the Internet* and *What Makes People Click: Advertising on the Web* were natural sequels to *World Wide Web Marketing*. Once you've launched a site, you have to be prepared to treat customers with care. Once your team is able to brave the slings and arrows of outrageous e-mail, it's time to buy banners to get even more people to come to your site.

But enough time has passed, enough mistakes made, and enough lessons learned that it's time to head back to the start and freshen up. Those of you who are looking for a beginner's guide will not be overburdened with jargon. This is not a technology treatise; it's about marketing. Those looking for advanced thinking about using the Web for business and where the Web is headed will not be disappointed. You'll find plenty of vision and lots of examples. Those who face the task of building and maintaining a Web site for their companies have come to the right place.

If you've been at this Web thing for a while or if you read the original edition, you will find lots of valuable insights in the first five chapters to help you explain this stuff to others. Then, starting at Chapter 6, "The Usable Web—Be Kind to Your Users," you'll find a whole new world of examples and the assumption that there are some lessons we've already learned.

Go to any Web site the second time and you'll be looking for the What's New button. Well, here it is. What's new in this book is that, as predicted, the world really has changed. We really are conducting business on the Internet; it's not just hype and in-flight-magazine fantasy. The Web has spawned a whole new industry and rocked the foundations of all others.

So, here it comes: my current outpouring of surprise, delight, disgust, and (if we're lucky) common sense about life on the Internet just before the Millennium bug comes along and turns our carefully constructed electronic customer relationships into a steaming pile of melted modems.

This is a look at today, fixed on a foundation of four years of Internet marketing strategy consulting, with a view into the future from a perch high on the shoulders of others who have done good, done bad, and done ugly.

Think of this book as the next frame in an ever-lengthening film about the development of the World Wide Web from the marketer's perspective.

I'm just gratified that I've been allowed to watch.

If you come up with something fresh, daring, breakthrough, and just a little mad, send me an e-mail. I'd like to hear about it.

Jim Sterne <jsterne@targeting.com>

Acknowledgments

My thanks to all those hardy souls who braved the misgivings of their peers and the mistrust of their managers to create Web sites that offer value to their customers. The result is nothing less than a new way to conduct business.

Thanks also to my wife and my father for their unflagging support.

About the Author

In 1993, Mosaic was released, and the world was changed forever. In 1994, Jim Sterne cofounded a regional Internet access provider and launched a "Marketing on the Internet" seminar tour of eight cities in the United States. Since then, he has been an Internet marketing strategy consultant, offering advice to the Fortune 500 and to Web-based start-ups. His consulting practice focuses on electronic customer relationship management, helping his clients grapple with the brave new world of online advertising, marketing, sales, and customer service.

Mr. Sterne has written two other books, *Customer Service on the Internet* (John Wiley & Sons, 1996) and *What Makes People Click; Advertising on the Web* (Que, 1997). He is a columnist for *CIO Magazine,* and his articles have appeared in *Network World,* in *WebWeek,* and on numerous Web sites. He is an internationally recognized speaker who has earned "best of show" for several years running at Internet World. He has been introduced to audiences in Germany as a Web-Meister and to audiences in India as a Web-Guru.

While Mr. Sterne admits to being enthralled by technology, his main interest is divining how it can best be used to achieve business objectives. His company, Target Marketing, is dedicated to helping companies understand the possibilities and manage the realities of conducting business online.

Introduction

The World Wide Web is the most important invention since Velcro.

Business Week **(February 27, 1995)**

A corporate presence on the Internet is now a necessity. In 1995, I claimed that it could greatly enhance a company's sales and marketing efforts. It could widen a company's circle of influence by providing yet another way to communicate with its clients, prospects, and the public. Today, things are different.

The power of real-time interaction with prospects and customers has created not just a whole new way to communicate, but a multibillion dollar business in hardware, software, and services. And that's just the industry feeding fuel into the Internet engine.

The Internet has even been credited with being a major cause of the United States' economic strength of the late 1990s. Low unemployment, high profits, and increased business and housing starts are laid at the feet of technology. Silicon Valley experienced a slump in the late 80s and early 90s that threatened the best and the brightest of the technology industry. But even the Asian economic crisis couldn't put a damper on the continued growth of the U.S. economy, spawned by a new marketplace called the Web.

It is a rush unlike the Oklahoma Land Rush or the California Gold Rush. It is far beyond those, and it is global. People, companies, and governments are jumping on the Internet faster than they have acquired any other new communications medium. Clearly, being connected is better than being disconnected. It is better to communicate than to stay isolated. There are dozens of reasons to be on the Internet today, and those reasons will increase tomorrow. For now, it's enough for today's business to want all these advantages:

- A leading-edge corporate image
- Improved service for current customers
- Increased visibility
- Market expansion
- Online transactions
- Global information distribution
- Lower communications costs

BE ON THE WEB OR BE OUT OF BUSINESS

"Be on the Web or be out of business" would have been an over-the-top statement in 1995, even for me. Today, it's right on the mark. Think about how well you could compete today without a fax machine or voice mail. Your company would be hurting.

The Internet was enjoying the spotlight in 1995, and not participating was to hide one's head in the sand. It would be like having a booth at a major trade show in your industry—you may not receive millions of leads or make thousands of sales, but not participating would make your company conspicuous by its absence. Yesterday, we began to see changes in the landscape.

"No Web site, huh?"

"What? You mean your information is *not* available electronically?"

"I've already downloaded product information from your competitor."

Today, it's hard to justify doing business with a company that isn't aggressively using the Web to recreate itself.

When National Semiconductor says it's saving its customers $100 million a year because of the new buying techniques its Web site has made possible, it means the competition has heated to the boiling point. There's no time to decide if the Web site you put up a couple of years ago might be worth serious investment. We're past that.

With its multimedia capabilities, the World Wide Web captured the imagination of computer users everywhere, and corporate marketers rose to the challenge. Today, the marketing department is teaming with the information systems people; together, they are leading the company into a whole new era.

Sound trite? Maybe a little.

But realize that with the wholesale reduction in the cost of communication and the speed at which global commerce is creating new ways of doing business, the word "revolution" isn't hype anymore.

WHO IS THIS BOOK FOR?

If you are like thousands of others who are looking for ways to improve your company's electronic presence, you will find advanced techniques and philosophical perspectives in this book that will vastly improve your chances for success. There is a healthy amount of how-to, what to avoid, and, above all, how to think about electronic marketing on the World Wide Web.

Enough smart people have spent enough time making mistakes reinventing the wheel that is no longer necessary. Whether you are putting up a Web site for your fledgling company, responsible for a specific content area on your company's Web site, or in charge of a multinational Web effort that crosses all your corporate divisions, you will benefit by learning from the successes and failures of others.

Students, managers, Web development firms, and those who are merely curious will find straight, business-oriented descriptions, advice, and examples of what's happening on the World Wide Web.

This is not a book about tools. It's not a step-by-step, how-to manual for building your own Web server. It's about technique. How you implement these techniques will change as the pace of new technology continues to accelerate.

This book isn't for programmers, unless, of course, they are interested in using the World Wide Web to market their software. This book is for big business as well as small business. This book is not for dummies.

CHAPTER 1

Introduction to the Internet and the Web— An Executive Summary

The Internet can be put to use in a business environment in various ways. As wonderful as the prospect of global communication may be, and as exciting as this technology appears from the gee-whiz perspective, its value to business is measured strictly by its impact on the bottom line.

That impact will depend on the goals of the organization that plans to make use of the Internet and the World Wide Web. Some firms will benefit more by using this new communication tool for direct sales. Others will see an immediate reduction in the cost of customer service. Still others will view the Web as an opportunity to create and sell new services altogether.

Businesses will find many uses for electronic communication over the Internet, from lowering the cost of sending faxes and overnight packages to superior internal communications. Improved internal communications will lead to faster time-to-market. Improved customer service will engender greater client satisfaction and better feedback to product managers.

You must understand the Internet before using it. This is not to say that you need a deep technical understanding, but rather an understanding of its capabilities and, most important, its limitations. You don't need to know the intricacies of an internal combustion engine; it is enough to know that it requires oil at specific intervals.

It is critical, however, that you understand the rules of the road. A feel for navigation and the ability to read a map won't hurt. You must know how fast your car can accelerate, or you'll never get on a freeway without a panic attack or an accident. You must know how long it takes to stop your car in the rain and how long the needle can point to Empty before you need to get gas.

Understanding the Internet from a bits-and-bytes perspective may be fascinating, but only a handful of technical details are required to avoid the pitfalls. These are presented in plain terms in Chapter 2, "Getting to Know the Internet."

INTRODUCTION TO THE WORLD WIDE WEB

The World Wide Web is a software application that runs on the Internet. If the Internet were the Microsoft MS-DOS operating system, then the World Wide Web would be Windows. It is the graphical interface that incorporates underlying functions in an easier-to-use manner.

The Web's technical capabilities are changing at a phenomenal rate. New features are proposed and implemented with breakneck speed. Your technical team will have to work overtime just to stay current, and they will keep you apprised of the latest and greatest to ensure that your corporate Web site doesn't get stodgy and boring.

A quick word to the wise: A technically boring Web site might be just the thing you need. I think it was the April 1998 issue of *Wired* that showed, in its monthly table, "Tired: more bandwidth, Wired: skinny Web sites."

Yes, some changes will be required to prevent technical stagnation. You will install seat belts. You will switch to unleaded gasoline. You will install air bags. You will have to keep up to date. But don't let the techno-maniacs get the better of you. It may embarrass them to look a little behind the times in front of their peers. But you can lose the potential return on your Web investment if you get too far out in front of your customers.

The Web has caught on so quickly because it enables you to present information in a myriad of media: hypertext, graphics, video, sound, and so on. Chapter 3, "Welcome to the World Wide Web," explains the Web and how it is changing our perception of computer communications from Figure 1.1 to Figure 1.2.

USING THE WORLD WIDE WEB FOR MARKETING

A business prints a variety of documents to help move a prospect through the sales cycle. Each document has its own purpose and life expectancy. Each document is crafted to achieve a specific goal.

A flier handed out at a trade show, an ad placed in a newspaper or magazine, and a direct mail piece are each designed to do one thing—hook

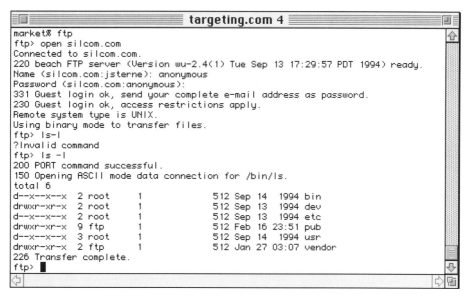

```
═══▨══════════════════ targeting.com 4 ═══════════════════▨═══
market% ftp                                                    ⇧
ftp> open silcom.com
Connected to silcom.com.
220 beach FTP server (Version wu-2.4(1) Tue Sep 13 17:29:57 PDT 1994) ready.
Name (silcom.com:jsterne): anonymous
Password (silcom.com:anonymous):
331 Guest login ok, send your complete e-mail address as password.
230 Guest login ok, access restrictions apply.
Remote system type is UNIX.
Using binary mode to transfer files.
ftp> ls-l
?Invalid command
ftp> ls -l
200 PORT command successful.
150 Opening ASCII mode data connection for /bin/ls.
total 6
d--x--x--x   2 root      1              512 Sep  14   1994 bin
drwxr-xr-x   2 root      1              512 Sep  13   1994 dev
d--x--x--x   2 root      1              512 Sep  13   1994 etc
drwxr-xr-x   9 ftp       1              512 Feb  16 23:51 pub
d--x--x--x   3 root      1              512 Sep  14   1994 usr
drwxr-xr-x   2 ftp       1              512 Jan  27 03:07 vendor
226 Transfer complete.
ftp> █                                                         ⇩
◁                                                            ▷ ▨
```

Figure 1.1   A standard file transfer protocol (FTP) session grabs files from a remote computer.

the reader into wanting more information. Your goal is to entice the recipient into a relationship that will culminate in the purchase of a product or service, perhaps on first contact.

The four-color, eight-page brochure gives prospects a taste of your quality, a picture of your product or people, and something they can show to the manager who approves the budget. If they like the brochure, they will want to know more.

Firms selling complex equipment or lengthy consulting services often use some sort of concepts and facilities guide. This document outlines the company's approach and provides detailed specifications. It lets the prospect fully understand what is being sold in order to make a more informed decision.

Finally, the product or service might be tested on a trial basis to ensure a good match and reveal any unforeseen incompatibilities between buyer and seller.

What if all these documents, all these steps, all these interactions, could be managed online, interactively and untouched by human hands? What if your prospects could reach into your organization and take the information they want? What if they could educate themselves? What if you could

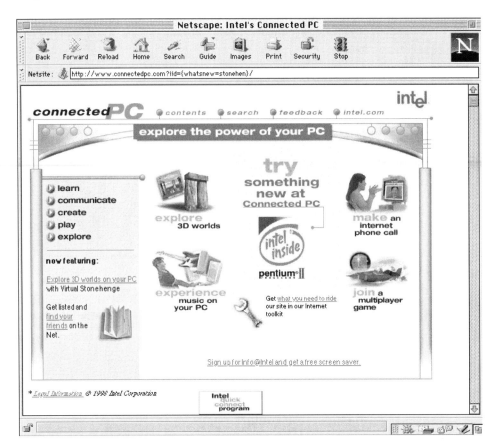

Figure 1.2   Intel shows the wide range of possibilities on today's Web.

instantly deliver promotional materials to a worldwide, growing population of self-selected prospects?

What if they could place the order, track the shipping, answer the
tough questions, and get the help they need online?

This is the promise that the World Wide Web holds. This is what is
making companies all over the world rush to implement back-office connections to their Web sites.

All that remains is to do it well. Doing it well depends entirely on your
definition. Being successful at anything requires a means to measure that
success. Without clear goals, you will never know if you have achieved
your end. Each association, group, society, or business that sets out to create
a presence on the Web must first know why it wishes to invest the resources.

Selecting reasonable, achievable, and measurable goals at the start is the only way to be sure your efforts have paid off at the finish line. Chapter 4, "Using the World Wide Web for Marketing," provides some pointers in determining your Internet marketing goals—the first step toward a successful Web site.

CUSTOMER SERVICE

The best marketing ploy on the World Wide Web may well be a strong customer service offering. It doesn't need to be cool, hip, sexy, or cutting-edge. What people want is more value for their money. If your new garden tool is backed by a Web site full of tips, tricks, and gardening traps, it has more value than the one that just comes with a price tag. If your site offers numerous ways to acquire your products, people are more likely to do so.

If you are successful at promoting and selling products and services on your Web site, you have to be prepared to manage the needs of your new customers. They come to the table with high expectations, having been taught the possibilities by all the other Web sites they frequent. Chapter 5, "Customer Service First," suggests numerous ways to support an electronic clientele.

THE KEYS TO SUCCESSFUL WEB SITE DESIGN

For people surfing the World Wide Web, viewing a corporate Web site is the electronic version of visiting the company. What does the building look like? Is there enough parking? Is the door so heavy it's impossible to open? Does somebody greet them in a professional manner? Are they treated as though they were expected and welcome?

Creating a Web site is similar to creating a demonstration diskette or an infomercial CD-ROM. It requires the same care in copywriting and graphic design, with particular attention to the prospect's viewing experience.

The challenges to the Web site designer are threefold: providing adequate navigational tools, creating sufficient interactivity, and successfully soliciting feedback from those who take the time to visit.

Navigation

We have all experienced the frustration of dropping a book and watching our bookmark flutter to the floor. Finding your place in a book is an inconvenience. Due to the linear nature of bound pages, this task is annoying, but not difficult. Finding your place in an electronic medium is much harder and much more frustrating.

A software package I ordered arrived in a large box containing 12 pounds of documentation and no fewer than 20 disks for installation. Upset at the prospect of spending so much time loading plastic squares into a computer one by one, I sent the package back. Two days later, a small box arrived with the coveted CD-ROM in it—but no paper documentation. All the documentation had been digitized.

After installation, I tried valiantly to read through the online Help screens to get acquainted with the software. After a diligent effort, I put the CD back in the box and exchanged it for the disks. Now I have a complete set of manuals to mark up, infuse with yellow stickies, and take on the train, bus, plane, and into the bathroom.

Electronic information is difficult to navigate. Without proper signposts, it's very easy to become lost, turned around, and disgruntled. This makes electronic documentation for software difficult to use and a poorly designed Web site a disaster. People will come, look, and tell their friends not to waste their time. They will never come back.

Chapter 6, "The Usable Web—Be Kind to Your Users," points out some of the rules of the road for keeping people from getting lost, getting frustrated, or just getting gone.

Interactivity

If you remember nothing else about building a successful Web site, remember this: Your Web site isn't something people read, it's something they do. Visiting your site is an activity. A Web site should interact with the visitor.

When prospects read your brochure, they receive information in a passive manner. It is often said that if you read something you are aware of it, if you see something you can understand it, and if you do something you can master it. Involve your viewers in the information you are providing.

An electronic page of text is read in a passive manner. A Web site that makes the viewer think and make choices, decide and take action, participate and learn will be much more successful. It will engage the audience in the activity of learning about your products and services, and the result will be longer participation (exposure to your message) and higher comprehension.

A growing number of organizations are taking these lessons to heart. Current studies in man/machine interface theory are reviewed in Chapter 7,

"Interactivity Goes with the Flow," and applied to the process of Web site design.

Feedback

The Internet isn't a broadcast medium. Although it is technically possible to send a message to millions of people at the same time, doing so is a cultural mistake and a business disaster of immense proportions.

Instead of being used as a broadcast tool, the Internet can be put to better advantage as a means of multidirectional communication. As long as you are going to the effort of creating a Web site to disseminate information, you should also solicit the opinions of the recipients.

The costs of customer surveys and focus groups are very high. Learning what your customers feel about your products is central to improving the product line. The Internet provides a wonderful mechanism for getting information back from the masses. Do it well, and they will tell you what they like and don't like, what they want and don't want, and what they will buy.

Techniques in use on the Internet today (and a few that will be soon enough) are discussed in Chapter 8, "Feedback."

VALUE-ADDED MARKETING

The Internet was born and grew up nurtured by a gift economy. In the beginning, the Net was hard to use, and the people using it were happy to help each other. Someone stranded on a desert isle is very happy to help a newcomer in any way, just for the company. The same was true online.

Programmers came up with nifty utilities to help accomplish specific tasks. They made these programs available to everybody on the Net and offered advice and support when needed. In return, they had access to other programmers' creations. Soon, scholars made their information freely available to any who cared to download it. In return, they had access to libraries and academic archives around the world.

The key secret to success on the Internet and the World Wide Web is to provide value-added marketing: offering something of value for free. It is proving your worth as a vendor. It is delivering exceptional service and valuable products before making the sale.

There are many examples of value-added marketing on the Web. The best approach for each company depends entirely on its products, services, and areas of expertise. Somewhere in your organization is a unique body of information. That information is powerful enough to draw people to your Web site, where they will be exposed to your message and compelled to tell their friends to visit as well.

What's new and what makes your site all the more interesting to the visitor is its ability to recognize that visitor. As we approach the year 2001, Web sites *are* able to say, *"It's good to see you again . . . Dave."* Personalization, customization, and one-to-one marketing are now part and parcel of life online. Getting comfortable with that idea, getting familiar with some examples, and getting to understand the value it adds to your customer relationships is what Chapter 9, "Value-Added Marketing—It's Personal," is all about.

ATTRACTING ATTENTION

A World Wide Web site is just like a toll-free telephone number. On one end are people hungry for information; on the other end are people trained to provide that information. It is a painless way for potential customers to reach you. It is also completely useless if they don't know you're offering something worth seeing.

When there were 1000 Web servers to choose from, it was possible to visit them. Now, instead of 500 cable channels to click through with our remote controls, we have millions of Web sites, each acting as its own channel. You will not attract attention just by being online. You will attract it in the same way you have always attracted attention: in print, in the mail, on TV, and so on. You can also attract attention online.

There are several ways to announce your Web value on the Internet itself. When you do, you will experience a rush of electronic visitors—the curious who want to see what's out there. You will also be able to reach people you cannot reach via other media.

Your long-term customers will not come from the ranks of casually curious Web surfers. They will come from your steady efforts using old methods of communication to promote your new method of communication. Chapter 10, "Attracting Attention," focuses on ways to get noticed online.

HOW ARE WE DOING?

With the time and effort you have put into your Web site, with the time and effort you are going to put into your Web site, with the blood, sweat, and tears you have shed getting upper management to give you more funding for your Web site . . . how do you know you've done a good job?

A magazine ad pulls in phone calls. A mailer returns business reply cards. A trade show generates business cards. All of these can be counted and the effectiveness of the promotion measured.

Measuring electronic visitors to a Web site seems simple at first. Automatic logs make a record of every request and every electronic document sent in response. Some of these numbers are very helpful, but the most obvious are next to useless. I've heard hits defined as "how idiots track success."

Evaluating the number of times a particular document is requested is more informative. Calculating the amount of time people spend on each document can be illuminating. The most valuable measure of success, after tallying sales, however, is the number of written responses your Web site elicits. How much two-way communication can you inspire?

Chapter 11, "Measuring Your Success," offers a variety of metrics that will help you check your progress, maintain your self-respect, and show the boss you're headed in the right direction.

HATH NOT THY ROSE A THORN?

Maintaining a corporate Web site includes a few hazards. Some are minor, some are considerable, and some will take years to alleviate. All of them should be taken seriously. Several of the most important issues are covered in Chapter 12, "A Few Thorny Issues."

Chapter 12 takes a swing at determining if your customers are online. They are. It discusses the very real issue of Web site security. It raises the specter of channel conflict, the problem with global pricing, the fear of international trade law and culture, and the concern over intellectual property.

And you thought the Web was a happy place.

GETTING STARTED

Knowing everything in this book is great. Memorizing it word-for-word would be a nifty accomplishment. But taking that next step and actually getting started—that's a neat trick.

Chapter 13, "Where Do You Start?," gives you a map, a compass, and a flashlight. You still have to pick your own destination, but at least you'll have a guide that will point you in the right direction. The rest is up to you. Chances are you've tackled one or two of these points already. It's time to revisit them.

LOOKING TOWARD THE FUTURE

The Internet is changing faster than any other medium we have experienced to date. The potential to make money selling tools to make it better, faster, and cheaper has drawn thousands of companies to the race and caused more than a few to go public. As a result, it is hard to predict what will happen when browsers disappear because all applications can surf the Web. It is difficult to guess how the commoditization of goods and services will be handled in five years.

At this point, however, everybody agrees that interactive, online, many-to-many communication is here. It is being used for advertising, marketing, sales, and customer service. Those who embrace it as a new way of doing business will be more likely to stay up to date and continue to take advantage of it in the long run.

The entry barriers to this marketing technique were surprisingly low for several years, but those days are gone. The learning curve is steep, and it is sure to become precipitous. Now is the time to learn, implement, and benefit from marketing on the Internet. What the future holds is up for speculation in Chapter 14, "Looking Toward the Future," and is in your hands.

CHAPTER 2

Getting to Know the Internet

"What hath God wrought?"   *First words sent over the telegraph*

"Watson, come here. I need you!"   *First words spoken over the telephone*

"Are you receiving this?"   *First words sent through the Internet*

New technologies periodically cause major shifts in the way we do business. The telegraph, the telephone, and the fax machine have all left their marks on commerce. It is impossible to imagine doing business without any one of these devices. Today, the Internet is shaping up as the latest technology to alter the way business is conducted, and it is remarkably simple in how it works and extremely exciting in its usefulness. People are finding new ways to use the Internet every day, and the majority are using it for business.

HOW THE INTERNET GOT STARTED

The U.S. military wanted to be sure networked computers could talk to each other even if some of them went offline (in other words, if they were vaporized in a nuclear attack). They needed a network that wouldn't be vulnerable to a direct hit on a central point of control. The RAND Corporation devised a concept that was as unique in computing as it was in general management: A network should be built that was expected to be unreliable and without a central point of control. Data would flow freely around downed lines and missing components. Each computer on the system would share the same degree of responsibility as all others.

In September 1969, "Are you receiving this?" was sent from Boulter Hall at the University of California at Los Angeles across a four-node network: UCLA, Stanford Research Institute, UC Santa Barbara, and the University of Utah in Salt Lake City. The Internet worked.

As the engineers working on the project added more and more computers to the network, they improved its stability. The TCP/IP protocol allowed this conglomeration of computers to grow without any detriment to its capability.

The ability to send a message and fetch a file turned out to be very useful. Soon, researchers associated with universities under government contract began using this network to great advantage. Their latest advances could be propagated around the network in a matter of seconds. Their immediate questions about their work could be broadcast to those most likely to have the answers. Long documents could be made available to everybody who was connected.

The original intent of the Internet was safeguarding military data. Later, in 1984, the National Science Foundation (NSF) saw that the Internet protocols were a great way to distribute expensive supercomputer power. A scientist predicting the weather in Illinois could use time on a supercomputer in San Diego if the local machine was busy modeling molecules.

The NSF built a national backbone of high-speed communication lines known as the NSFNET (Figure 2.1). The Department of Energy, NASA, and the National Institutes of Health saw the value and donated their resources as well. As these were government agencies, they created the Acceptable Use Practices, which clearly stated the Internet could be used for research only. Commerce was clearly excluded.

Universities and research companies under contract to the government found the Internet very useful. They used the Internet to trade information on specific bids, projects, and basketball scores. Topic-specific electronic bulletin boards sprang up. E-mail lists allowed distribution of electronic duplicates of newsletters, memos, and recipes.

For these companies the value of being connected to the Internet was high enough that they were willing to commit computer and human resources for the privilege. Companies merely needed to dedicate a computer and a telephone line and find somebody who understood the UNIX operating system to be in touch electronically with their wired colleagues.

Tim Berners-Lee at the European Laboratory for Particle Physics (CERN), near Geneva, thought of a new way to use these file transfer func-

Figure 2.1   This is the Internet backbone as seen by the National Science Foundation in the early 1980s.

tions. He figured that people would want to link multiple documents through hypertext. He knew how helpful highlighted words in a document would be if they acted as electronic reference pointers to additional information.

Tim Berners-Lee created the Web for internal use at CERN in 1989, but it was so popular and worked so well that it was let loose on the Internet as a whole and became the World Wide Web. Suddenly, a document written by a graduate student in Ann Arbor could point directly to a research paper in Cambridge. The bibliography became a gateway to each referenced treatise.

By 1992, serious commercial traffic had crept onto the Net. The NSF had been contracting the operations of the backbone to companies that wished to offer commercial access. Knowing that its funds were limited, the NSF saw an opportunity to narrow its responsibility to its own network.

Users of the Internet were outraged that their special means of communication, intended to further the knowledge base of mankind, so unsullied by Madison Avenue, could succumb to brash capitalism. They argued against the fall of the only undefiled medium from the hands of the people to the hands of the corporate money grubbers.

> One hundred and one years ago, Joseph Pulitzer developed color presses so that *The World* could bring famous European paintings to the masses. The result was a polychromatic eyesore—but the presses were perfect for printing color cartoons.
>
> *The New Yorker*, December 26, 1994

In the fall of 1992, Marc Andreessen at the University of Illinois conceived Mosaic, the graphical user interface to the World Wide Web. In early 1993, he developed it with a team from the university's National Center for Supercomputing Applications in Champaign, Illinois. The potential to include images, video, and sound, coupled with the truly wild growth of personal computers, propelled the World Wide Web, and the Internet itself, into public view.

Business had discovered the Internet, and the Web has grown at incredible rates ever since.

HOW THE INTERNET WORKS

Successful direct mail campaigns depend on an understanding of how the physical process works. Knowing how to deal with the list vendors, the printers, the mailing houses, and the post office is essential. You really need to know the piece size limitations and the trade-off of postage cost versus speed of delivery.

You may not need to understand how a printing press works or the process of ink sublimation onto paper. Plenty of people can help you avoid mistakes by lending you their years of experience. On the Web, there are very few people with more than five years of experience. It helps to know some of the technical background so you can take full advantage, without being taken advantage of.

GETTING DATA FROM HERE TO THERE

When you send an e-mail message across the Internet, the network protocol chops it up into packets of information. Each packet includes the "from" address and the "ship-to" address. Every computer on the Internet acts as a post office. It receives each packet, reads the address, and determines whether to keep the packet or pass it along.

Packets travel individually (Figure 2.2). While computer A is sending a steady stream of packets to machine B, machine B may suddenly be called on to run another program at the same time. B will send a message back to A telling it to stop sending packets for the moment. A then starts to send packets to C instead. B and C are likely to be in very different geographic places. They will also send packets along to whichever machine is ready, willing, and able to accept them. As a result, packets from one e-mail message may end up taking many different paths to reach their destination. The destination computer collects all the packets and reassembles them into a cohesive message for delivery to your mailbox.

As the destination machine receives packets, it sends word back to the originating machine that it has or has not received all of them. The originator can then resend missing packets, and eventually the e-mail, or Web page, is complete.

Imagine that the lights went out at half time at the Superbowl and the game was moved across town. The players, the reporters, the hot dog vendors, and thousands of fans would stream out of the stadium, get into individual cars, and make their way to the new venue. Those who hopped on the freeway first got there in plenty of time; others were stuck in traffic. Many took alternate routes across the network of streets, boulevards, and highways. In the end, they all arrived at the same place and were reassembled into the football game.

Thinking of that football game as a home page and the cars as data packets, you now have a clear picture of how the Internet works. Even if roads are closed or the freeway is jammed, eventually the page is delivered and reassembled.

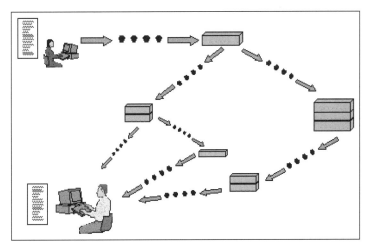

**Figure 2.2   A message might be sent over a number of
paths to reach your computer.**

As ingenious as this sounds, it is exactly how your telephone works. Your boss's voice is packetized and traded between distributed telephone switches. The packets are reassembled at your desk, where they sound very much like continuous speech asking for the latest expense reports. The difference between the telephone and the Internet is that the phone system holds a specific electronic path open between you and your boss. The Internet just lets the packets fly, knowing they'll make it to their destination sooner or later.

This system works astonishingly well because it doesn't depend on one central computer or any one particular transmission line. The designers intended the Internet to be self-healing and autonomous. It is the military experiment that escaped the laboratory, has mutated, and has grown with unimaginable speed. It has engulfed the globe and cannot be stopped.

NON-WEB TOOLS ON THE INTERNET

The World Wide Web has caught the public's and the marketing professional's attention with the flash of multimedia. Although multimedia is exciting, older Internet tools prove very valuable for marketing. They must be understood and put to use in conjunction with a Web site if that site is to be successful. From a marketing perspective, there are two classifications of Internet mechanisms: communication tools and information vending machines.

Communication tools are used to transmit specific messages to specific people. They are a means of electronic discussion. The three primary tools are e-mail, newsgroups, and lists.

E-Mail

Electronic mail allows a computer user to type a message and send it to another computer user. The message can arrive in seconds, and the recipient can edit it and send it back. An e-mail message can be sent to multiple individuals with a single click. It can be electronically stored or printed. It takes the art of written communications and accelerates it to the speed of light.

It's no surprise that e-mail is so popular. Its convenience is far superior to that of voice mail, letter writing, fax communications—you name it. The asynchronicity allows people to create or respond to e-mail messages when it suits them, rather than on-call. Forrester Research estimates that 50 percent of the U.S. population will be using e-mail by 2002.

Newsgroups

Many local grocery stores have large cork bulletin boards near the door. Lengths of yarn divide the board into vertical strips with "Baby Sitting," "Cars," "Furniture," and so on posted at the top of each strip. This is the community version of the classified ad section of the newspaper. Local shoppers post their messages on the board for all to see.

On the Internet, we add a few twists to this time-honored method of communication. First, the board is now ten miles long and is divided up into a thousand sections per mile. Second, people can read it from the comfort of their own computers. Finally, the culture of the bulletin board becomes interactive.

Rather than simple advertisements, the messages may ask questions, seek advice, and petition for assistance. Instead of merely copying down an address or tearing off a piece of paper bearing a phone number, people reply to the messages they see by posting their own.

Due to the many different newsgroup categories, you are sure to find several groups of personal interest. More importantly, you are sure to find groups of professional interest. Lists about bicycle racing will be of interest to the makers of sporting goods. A newsgroup on the topic of health will be of interest to vitamin companies.

Lists

Lists are a combination of e-mail and newsgroups and are growing in popularity. When a message is posted to an electronic bulletin board, it must be "visited" by the reader. The reader must actively go to the newsgroup to see what's been posted.

When a message is posted to a list, all list subscribers receive a copy in their private e-mailboxes. As a reader of a newsgroup, you may take a look every now and then. As a list subscriber, the messages come right to you. Some people must still sift through the list postings to find any personal mail sent to them, but most are making use of e-mail filtering software. The computer sorts out the list mail from the personal mail and keeps it in a different directory or folder. That makes subscribing to lists a tad easier.

Newsgroups and lists come in two flavors: moderated and unmoderated. A moderator may assume a dictatorial role, determining which messages are of value and posting only those. A moderator may assume a more avuncular position, steering the discussion if it gets off-topic or is taken over by a flame war. These individuals provide an inestimable editorial eye.

We all have the ability to receive direct feeds of news from the wire services, but we don't. There is simply too much information, and not all of it is valuable. Some want more emphasis on sports and buy sporting magazines. Some want a more liberal or conservative view; they subscribe to the newspapers and magazines and listen to the talk shows that are more to their taste.

The same is true for newsgroups and lists. Without a moderator, these discussion groups may do quite well, as they are self-governed. On the other hand, they may also deteriorate into a great deal of worthless babble by throngs of people who take great joy in expressing their opinion. Consequently, some lists are very good, and some swing back and forth between the thrill of enlightenment and the agony of cacophony.

E-mail, newsgroups, and lists come complete with a culture of use referred to as "netiquette." I strongly recommend reading other reference materials about the do's and don'ts of using these tools for business. I also recommend looking at the frequently asked questions (FAQs) associated with each group or list to get a feel for its micro-culture. A poorly phrased or misplaced message can have very detrimental effects.

In a nutshell, netiquette says that all users on the Internet deserve to say what they please as long as they don't inflict themselves unduly on others. Sending a commercial message to tens of thousands of people who did not request that information, posting a commercial message to a discussion list or newsgroup that is not designed for advertising, or peppering your posts with scathing personal attacks are all examples of netiquette breaches.

There is an entire section at Yahoo! (www.yahoo.com) for Web sites on netiquette. It's at Computers and Internet:Internet:Information and Documentation:Beginner's Guides:Netiquette, and it's well worth some time. You are venturing into a new territory, and it behooves you to get to know how the natives expect to be treated. You wouldn't charge into the home of your Japanese host without removing your shoes, so don't charge onto the Internet without taking some time to learn the basics.

E-mail, newsgroups, and lists are the communication tools. They let individuals talk to each other. There are also a set of tools for electronic publishing on the World Wide Web in a more classic, one-to-many method.

Information Vending Machines

Gopher, FTP (file transfer protocol), and Mailbots all fall into the same category. These tools all perform the same basic function: When a request for a file is made by somebody out there, these tools fetch and deliver. They are the fax-back programs of the Internet. They can be open to all or be password protected. They can contain as much or as little information as desired. They are the groundwork on which the World Wide Web was formed.

IRC, MUDDs, and MOOs

These more esoteric capabilities have not yet found their way into mainstream Internet marketing per se. As we can expect their capabilities to be incorporated into Web sites over time, you need to be aware of them. They may even be worth further study if your marketing team is willing to take on a live, out-of-control, un-focus group.

Internet relay chat (IRC) allows multiple individuals to type a live conversation. Imagine placing a microphone at each table in a crowded bar and having the conversations transcribed in chronological order. Person A may make a comment that person B responds to as persons C and D intersperse their own line of discussion. To make things more confusing, D, C, and all the way through Z can comment on anybody else's comments. It can be fun, but it creates a unique challenge to those who wish to accomplish a specific task.

Multi-user Dungeons & Dragons (MUDDs) are interactive games where players assume roles and the computer acts as arbiter of their actions. This type of role playing may quickly reach multimedia Web sites and be used to entertain while teaching prospects about products. Companies like OZ Interactive (www.oz.com) specialize in creating colorful, 3D virtual worlds that you can wander around in (Figure 2.3).

Multi-user object-oriented MUDDs (MOOs) are similar, but with a twist. The "players" may add their own rules and actions. This begets an ever-changing artificial environment in which the users themselves can make permanent changes. This is another technical capability you should keep in mind when looking for unique and creative ways to attract an audience.

These utilities, programs, and games have made the Internet a fun place to hang out. Students with Internet access but little cash, computer experts who like to show off their acumen, and hundreds of thousands of people who are more comfortable communicating from the safety of their dens have co-occupied cyberspace with researchers looking to share information with others in their field, academics looking for reference materials, and business people engaged in commerce. With all these uses, it's no wonder the Internet has grown so fast.

Figure 2.3   MUDDs get visual; OZ Interactive can create a 3D space where prospects can learn about your products.

THE INTERNET'S UNBELIEVABLE GROWTH

Before spending any time on Internet marketing, and certainly before spending any money, the marketing professional wants to know if this Internet stuff will still be around next year.

In 1995, the answer was a qualified "Yes." Today, it's a foregone conclusion. The Internet's worth is clear and present. It is better to be connected than not. Companies creating technical products have been using the Internet from the beginning and have found high administrative value at their fingertips. Planning meetings, distributing memos, and making policy information available online were just some of the ways these innovators found to make their business lives easier. As others saw what these folks were up to, they wanted these benefits as well. The Internet began to grow even faster.

This new communications medium is changing the way we do business, just like the phone and fax before it. Moving from carbon paper to copy machines boosted our ability to disseminate information faster. Moving from typewriter to word processor eliminated the secretarial pool. With the telephone companies fighting cable companies and even electric utilities over who will bring the Internet to our homes, and with reasonably powerful computer systems at the $500 price point, we soon will all have Internet access as we do telephone and television.

How Many Computers?

We know that the number of computer systems on the Internet is increasing by 5 to 10 percent per month. We can count them. We know that the number of companies jumping on the Internet is growing just as fast. How many is that? What's the date today?

We will not see a completely wired world within the next few years. Many places on the globe get along just fine without television, and 50 percent of the people on this planet have never made a telephone call. Nevertheless, the Internet's growth has been phenomenal and is worth noting.

When measuring the Internet, two numbers are worth review: the computers and the people.

A host computer is one that can be seen by other computers on the Internet. Computers behind a corporate firewall cannot be seen from the outside. (Firewalls are hardware and software constructs designed to keep people out of your internal computers.) As a result, these numbers (Figure 2.4) are much lower than reality. The final count is not as interesting as the continued growth. From 16 million in January 1997 to almost 30 million in January 1998 proves that the Internet hysteria in 1994 and 1995 wasn't just a fad. This one-year growth is evidence of wide-scale adoption.

How Many People?

The number of people on the Internet is pure speculation. How many people work at Microsoft? How many at IBM? In each case, only a handful of computers are visible to the Internet with microsoft.com and ibm.com as their domain names. That's because all of the individual company's computers are safely tucked behind firewalls. Regardless of the validity of each

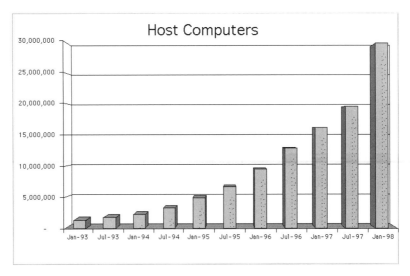

Figure 2.4   The number of computers (hosts) connected to the Internet continues to grow.

number, there is no denying that those numbers are increasing at a tremendous rate.

Every time a new survey is released, new numbers emerge. None of them ever agree, but all of them point to *very big numbers* and a serious growth rate.

In the fall of 1997 Nielsen Media Research (www.nielsenmedia.com) released its Internet Demographic Study in conjunction with Commerce-Net (www.commercenet.com). The highlights of that study of people over 16 in the United States and Canada look like this:

- There are 52 million Internet users in the United States, 6 million in Canada.
- 43 percent are women.
- 9 million Internet users are full-time students.
- 80 percent own or lease a home computer.
- 77 percent have a credit card in their name.
- 49 percent have at least a college associate's degree.
- 46 percent live in households with total annual income over $50K.
- 30 million persons used the Internet in the past 24 hours.
- There are 45 million Web users in the United States, 5 million in Canada.
- There are 10 million online buyers.

- Over 60 percent of online buyers live in households with total annual income over $50K.
- 12 million persons have never heard of the Internet.
- 48 million persons are not using the Internet because they don't have a computer.
- 30 million persons used e-mail in the past 24 hours—4 million of them are not Internet users.
- 57 percent of Internet users have never heard of HTML.

Nicholas Negroponte of MIT's Media Lab has said that by the year 2000 there will be a billion people on the Internet. At that rate, it's growing so fast we don't have a real grasp of its impact.

By the same token, Mark Gibbs, coauthor of *Navigating the Internet* (SAMS, 1994), recently stated, "When Elvis Presley died in 1977, there were 37 Elvis impersonators in the world. Today, there are 48,000. If the current trend continues, by the year 2010, one of every three people in the world will be an Elvis impersonator."

Finally, Michael Bauer, president of The Internet Group, lays the issue to rest by pointing out that at the rate it is growing, there will soon be more computers hooked up to the Internet than particles of matter in the universe.

Nua Ltd., an Internet consultancy and Web site developer in Dublin, Ireland, maintains a wonderful source of statistical information at its site (www.nua.ie). Its estimation of the worldwide use of the Internet is higher than most, and it proudly displays the differences (Figure 2.5).

For a wonderful compendium of statistics, demographics, and all-around numbers-of-the-Net, take a look at *The State of the Net, The New Frontier* by Peter Clemente (McGraw-Hill, 1997).

Oh—and yes, people are buying things on the Internet. Make no mistake.

Los Angeles County spends $627 million each year on office supplies and equipment and 80 percent of that purchasing will be online in 1999. The most populous county in the country (9.5 million people) is letting government workers buy computers and office and janitorial supplies on the Internet. Internet access is now the preferred method for filing your tax return. For those who feel the need for numeric proof of the Internet's longevity, there are plenty of measuring sticks.

The U.S. Commerce Department (http://ecommerce.gov) clocks traffic on the Internet as doubling every hundred days. In April 1998, its crystal ball said electronic commerce will grow to $300 billion a year by 2002.

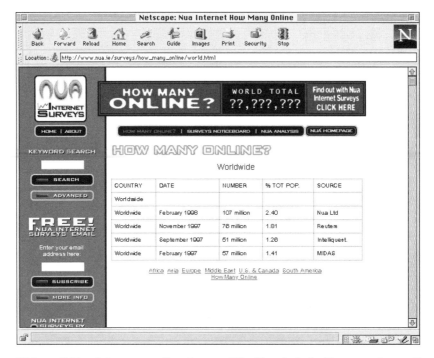

Figure 2.5   Agree or disagree with the total, the number of people on the Net continues to burgeon.

In a press release dated March 25, 1998, Price Waterhouse (www.pw .com) released its Technology Forecast: 1998, a compilation of technology trends and market analyses. In it, Price Waterhouse saw the growth of the Internet continue and a surprising growth in business-to-business electronic commerce. It expects revenues to double every few months in the next few years. By 2002, PW predicted online revenues of $434 billion. On the consumer side, PW expects revenues of $94 billion, compared to only $5 billion in 1997.

Forrester Research (www.forrester.com) predicted the end of 1998 would see 50 percent of North American homes owning a PC, 29 percent of them being on the Net, and 10 percent conducting online transactions.

A Deloitte & Touche survey at the beginning of 1998 found that half of top executives from the largest U.S. companies expect to get their news from the Internet. Around the same time, a survey of human resource executives from Ernst and Young found that e-mail was already their top means of workplace communications, beating out the telephone.

When Loral Space and Communications launched its CyberStar program of Internet access over satellite in April 1998 it spent $20 million just to promote it.

At last count (March 1998), Dell Computers (www.dell.com) was selling $4 million worth of PCs from its Web site—*per day.* Countrywide Home Loans (www.countrywide.com) funds $35 million in loans every month.

The Impact of What You Can't Count

You can see it on billboards. You can overhear it in coffee shops. You can smell it in the air. The Internet has caught on, and it's not going to stop.

Airports, shopping malls, and hotels are sprouting Web and e-mail kiosks that take credit cards. In-flight phones have dataports for laptops, and some business class seats have power outlets as well. Business offices are being promoted as being "Cyber-Ready" with high-speed Internet connections to all suites.

This week's mail brought me a flier from AT&T. "Save an additional 10% off the already-low price of every product at Spree.com through September 30. Simply return to this special AT&T Extras shopping page every time you want to shop and save at Spree.com. Your discount will be applied at checkout—watch for it!"

1998 saw the beginning of the electronic stamp (E-Stamp) for paper mail. What Pitney-Bowes has been offering through a private phone number its postage meters can dial, the U.S. Postal Service now says everybody can have. Download the desired value to a little attachment to your printer and you, too, can print an E-Stamp on your next envelope. (This explanation will look funny about six months from now because it'll be in such wide use. In 1998, though, it's a bold step for Uncle Sam.)

Why is the Internet growing so fast? What causes corporations to dedicate thousands of dollars worth of equipment and personnel to this connectivity? Simply put, being connected is better than being disconnected. Communicating faster is better. It was a status symbol; now it's a competitive necessity.

You can sell lemonade on the street corner without a telephone. You can run a restaurant without a fax machine. But somewhere out there is an enterprising ten-year-old who uses a cordless phone to invite his friends to come buy a cool drink. Somewhere, the local deli accepts lunch orders via fax and has the sandwiches made and ready to go when you show up. Ninety restaurants are listed on the Palo Alto, California, Chamber of Commerce Web site, and 17 list their own Web sites on Yahoo!.

There is value in being connected. The price is a telephone line, a connection to the Internet, and the time and energy (or cash) to create a decent Web site. The value is far higher than the cost.

THE GREAT TIMESAVER

The Internet may slow productivity at first. There is a little bit of a learning curve as you figure out the value of clicking the Back button on the browser instead of clicking on the "back" link on the page. The gee-whiz factor will waste a few hours while newbies gawk at the Louvre in Paris. Hours may get sucked up by items of personal interest such as the latest sports scores and long lists of things to make with loganberries. Finally, productivity will take a dip when people realize they can easily create their own pages and publish their baby's photos online.

The benefits of being connected so far outweigh the momentary decrease in productivity, however, that the temporary loss of efficiency is negligible.

A global firm with offices in San Francisco, London, and Tokyo can work its large documents around the clock. The London team creates a document draft between 08:00 and 16:00 Greenwich Mean Time and forwards it to Tokyo. The Tokyo team adds illustrations between 16:00 and 00:00 and forwards the project to San Francisco. The San Francisco team adds charts and tables between 00:00 and 08:00 and sends the package off to London. London may now format the entire document for final review and printing.

Three contractors team up on a project for the federal government. One is building the radar system, one is building the truck in which it is to be mounted, and the third is writing the software. Given the speed and cost-efficiency of electronic communications, they are able to create a better proposal with more detail than their competitors. They also have a better chance of delivering that project on time and under budget.

Technical standards committees, political associations, and whole communities of knowledge workers can plan, meet, and work together as never before. Graphic artists can e-mail finished brochures to the print shop for mass production. Engineers can pursue databases of the latest government regulations. Research and development departments can scour university archives for arcane information. Business leaders can form valuable relationships through e-mail.

THE GREAT MONEY SAVER

For those who need to see hard evidence of bottom-line value, consider the costs of two items:

- Production and dissemination of company policy documents
- Overnight delivery

Joel Maloff of Maloff Group International (www.maloffgroup.com) is a fount of knowledge about the size of the commercial Internet access business. In April 1994, Maloff predicted that the Internet access provision industry would grow to over a billion dollars by the spring of 1996. It turned out to be closer to $2 billion. His prediction was made before service companies like Prodigy and America Online (AOL) realized they needed to offer Internet access to their customers. His prediction was also made before Microsoft announced its intention to operate an Internet access service.

In his "1996–1997 Internet Access Providers Marketplace Analysis," Joel Maloff reported that, "The Internet exploded in 1996 and 1997, expanding to more than 4,000 Internet Service Providers (ISPs) in the United States, and accounting for annualized revenue from IP access alone of over $8.4 billion . . . This study does not consider revenues from sources other than Internet connectivity, such as consulting, training, security services, hardware, or Web hosting." With so much being spent on access, there must be some cost savings around here somewhere, right?

In his "Value of 'Internetworking' and the Internet" (*Internet World Magazine,* July/August 1994), Joel pointed out an additional commercial cost savings: rare, remote devices. These are pieces of equipment too costly to be duplicated that can be more valuable if they can be accessed by all. A high-speed printer, a lithography machine, or a massive hard disk farm can be made available to authorized people from around the world. The savings realized for capital equipment well outweigh the cost of Internet connections.

For the past several years products have been available that allow live voice transmission over the Internet. New compression technology allows conversations via computer. Companies quickly realized that a local flat fee for a connection to the world is less expensive than paying international rates for phone, fax, and document delivery.

This electronic movement of information is even more promising as a distribution medium for any company selling electrons instead of atoms. Creators of books, software, music, and video use the Internet to deliver their products as well as market them. The savings in shipping pale compared to the savings in packaging.

As long as the Internet continues to provide improved communications at a lower cost, more and more people will acquire Internet connectivity. As long as more and more people get on the Internet, it will become more and more entrenched in our business and personal lives. The more the Internet is entrenched in our lives, the more sense it makes to use it as a marketing medium.

THE INTERNET CULTURE OF GIVING

To grasp the culture of electronic living on the Internet, it helps to understand that it was born and bred in an atmosphere of sharing. When programmers began creating tools for using the Internet, they made them as fast and efficient as possible. They didn't always make them easy to understand. As players in a small but growing and very exciting game of computer communications, they were more than happy to help each other out.

"I'm trying to get VAX VMS to talk to my IBM MVS system. How can I use TCP/IP?"

"I'm having trouble getting a file from the university system. Can anybody explain FTP?"

Within hours, several helpful Internet users would respond with advice, software, moral support, and a recipe for some relaxing tea.

When being online was new for everybody, everybody was willing to help. Users made information or software available, and they could reasonably expect others to be as generous. If you spent a few hours a week helping other faceless, bodiless computer folk, you could feel free to toss a perplexing problem out into the ether and expect to receive help.

An Internet participant is willing to let you use his or her resources in exchange for being able to use yours, and his, and hers. Your computer is part of the whole Internet system. You are willing to donate its cycles for the good of the global network. You are also willing to spend some time helping others.

It was all supported by the National Science Foundation, which declared it couldn't be used for commercial purposes. Electronic Utopia. The Age of Aquarius had come to computer jockeys at universities and research companies all across the nation, and soon all around the world.

And then somebody figured out how to sell access to it.

AMERICA ONLINE AND OTHER ONLINE SERVICES

Take the Internet protocol, take e-mail, take bulletin board discussion groups, take the free exchange of information—and bottle it. Set up a private version and charge admission. Add some front-end software to make it usable by those who know their computers only from the outside. Offer additional fee-based services and quietly remove $20 a month from everybody's credit card.

Another money-making gambit for these online services is advertising. Logo space is sold, fashioned on the magazine model: The larger the logo and the larger the audience, the larger the fee. In addition, they take money for setting you up in an electronic, public forum. They take money for setting you up in their electronic mall. They also take a cut of everything you sell through their mall—an all-around moneymaker.

Then an interesting thing happened in the early 1990s. Subcontractors running the National Science Foundation Internet backbone saw there was money to be made offering these services to corporations. The NSF realized commercial for-fee use would overshadow the pure research use. If the contractors wanted to be in the business, they realized, then the NSF could stop spending millions of dollars every year on a telecommunications infrastructure. As a result, the NSF relaxed its rules about doing business on the Internet.

In the following months, commercial traffic blossomed, the Internet made the cover of *Time, Business Week,* and *Newsweek,* and a whole new industry of access providers was born. The Internet allowed everybody to be his or her own publisher. Public forums were free for the asking. Web sites were able to attract attention all by themselves and didn't depend on "foot traffic" from online services. Did this spell the end of America Online? No.

Online Services as Access Providers

In 1995 the online services completed their transition from private networks to Internet access providers. They still offer fee-based extras. They still charge their commercial customers for space in their electronic stores. But they opened the doors from their private networks to the rest of the Internet.

They began by allowing users to trade e-mail across the Internet, and they finished by allowing complete access to the World Wide Web. They don't have control over the content of Web sites, some of which are in direct competition with their fee-based services. However, in light of the Internet's growth into adolescence, in light of Internet access being sold by every telephone company *and* Microsoft, this is the only move online services could take and still maintain their growth rates.

Whatever the user access mechanism looks like, there is no question that the Internet is useful to business. Business depends on communication, and the Internet is very good at communication. As a result, it's changing the way we work, just as the phone and the fax machine have done. It improves research, speeds customer service, provides a competitive edge, and cuts time-to-market.

All, however, is not happiness and roses online.

THE DARK SIDE OF THE NET

There are enough negatives about the Internet to cause concern at the higher levels of any business organization. When you go to upper management for Internet resource allocation and describe all the marvelous marketing programs you can undertake, you will meet some trepidation. Upper management has been reading enough to have serious concerns.

Security

There are only so many ways to break into a house: through the door, the window, or a skylight, or just by bashing a hole in the wall. There are many ways to break into a computer, and new ones are dreamed up every day. This is a real problem, but there are some reassuring things you can tell upper management to keep your plans from the round file.

A good lock on a house, like a good lock on an automobile, will do the most good. Corporate network gurus should be up on all the latest in network protection anyway. It is their job to make sure internal snoops don't get into the payroll files. They are responsible for keeping the CEO's private papers private. As fast as new security breaches crop up, new security measures can be put into place.

Firewalls and network management tools are a growing industry. If the folk upstairs don't want to get into electronic commerce because it's too risky, you should introduce them to your network people, be they in-house or outsourced.

If upper management is still nervous, you have one ironclad, foolproof, nobody-can-argue-with-you security guarantee: Don't attach your marketing computer to the rest of the company. Create a corporate Internet presence on a machine that isn't plugged into your corporate network. Then, even if somebody did break into your server, the worst he or she could do is tear up a few electronic brochures. You do have backups, don't you? This method of disconnecting the public Internet server from the internal network is foolproof, but it puts up a barrier to real e-commerce.

If you're not doing it already, it's only a matter of time before you take orders over the Internet, provide customer service over the Internet, and let your employees buy things over the Internet. If your internal network is not connected to the Internet, you're going to miss out on some of the major benefits of being online. Invest in security systems for your network just as you have for your business.

Now that the specter of Internet hackers has been slightly subdued, and now that you have a fairly good idea about what the Internet is and how it works, it's time to focus on the World Wide Web.

CHAPTER 3

Welcome to the World Wide Web

The World Wide Web has changed the way wired individuals go about looking for information. As more and more people get wired, the rate of this change will increase. Consider the following before and after pictures:

Before:

Fred walks into a library and goes straight to the Business Reference Desk looking for statistics on commerce in Oregon. Fred finds a multitude of books that might be helpful. Each book contains some of what he wants. Each book also contains references to other books.

In time, Fred discovers a few publications with the most complete and current references to information on Oregon business. Each morning for the next two weeks, he browses the bibliographies of these books as the starting point in his quest.

After:

Fred logs onto the Internet and goes straight to Yahoo! looking for statistics on business in Oregon (www.yahoo.com/Regional/U_S_States/Oregon/Business_and_Economy/). Fred finds a multitude of links that might be helpful. Each Web site contains some of what he wants. Each Web site also contains references to other sites.

In time, Fred discovers a few sites with the most complete and current links to sites with information on Oregon business. Each day for the next two weeks, he surfs these Web sites as the starting point in his quest.

Fred is very happy to find the information he wants in a variety of formats. Fred finds the usual reports you would expect, but he also finds an audio recording of the governor of Oregon outlining the state's industrial policy. He finds color pictures of the agricultural landscape and individual towns, plus a satellite photo highlighting Oregon's waterways. He also finds charts depicting the monthly rainfall by region and population density by square mile. Finally, to complete the research he's doing, Fred downloads a video clip of a helicopter flight along the coastline.

The World Wide Web has done a great deal to promote the use of the Internet. Its ability to transmit images, video, and sound has captured the imagination of the world. This has caused a growing number of organizations to develop Web sites full of information, pictures, and product descriptions.

As a consumer, you can access all the information you want, when you want, for as long as you want, without having to speak fluent UNIX. As a marketer, you have a way to sell while you sleep. A remote-controlled information vending machine dispenses product brochures at the speed of light, while your salespeople spend less time explaining your goods and services, letting them spend more time closing deals.

THE BASICS OF HOW THE WEB WORKS

A brief understanding of this technological wonder is an important foundation on which to base Web site designs. You must be aware of some of the Web's limitations to avoid the technical pitfalls. You must also stay on top of ever-changing technical advances.

Global attempts are being made to standardize the Web's underlying technology. Teams of software gurus, network magicians, and policy wonks are trying to put together a document describing the specific functionality of the Web. At the same time, companies like Netscape, Microsoft, and Sun Microsystems are busy creating new functionality. A feature-hungry public is demanding products faster than developers can agree on standards.

We were once able to look under the hoods of our cars and identify all the parts. Today, this task can be accomplished only with the aid of a mechanic who has a degree in electrical engineering. Similarly, the Web's feature proliferation is sure to accelerate. Therefore, now is a good time to understand some of the basics.

The Home Page

Your home page (the first page of your electronic brochure) sits on your computer, waiting for somebody to request it. It is sent across the Internet to the requester's computer, where it is rendered. The text, graphics, and hyperlinks are displayed on the viewer's screen, and the connection to your computer is severed.

Your home page is stored like any other computer file. It can be protected from alteration and copied for backup. It contains HyperText Markup Language (known as HTML), which furnishes three important functions:

1. HTML dictates the format of your document.
2. HTML identifies additional files to be sent along with the one requested.
3. HTML contains embedded links, allowing for further file fetching.

The format of your document is critical to its success as an electronic brochure. You want to direct the eye and the mind of the Web site visitor as best you can. Type size, graphic layout, and link identification all help with this task.

The HTML file that defines your home page is an all-text file that includes pointers (references) to the graphics that you have carefully designed to fit just so. The requester actually pulls several files from your machine at the same time. First the text portion is sent. That, in turn, tells your server to send your company logo, followed by the photo of your founder and the dramatic picture of your new world headquarters.

The text portion also contains interactive references called hyperlinks. These allow the requester to select the next file. You may be familiar with hyperlinked Help programs in which the link is a word that shows up underlined and in a different color. The principle is identical. While viewing a document, you may drill down into it for more detailed information.

Viewing a Home Page

When all these files reach the requester's computer, they are rendered by the browser. The browser is a software package that interprets the HTML tags and makes sure the text and pictures all show up where intended. This is the software that is changing faster than standards can be written. It is as if the railroad train evolved into an automobile and then a helicopter within a few months, while the engineers were still trying to agree on a standard distance between the tracks.

When the viewer clicks on a particular hypertext link (a word or image designed as a selection opportunity), he or she is requesting another file from your computer. This next file contains more text, graphics, audio, video, and links. The links point to more files, some of which are located on computers in different companies and in different countries. Because all HTML pages are intertwined, this electronic quilt has been named the World Wide Web. Because of its ability to transfer multimedia, the World Wide Web has captured the attention of artists, politicians, writers, and marketers the world over.

THE WEB AS ENTERTAINMENT

Bear in mind that a large number of these servers are set up by graduate students who want to see if their favorite flavor of soda is still available in the vending machine downstairs. In January 1995, there were ten such soda machines, and you can find them on the Yahoo! list (www.yahoo .com/Computers_and_Internet/Internet/Entertainment/Interesting _Devices_Connected_to_the_Net/). In March 1998, only two remained. The soft drink distributors of the world felt that a little too much information was being given away and, of course, their lawyers had a word or two to say about discouraging college kids from tampering with their clients' equipment.

A wide variety of silly devices are hooked up to the Internet. You can see live pictures of the weather in San Diego Bay, see if a pet iguana is sleeping, or check the amount of coffee left in a lunchroom in Cambridge.

The Web is full of such surprising, endearing stuff, which provides hours of entertainment. This raises a common concern among the profit-motivated. If employees are given access to the World Wide Web, they will waste valuable time surfing instead of working. Productivity will be compromised. Any expected benefit from being wired to the world will be lost to workers playing with telerobots and checking out the temperature of Paul's extra refrigerator (http://hamjudo.com/cgi-bin/refrigerator). There is some cause for concern. Two factors, however, will mitigate this danger to productivity: company policy and human nature.

It is common corporate policy to limit the use of company resources to company purposes. It isn't permissible to use the company telephone to call 900 numbers, talk to old friends from high school, or spend an inordinate amount of time talking with a stockbroker. You don't use the company copy machine or fax to duplicate and distribute notices of a child's piano recital. You don't use the company computer to play endless games of solitaire.

Yes, some of these infractions occur on a regular basis, and the rules shouldn't be strictly enforced. We all understand that abuse of these privileges is suitable grounds for dismissal. Your firm should establish an "acceptable use" policy before handing out unlimited Internet access to employees, who have every right to expect guidance from management.

In a paper written in 1994 at the Owen Graduate School of Management at Vanderbilt University (http://colette.ogsm.vanderbilt.edu), Donna Hoffman and Thomas Novak suggest that human nature will also alleviate the surfing syndrome:

> We anticipate that early interactions in the hypermedia CME (computer mediated environment—the Web) are characterized by a "time-passing," ritualistic quality. Over time, ritualistic use evolves into instrumental use as consumers become bored after they accumulate experience navigating within the medium. This experience is likely to be accompanied by an increase in skills the consumer develops to meet the challenges presented by the environment. In other words, learning occurs and consumers begin to seek higher challenges. Thus, an instrumentalized orientation is likely to dominate a consumer's later interactions in the environment, although both orientations may be present at different points in time, depending on consumer characteristics.

The joy of surfing is intense, but it wears off as the surfer becomes more skillful. Once they've determined which $100 bill is a fake at Legal Tender (www.counterfeit.org), checked out the Amazing Fish Cam (Figure 3.1) (http://fishcam.netscape.com/fishcam/fish_refresh.html), and been insulted by William Shakespeare (http://alabanza.com/kabacoff/Inter-Links/cgi-bin/bard.pl) (Thou tottering unchin-snouted giglet!), they will grow tired of the novelty.

During this entertainment surfing, they will pick up the skills needed to find information and make contacts. These skills will directly improve their efficiency. Just as Microsoft's solitaire game on Windows helped people master the mouse, touring Stark's Museum of Vacuum Cleaners (www.reed.edu/~karl/vacuum/vacuum.html) or watching the earth tremble on the Hayward Fault above University of California at Berkeley on a Streckeisen STS-1 seismometer (http://memento.ieor.berkeley.edu) will help them understand how to navigate in cyberspace.

THE RISE OF MARKETING ON THE WORLD WIDE WEB

The World Wide Web was created to help physicists communicate better at a laboratory near Geneva. As it grew in range and ability, two groups of people discovered its value: computer scientists and librarians. Librarians are students of information retrieval. Library science has changed remark-

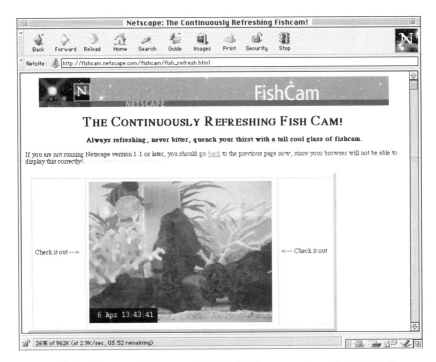

Figure 3.1   Every office needs the Netscape Amazing Fish Cam.

ably since the first days of the Dewey decimal system. Librarians across the country and around the world had been electronically cataloging books and periodicals for dozens of years. They took to the Internet immediately.

Computer scientists, computer programmers, and people working in the MIS (Management Information Systems) departments of companies around the world read about the Internet in their computer journals. The Internet was viewed as the poor man's network and not robust enough to entrust with corporate data. On the other hand, it was useful for more difficult connections, especially temporary and global connections.

When Mosaic transformed the Web from a moderately useful utility into a storehouse of multimedia fun and games, computer devotees became very excited. Here was an uncontrolled, no-holds-barred, global outlet for personal expression. Their words and pictures could stand as testament to their technical skills and cutting-edge awareness.

The most common forms of personal declaration were the photo and the blue page. The picture was placed for all to see because it was possible to do so. The blue page was a long list of other interesting things to see on the Web. (Internet Explorer and Netscape display unvisited links in blue—hence, the blue page.)

In time, these capable and cutting-edge programmers realized they could represent their companies on the Web. They correctly envisioned positioning their firms as progressive organizations. Perhaps it was a conversation overheard in the hallway or a phone call from a friend. It might have been a staff meeting where the technical manager proudly announced the progress made with the home page. Whatever the cause, the marketing department discovered the World Wide Web.

The marketing department exhibited three successive reactions: disbelief, excitement, and horror.

A marketing manager allocates his budget between buying magazine space, mailing lists, air time, and booth space. The concepts "free access," "unlimited copies," and "with millions of people" are such non sequiturs that they require a good deal of explanation and some aspirin. To an executive raised on run rates and statistics, an unconstrained, no-cost message delivery system sounded like science fiction. Disbelief reigned until the manager saw a demonstration.

Once the marketing manager saw a demo, reached out and touched AT&T (www.att.com), and heard Socks the cat meow from the White House (Figure 3.2) (www.whitehouse.gov), there was no choice but to become enamored with the possibilities. Electronic brochures flying off the computer without paying the post office! Instantly updatable product data sheets! Prices that can change on a daily basis! Video clips of the product in action!

The third reaction, horror, struck the marketing manager in mid-epiphany. For some undetermined amount of time, the company, its founders, its products, and its services had been portrayed to the world as seen through the eyes of the data processing department. The careful wording in press releases, the affectionate lighting in product glossies, the delicate manipulation of emotions, were all ignored in favor of the specifications found in the user manual.

The logic of those in the data processing departments of technical companies was impeccable: "We sell technical products to technical people. We are technical people. We know what technical people want to know about technical products."

"But it must be an interesting and appealing Web site to attract them," opined the marketing department.

"But, of course!" gloated technical. "That's why we've added this section on our favorite coffee blends, this link to the Dilbert cartoon strip (Fig-

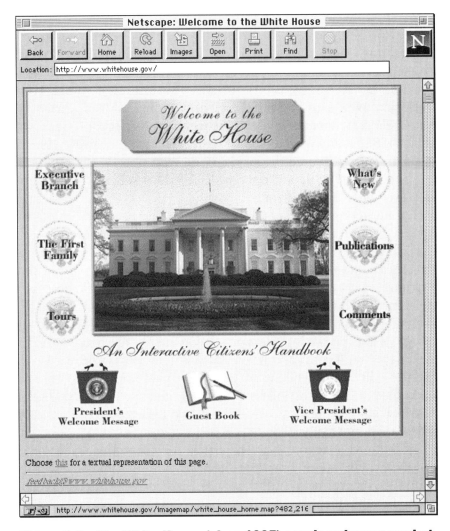

Figure 3.2   The White House (circa 1995) convinced many marketing managers that the World Wide Web was a mainstream phenomenon.

ure 3.3) (www.unitedmedia.com/comics/dilbert), a newsgroup listing computer viruses (alt.comp.virus.source.code), and all these links to all sorts of really cool stuff on the Web!"

And so, the first version of the electronic brochure for most companies had more information about the Internet than its own products and services.

DILBERT ZONE reprinted by permission of United Feature Syndicate, Inc.

Figure 3.3   Any engineer worth his or her salt will try to incorporate the original gray-backgrounded Dilbert Zone into a Web site.

BUILDING A WORTHY WEB SITE

The World Wide Web is a new communications medium. It has miraculous capabilities and aggravating limitations. It is up to the site architect and developers to create the best possible experience for the prospect or customer.

It isn't enough to repurpose your tried and true literature for the Web. People expect a great deal more on the Web than they do on paper. They discovered early on at the *Wall Street Journal* (www.wsj.com) that visitors read fewer articles, but they read a great deal more of the background material. The experience of visiting a Web site is very different from that of reading a brochure or a newspaper.

Engaging the Audience

The goal is to make the viewer an active participant in the action. Capture the viewer's attention and hold it.

> Tell me and I will hear.
> Show me and I will understand.
> Let me do it and I will learn.

If you sell software, let viewers see what it's like to run it. If you sell hardware, let them test drive your equipment. If you sell information, engross them in a sample of your work. If you sell services, enthrall them with an electronic evaluation of their needs.

Foot Traffic on Your Web Site

If you publish a magazine, you try to improve circulation. If you produce a television show, you try to increase ratings. If you own a shopping mall, you try to increase foot traffic. In these cases, the purpose is to deliver more people to the advertiser or store owner. Increased traffic allows you to charge more for the ad space, air time, or storefront.

Shopping malls and publishers of electronic magazines both try to deliver more foot traffic to their clients, the advertisers. This is a daunting task, and one that requires the best innovative thinking. Giving away a free car on DealerNet (Figure 3.4) (www.dealernet.com) was good for that market and got a lot of attention back in 1994. But a magazine like *Time* (www.pathfinder.com/time) or even *Wired* (www.hotwired.com) must constantly provide fun, interesting, or useful information and activities to keep people coming back again and again.

Figure 3.4   DealerNet gave away an automobile to attract people to its Web site.

Value-Added Marketing

The gift economy of the Web requires a vendor of goods and services to offer something of value to the visitor. A white paper, a searchable index, or a list of stores in your area might be enough. Perhaps a discussion group on current events in your industry or a page of pointers to other topic-specific sites on the Web will be sufficiently enticing.

Somewhere in your firm, there is information that is valuable to people trying to buy the products you sell. Offer that information to the world.

Now that you're oriented to the Web, it's time to put its magic to work for marketing. You'll find that marketing changes in important ways on the Web.

CHAPTER **4**

Using the World Wide Web for Marketing

Marketing on the World Wide Web finds us stepping off the highway of 500 cable channels and into a quiet field of 5 million channels. These aren't broadcast channels. They don't spew reruns, sitcoms, and talk shows. These are messages patiently waiting for us to interact with them.

The World Wide Web is a pull medium, not a push medium. The Web cannot be used to propel messages out to the masses in hopes that somebody will catch a glimpse while spinning the dial. The only two exceptions are spam (don't!) and banner advertising on other Web sites.

Advertising is a different subject and one I've already written about. Take a look at *What Makes People Click: Advertising on the Web* (Que, 1997) for a good dose of that. This book is about marketing. Let's stick with that.

The Web offers information to people who might be willing to reach in and pull it out. Kristin Zhivago, publisher of the *Marketing Technology* newsletter (www.zhivago.com) understood this difference and clearly illustrated it in the February 1994 issue:

> If your delivery medium was water, broadcasting would be like using a big hose to spray a crowd of prospects, hoping some of them will enjoy getting wet. Narrowcasting, a term used by producers of specialized cable TV programs, is like using a smaller hose and only aiming it at people who have already expressed an interest in getting wet. Cybercasting (marketing online) is the act of creating a pond of water in cyberspace, telling people that you now have a pond, and inviting them to come for a swim. Prospects can visit your pond anytime they want, stay as long as they want, and dive in as deeply

as they want. The extent to which they immerse themselves in your pond is determined completely by their own personal interest.

Some people may come just to look around. Some may take a dip. Some may swim and some may stay submerged for days at a time. The better looking, easier to navigate, more fun, and more informative your Web site is, the more likely it is that people will want to come back—and even bring their friends.

The World Wide Web allows an organization to create a library of materials anybody with an Internet connection can access. The Web's multimedia capability means that library is almost more restricted by the limits of imagination than technology. Therefore, the first step toward marketing on the Web is to get a handle on realistic goals.

SETTING REALISTIC GOALS

Each establishment, be it corporate, not-for-profit, or entrepreneurial, must determine what it hopes to gain by implementing a global, electronic presence. You undoubtedly spend a great deal of time and effort on every magazine ad or direct mail project. Maintaining this level of effort is even more critical on the Web. Your message may be read by millions, so special care is required to create a Web site that will elicit the desired response. Knowing what you want out of your site in the first place is the only way to ensure you might get there and have a chance at measuring your success.

There are many benefits to be enjoyed by connecting to the Internet. When asked why they wanted to learn more about using the Internet and the World Wide Web, an audience at DCI's Web World Conference in February 1995 said they wanted to:

- Improve corporate image
- Improve customer service
- Find new prospects
- Increase visibility
- Perform transactions
- Expand their market
- Meet their customers' expectations
- Reduce costs
- Get up to speed before it was too late

Back then, creating an image as a cutting-edge, technically savvy corporation was the most compelling reason to throw up a Web site for the majority of Web builders. Many Web sites were created just so the CEO could say the company had a storefront on the information superhighway. One by one, these one-dimensional billboards were revisited by their owners. Companies large and small are taking the time to populate that storefront with worthwhile images, documents, and, most importantly, activities. They know they must to keep up with other companies that devote serious resources to this new medium and to cope with their customers' growing expectations.

THE LEADING-EDGE IMAGE

Deciding between an empty storefront and a delayed storefront is a tough choice. If you take the time to build a robust Web site, your competitor may steal your thunder. Put up a site too quickly, and you take the chance your public will be disappointed by your hasty efforts. News of a new, exciting, intriguing Web site travels only slightly faster on the Internet than criticism of a site that is devoid of content.

There was a time when just putting up a Web site at all was cause for celebration in the nation's press. Next, you had to be first in your industry, first with new technology, or first with a unique service.

Today, having a site is a foregone conclusion. Having a site that's cool is fine if that's what your audience is really after. The game, though, will go to those who come up with unique services. If you have to choose between fun, interesting, or useful, useful wins every time. Hands down.

If you create the impression of a leading-edge company, you also create the image of a company that cares about its customers. Your company cares enough to explore new technologies and master them for the benefit of your clients. A leading-edge image also informs your clients that your company is financially strong. It is willing to take on new projects that relate more closely to service than profit. Superior service is said to bring superior profit; inferior service will certainly have a negative effect on the balance sheet. If your competitors have robust fax-back systems, sophisticated voice mail, and efficient Web sites and you don't, the marketplace will assume you are not profitable. You must not have enough resources to support your clients in the manner to which they have become accustomed. Or you simply don't care.

Yesterday, a firm could get away with not having a Web site by claiming its clients weren't on the Internet. Yesterday, the World Wide Web may not have been the best place to convince hair-styling salon owners that your new shampoo will make their customers look 10 years younger. Today is different. Today, every computer comes equipped with all the hardware and software necessary to access the Internet.

The trend has always been to identify the most widely beneficial software applications and bundle them with each new computer system. A computer purchased today includes Windows, which includes the Internet Explorer browser in spite of the best efforts of Scott McNealy (Sun Microsystems), Jim Barksdale (Netscape), and Orrin Hatch (U.S. Senate). There is no doubt that tools to access the Net will become more prevalent and more deeply embedded.

We can expect Internet access to become a part of every application, much as spell checking is today. Once, spell checking was an add-on program. Later, it was bundled with only word processing programs. Now, spreadsheet, database, and presentation software all include a spell-checking capability.

Today, a leading-edge image is hard-earned through the implementation of things that make life easier for customers. That means some serious investment in your Web site rather than mild experimentation funded by curiosity and spare time.

A company with a leading-edge image becomes a magnet for leading-edge employees. Don't forget to post your job openings on your Web site to attract talented staff members. It may seem that this task belongs more to the human resources department than the marketing department. Consider, however, that job postings give your prospects the impression of a vital, growing, successful organization.

PUBLIC RELATIONS

The days are gone when you could make a big noise and garner editorial attention just for being on the Internet. At first, editors were pleased to write, "A Flower Shop in Cyberspace," "Digital Equipment Corp. Offers Online Test Drive," and "B of A First Bank on the World Wide Web." Just being on the Web is no longer cause for this type of general attention. It's no longer cause for attention in your industry.

If you are the first one in your niche to go online or if your Web site offers something unique, you can still get some attention in the trade press in your industry. This sort of mention lets the rest of the world know your firm is a cutting-edge organization with a crack team of advanced thinkers on board. This is a distinctive measure of successful Web marketing.

A well-positioned Web site may harvest ink in your industry trade journals for being technically fashionable. It is also a great place to communicate with the press. A "What's New" section is a standard selection on most corporate Web sites. This is the area that shows off new products, your latest announcements, seminar schedules, and news. News and announcements lead to press coverage.

Letting Them Know

Mass e-mailing press releases directly to editors and writers may not be the best approach. In February 1995, Kim LaSalle of LaSalle Communications in Indianapolis posed the question to a number of journalism discussion groups. The results were mixed. The majority of those responding didn't care to have their e-mailboxes filled with unsolicited releases that didn't pertain to their specific focus. The same can be said about their fax machines and in-boxes. If it's a well-targeted item, within their area of expertise, they want to know. They all agree, however, that electronic mass mailing is more bane than boom.

E-mail systems are getting smarter these days, and editors are learning how to set up filters to keep from being drowned in electronic press releases. So how do you get your message to the right reporter at the right time? If your product or service revolves around the Internet, try Eric Ward.

Eric has been in the online world of public relations since the start of the commercial Web. At first, he focused on helping large companies figure out how to get links on other Web sites to point to their home pages. He soon found himself competing with Web sites offering automagic services. Those sites let you type in a description that is blasted out to hundreds of other sites, letting them know you had something of interest on your site.

Eric is more of a relationship manager than a technologist, and when he expanded into the press release business, he kept it that way. Here's how he describes what he does:

> Services like PR Newswire, Internet News Bureau, or Gina do a fine job of mass broadcasting press releases. I take a very different approach, non-automated, relationship built, sending news only of Web site launches, events, and happenings matched to my media contact's exact coverage interests. I have new media contacts in over 100 subject areas in 10+ countries, and I send Web launch news for clients like Microsoft, VISA International, ZDNet, and Internet WORLD. My sole mission is to match Web launch and/or event news with the exact new media editors, publishers, writers, reporters, and site reviewers that want it and can cover it. I'm cautious about which clients I take, and which editors I send news to. The goal is very clear-

cut: send news about major Web launches, events, and happenings to those who earn their living covering such things. Period.

My service is purposely non-automated, using the personal power of e-mail to and from a familiar person. Because e-mail is about connecting with people. My media contacts know me, trust me, and cover the Web related news I send them. Like I have been since 1994.

Eric Ward made a name for himself because he focused on the Internet industry. Whatever industry you're in, you should be able to find a PR company that knows the editors and knows whether they like paper, fax, or electronic press releases.

Filling Them In

Once notified that something is worth looking into, editors can check your Web site and read all about your latest endeavors. They can also copy your text and paste it directly into their articles. This is a wonderful time-saver for them. It might also increase the likelihood of your message's duplication, rather than its interpretation.

As more and more companies set up Web sites, more and more journalists are visiting for the latest news. Journalists also find your site useful for background information. Your description of the company history, your presentation of the corporate mission, your gallery of the senior executives, and your electronic links to other Web sites of interest can all contribute to any given editorial mention.

IBM had a quandary when it acquired Lotus Development Corporation. How much do we put on our Web site about this acquisition? How widely do we open the kimono? How much do we hold back to hand out as special favors—exclusive tidbits—to special friends in the media?

IBM chose to publish all and do it at the very moment the press conference started. The sentence, "You can get that document/spreadsheet/report on our Web site," was heard again and again.

The results were surprising. Knowing that the hard-fact details could be had at the end of a modem, the members of the press in attendance were able to focus more on the personalities in the room and the atmosphere of the event.

IBM had been worried that a tell-all Web site would keep reporters from writing about what was already "published." In fact, it gave them enough information that each reporter could write his or her own story, his or her own way. Reporters came up with the angles and found the background they needed online. Win-win.

If press relations is one of your goals, consider the types of publishers who would access your site. Provide them with the appropriate electronic components—text, images, sound bites, and video clips. The easier you make it for editors to put together a story, the more often you'll appear in print.

INVESTOR RELATIONS

For some companies, investor relations is a significant affair. The marketing department often has a hand in generating the annual report. It must look sharp, be readable, and present the best possible picture, no matter how grim the financial situation. A Web site can easily include an area for stockholders and industry analysts alike. Determine the depth of information you provide by balancing the investor's desire to know and your desire to withhold competitive information with the Securities and Exchange Commission's rules and regulations. Publicly released financial reports certainly belong on a corporate Web site. You may consider adding product progress reports, contract announcements, and corporate sponsorship stories.

Most public companies provide up-to-the-minute stock pricing on their home pages, and some offer links to the many financial services sites, allowing investors to view an up-to-date graph of a stock's price and volume. This sort of interactive, live communication used to be a sign of technical leadership and strength. Now it's a sign of understanding the needs of Web site visitors and giving them what they want.

CUSTOMER SERVICE

One of the best uses for a new communications medium is customer contact. The customer service department should always be the first to receive new methods of information exchange. The telephone, the telex, the fax, and voice mail all began as curiosities, then found their way into more and more companies. Before long, they became a requirement for helping and keeping customers. The World Wide Web belongs on this list as well.

Customer service desks and help desks have already discovered the value of the database. With telephone headset in place and hands on the keyboard, the freshest recruit can provide the most detailed explanation and answer the toughest question. The bottleneck has been information delivery. The World Wide Web offers a method that is faster and more direct than fax-back. This meaty subject is covered in more detail in Chapter 5, "Customer Service First."

PROSPECT QUALIFICATION

It is possible to make a profit through all selling and no marketing. It is possible to make a profit through all marketing and no selling. A salesperson can walk door to door with a case of samples and sell them without spending a dime on marketing. A pizza company can bake and deliver truckloads of pizzas through ads in newspapers, the Yellow Pages, and direct mail without any salespeople. Most businesses, though, fit between these two extremes and will greatly benefit from a well-designed Web site.

The cost of an hour of a salesperson's time differs for each firm and for each product. Without a doubt, a major part of the marketing function is to find the largest number of the most qualified buyers. Marketing tries to keep the salesperson selling instead of prospecting. For a company involved in the sale of a sophisticated product with a long lead time, the most attractive goal of an Internet Web site is to shorten the sales cycle. A prospect may require a good deal of education before understanding and appreciating the product and making a reasonable buying decision. If so, the World Wide Web is a wonderful place for promotion.

Your prospect can electronically retrieve education, understanding, appreciation, and more—while you sleep. Photographs, technical detail, and the answers to the most frequently asked questions are available at any time of day or night. Every time somebody understands the electronic answer to a pressing question, he or she has saved your salesperson five minutes of telephone time and who knows how much time tracking down the answer. As a result, the salesperson spends more time with prospects toward the end of the sale's cycle, instead of at the beginning, in the education phase. The Web site has become the prospect tutor, and the salesperson can concentrate on making more sales.

PRODUCT SALES

Technical companies were successfully using the Internet for marketing long before the World Wide Web arrived. Their Gopher and FTP (file transfer protocol) servers performed much the same function as the Web information vending machines. Information is made available, and people will fetch it as long as it has value. Depending on the product, the results can be surprising.

Your Web site might be able to close the deal without help from a salesperson, depending on the products you sell. Your Web site might allow prospects to select colors, styles, configurations, shipping methods, and payment terms. Your system can then print pick lists, shipping labels, and invoices without human intervention.

InterCon Systems Corporation in Herndon, Virginia, makes networking software for Macintosh and Windows platforms. Granted, it has a built-in audience on the Internet, but its experience is still interesting. Several years ago, Jeff Osborn, then vice president of sales at InterCon, decided to try putting up an FTP server. He populated the directories with descriptive documents and trial versions of InterCon's software. The software would run for 30 days and then quit unless the keycode was provided via e-mail.

Jeff set the system up on a Friday afternoon and went home for the weekend. He accessed his server several times over the next two days to test it and to marvel in the ability to publish his promotional materials worldwide. On Monday he checked the logs to make sure his transactions were recorded. He discovered that 500 people had logged onto this unannounced, unpublicized machine and had taken a look at the software.

Two weeks later, InterCon received a wire transfer from the Republic of Kazakhstan for more than $10,000 for software that had been downloaded via FTP. InterCon e-mailed the customer the 20-digit code to unlock the software. InterCon is still trying to calculate the cost of goods sold.

As exciting as this may be, companies face a number of troublesome issues when selling online, which are reviewed in Chapter 12, "A Few Thorny Issues."

CUSTOMER INTERACTION AND FEEDBACK

Web sites can contain forms to fill out, including long text blocks for lengthy comments. In this way, they are like e-mail. A Web site can also contain areas where visitors can post comments to be read by all. In this way, they share attributes with newsgroups. Web sites can include questions that can be answered with a click of the mouse. In this way, they are like surveys.

Online, interactive communication with your customers and prospects allows more direct feedback than ever. Each phase of product development, positioning, and promotion can include the most intelligent, experienced, and expert resource on earth—your customers. They become part of your team.

INTERNAL COMMUNICATIONS

The marketing task is not directed entirely outward. A great deal of time is spent communicating within the walls of a corporation. Getting everybody to understand product positioning or corporate vision can be daunting. Keeping the sales force aware of product line changes and pricing updates is a monumental task. Just as the Web offers better communications to prospects and customers, it can offer better communications internally.

There are many good books on creating intranets for your company; this one is about marketing. But it's worth a moment to think about how an intranet can benefit the marketing department. If you're not using Web services inside your company for internal communications, your competitor is about to eat your lunch.

Here's an article I wrote on the subject for *CIO Magazine:*

For Internal Use Only
CIO Magazine, February 1998

Marketing people are extroverts. They have to be. It's their job to view the company from the outside and project the right corporate image into a world that doesn't understand the intricacies of the company's products, the structural nuances of its politics or the arcane terminology of its industry. When marketing people think of the World Wide Web, they generally think in terms of creating a Web site. But the marketer's purview includes more than just publishing content, and some marketers are now beginning to investigate how intranets and extranets can improve their ability to communicate within and without. Marketing has the same information publishing requirements everybody deals with: phone book listings, scheduling, expense reporting. And just as all departments have insatiable mouths to feed with data, so marketing has an exceptionally hungry crew to contend with in sales. Salespeople will eat every bit of information you can give them and still be sniffing around the development labs for a morsel of a release date, begging a crumb of competitive insight from the market analysis team, and mooching month-to-date sales figures from finance. At least the good ones will.

MARKETING COLLABORATION

Understanding that the Web is changing the way the world does business, Case Corp., a Racine, Wis., manufacturer of earth-moving

---

and farming equipment, decided a few face-to-face meetings were required to make sure it was plowing the right fields. Thereafter, the company's deliberations were augmented with collaboration tools. By ranking the relative importance of possible online features, tracking assignments doled out during meetings, and openly discussing the merits of different options, Case's team learned to use the tools they could later put to use on other projects.

Case used collaboration tools from Radnet (www.radnet.com) that were designed for software developers. Your marketing team may not need the problem tracking module, but the contact management, discussion forums, document management, and calendar modules are so generic, anybody can use them. Or you can look into tools created just for marketers.

Marketsmarter LLC (www.marketsmarter.com), for example, has encoded its PRAISE process into customized intranet applications for its clients. PRAISE stands for Purpose, Research, Analyze, Implement, Strategize, and Evaluate.

Marketing and sales personnel are out in public collecting information on competitor surveillance, potential product development projects, and research tasks. The PRAISE system makes it easier for them to share that information and includes time-sensitive accountability for results. Face it, the hardest thing about collaboration tools is getting people to collaborate. Why not automate?

SETTING STANDARDS

Given a common goal across all departments and divisions, a Web site has to have a common look and feel to be cohesive. Since content owners are located in every division and at every level of a large company, the intranet is the best place to publish standards and procedures for posting material on the corporate Web site.

One company that does this well is Sprint Communications Co. When it isn't flipping dimes at us, the company does a comprehensive job of making necessary information available to content owners at all times. Sprint realizes that a common online brand provides customers with a more intuitive interface, which in turn makes them happier customers. So its marketing department offers content owners an online tool kit complete with "graphic elements designed to utilize the advantages of electronic media, while retaining and enhancing the value of Sprint's brand."

(Continued)

Sprint's marketing department doesn't just publish a style guide; it backs it up with graphics standards, including examples to ensure swift downloads. It outlines what it takes to get a section added to the corporate "What's New" page and how to place a promotional banner on the Sprint home page.

Besides the standard telephone/e-mail/cubicle guide, the Sprint intranet hosts a document sharing library to allow uploads and downloads of marketing plans, PowerPoint presentations, graphics, and software. This is no standard text-based FTP server, but a simple fill-in-form and push-button process. No need to speak Unix.

STAYING ON TOP OF THE NEWS

Sprint content managers from all over who are interested in the impact of their work (read: all of them) can access month-to-date and year-to-date Web activity data. What are the site's most popular pages? How many people pass through? At what time of day? How do they get there and what path do they take once they arrive? What search words do they use? Which special offers catch their eye? What sort of transactions do they conduct?

This is the marketing department's dream come true: the ability to measure the effectiveness of your work as it happens, to see the results of minor adjustments to verify that you're moving in the right direction, and to prove to the powers that be that your efforts are actually having a positive effect.

Sprint defines value added as "a Web site transaction calculated by attributing the cost of performing the same transaction through one of Sprint's other channels. A negative value means incremental costs are associated with the transaction." On the Sprintranet, there's a report that shows the month-by-month value added by using the Web to send out annual reports, process orders for calling cards, deliver press releases, sign up new customers, and handle myriad other marketing tasks.

ONLINE REAL-TIME

Sprint's marketing department also gives its advertising team the kind of insight needed to manage an ad budget well. When an ad person places banners on other people's Web sites, Sprint shows on its intranet each banner next to its performance stats from each of the Web properties. The same banner on different sites and different banners on the same site can yield surprisingly divergent results. As long as those results can be reviewed in almost-real-time, an advertising professional has a chance of controlling a budget to best advantage.

There's another way marketers are making use of intranets—they're using other people's intranets. It started out with the idea that one could buy advertising space on another company's internal Web. You want everybody at GiantCorp to know you have a special offer just for them, don't you? But why would GiantCorp allow such a thing? Well, paying for infrastructure isn't easy. If it can generate income while lowering expenses, why not?

If that sounds a bit vulgar, consider a method in use by AT&T. When it wants to make a proposal for a large network installation, it sends it on CD-ROM. All singing, all dancing multimedia? Nope. Show-all, tell-all HTML.

An installation project of that size requires the review of dozens of different people with different responsibilities in different offices in different time zones. Make multiple CD-ROMs and ship them out? Nope. Send one, with instructions that it is to be installed on the company intranet for all to see.

The opportunity is tremendous. Give prospective customers all the information any of them could want at gigabit speeds. And then give them some collaboration tools. The art of the deal becomes the automation of the deal when the application helps the prospective customer select options, approve configurations, and arrive at conclusions. Give them spreadsheets for competitive comparison. Design a process for balloting. Orchestrate the internal decision-making process. And then make the sale.

Astute marketers are also finding ways to incorporate not just their message but their whole ordering process onto other companies' intranets. If you ran a travel company, for example, you could offer great discounts on a client's intranet pages. You could incorporate all of your client's internal business rules in the bargain. They'd get automated travel policies that ensure coach seating and low fare scheduling. If you ran an office supply business, your client would get routed supply orders that were work-flowed through the approval process and aggregated for best discounts.

Vendors have become software purveyors as the offspring of EDI turns marketing extroverts into "intraverts." Just wait until the competition heats up.

WEB SITE TRAFFIC AS ITS OWN REWARD

The billboard philosophy tells us to place our names in front of people as often as possible. The more product impressions people see, the more likely they are to remember, trust, and buy the product. Some Web sites are designed with foot traffic in mind. Internet shopping malls and periodical e-zines (electronic magazines) are trying to sell advertising space based on the number of people who visit their sites.

Causing people to make a habit of visiting a particular Web site is a unique challenge. If your purpose for a public Web site is to disseminate technical information, the number of new visitors may not be important. If your goal is a high number of impressions, you can use techniques that encourage repeat visits. Or you can simply buy space or sponsorship at other sites.

Determining your goals from the outset is half the battle. The options are many when it comes to execution. The novelty of this new communication medium, combined with its seemingly limitless possibilities, causes creative excitement. That excitement can generate a very successful Web site.

CHAPTER 5

Customer Service First

Stripped to its bare essentials, the Web is an information vending machine. Just like Gopher and FTP, on the Web people ask for files and the computer sends those files back. But the Web has taken on the abilities of other communication tools—e-mail, newsgroups, and lists. These other communication tools are important to the design of a successful Web site. Your Web site is a two-way street, not a one-way broadcast. E-mail, newsgroups, and listservers are critical tools in your marketing arsenal on the World Wide Web.

Although I've written an entire book on this subject since *World Wide Web Marketing* was first published in 1995, *Customer Service on the Internet* (John Wiley & Sons, 1996), this chapter is very important to the Web marketer. Understanding the possibilities of customer service helps the marketer understand the meaning of communicating with prospects.

CUSTOMERS ARE WHERE THE MONEY IS

More important, by now you've all read *The One to One Future* and *Enterprise One to One* by Don Peppers and Martha Rogers (Currency/Doubleday, 1995, 1997). What? You haven't? Well, as soon as you're finished with this one . . .

The main premise of one-to-one marketing is that it has always been easier (cheaper) to sell something to a current customer than to find and hook a new one. Yet most of the sales compensation plans out there pay off big when new customers are signed. Most marketing plans are geared toward bringing fresh blood to the table.

According to Peppers and Rogers, if it's less expensive to sell something to current customers, and because you know so much about them, you should create marketing projects that cater to and extract dollars from your very own customer base.

YOUR BEST MARKETING IS GREAT CUSTOMER SERVICE

If this comes as a surprise, you simply haven't been wearing your customer-colored glasses enough. Think about it: You visit two different Web sites that have the same products. At about the same price. At about the same availability. With about the same warranty. Which do you choose? All that's left is to look at the label and pick the brand you trust the most.

But what if one of the sites has lots of information on how to use the product? Has lots of information on how to fix problems? Has lots of ways you can contact the company and talk to somebody? Now the scales of value are clearly tipped. You buy from the company that offers more value for the same product.

Therefore, every marketer should understand what the electronic customer is all about. And we start simply—with e-mail.

USING E-MAIL FOR CUSTOMER SERVICE

E-mail provides a wonderfully frictionless way to communicate. A message comes to the desktop. The reply is written on the same screen, and out it goes at the speed of light. No paper trays to fill, no fax machine to run out of paper, and the response is delivered directly instead of sitting in interoffice mail. An e-mail can contain more detailed, specific information than can be written on a "while you were out" note or left in voice mail. Answers to questions that come up again and again can be stored for quick retrieval.

Arming your customer service department with e-mail gives your customers one more method of corresponding with your firm. More sociable people like speaking on the phone. More formal people prefer writing letters or sending faxes. Some prefer e-mail. With so many people using e-mail in their homes and offices, it behooves you to cater to them.

In a report released at the beginning of 1998, Forrester Research predicted that 50 percent of the people in the United States would be using e-mail in five years. No surprise. Students are given e-mail accounts the moment they enter a university. When these people enter the workforce, e-mail will be a requirement.

You wouldn't consider running your company without a fax machine. Customers won't consider doing business with a company without an e-mail address—and the skills to use it wisely.

Basic Training

Responding to a customer comment, question, or complaint via e-mail requires the same care used when responding over the phone or in writing. Inflection and attitude are critical to maintaining a happy and healthy customer/vendor relationship over the phone. The correct answer, spoken in the wrong manner, can have a negative effect. On paper, the wrong words can return to haunt the well-meaning customer service representative over and over again. Those words may even show up in court.

E-mail falls between the spoken word and the written word. It is fast; it is spontaneous. When an e-mail beeps onto your desk, you get a feeling of instant communication—somebody wants to tell you something right now. The natural reaction is to respond at once, with the same informal manner used when passed a note in school. This casual regard for the written (but e-mailed) word is creating a middle layer of communications. Companies will have to protect themselves from employees being overly informal.

Let's Be Careful Out There

I recently consulted at a large software company in Chicago, which will remain nameless because they don't want to appear in next Sunday's Dilbert strip. This company pulled off one of those classic e-mail goofs.

I was working with one gentleman—let's call him Mike. We were sending e-mail back and forth, and he was copying some others on the project to keep them in the loop. True to proper netiquette, I made sure they were all included in my reply. Mike inquired if I could come out right away, within the next couple of weeks. I replied that I had only one day open and it would mean taking a red-eye to get there. "In order to be non-comatose, I'm going to have to request business-class travel." Within a couple of hours, I got a response from somebody I'd not come across before, nor even heard of before. We'll call her Michelle. Michelle's message was a copy of my message with the following at the top:

```
Wow. what a woosiekins. Can't believe he's requesting
business class travel. Funny stuff. Let's put his email
on the Web and see what it does for his career...
```

I was nonplussed. I reacted the way I have trained myself to do whenever a particularly upsetting message hits my screen: I sat on it for 24 hours. My wife got an earful. My brother got an earful. I was livid. But I sat on my hands.

The next day, as I carefully started constructing an additional 10-minute seminar segment for my consulting trip that would include e-mail do's and don'ts, Mike called. Understand, this was the first time I'd ever spoken with the man on the telephone.

"Uh, Jim?"

"Yes."

"This is Mike."

"Hi, Mike," in slightly frosty tones, "How are you?"

"Great, great. Thanks. Uh, Jim, did you get an e-mail from my boss?"

"I'm not sure. Who's your boss?"

"Michelle."

"Yes."

"Uh, well, uhm. Heh-heh. You see, uhm. She's got a really wry sense of humor and, uh, well, heh-heh, you know, and uh, so I just wanted to, sort of, well . . . We'll be seeing you on the 6th, right?"

"Yes, Mike. I'll be there."

"Oh, great! That's real good. OK! Well, I'm glad we got that cleared up. Thanks, and, uh, see you on the 6th!"

I looked at the dead receiver in my hand. Whatever happened to "I'm sorry"? What the heck happened to Michelle? That 10-minute segment was now going to be a half hour. Not only did she send it to me, but she took away the element of surprise—I was going to flash her name up on the big screen in front of their whole marketing department.

It wasn't until five days later that I received the following:

```
Date: Tue, 26 Nov
From: Michelle Xxxxxx <xxxxxx@xxxxxx.com>
To: jsterne@targeting.com
Subject: So, what have I learned pre-seminar?

I posed my obviously beyond stupid self-imposed dilemma
to my former sixth grade teacher, who suggested the fol-
lowing retribution:

(in lieu of chalkboard)
```

```
I will never thoughtlessly hit the send key
I will never thoughtlessly hit the send key
I will never thoughtlessly hit the send key
I will never thoughtlessly hit the send key
I will never thoughtlessly hit the send key
...
```

[Yes—there were 100 of them.]

```
...
I will never thoughtlessly hit the send key
I will never thoughtlessly hit the send key
I will never thoughtlessly hit the send key
```

```
Please fly out here first class on us. We will also pro-
vide limo service. All this is paid for under a grant
called the Michelle's-An-Idiot Fund (it's not a big
fund, but an incredibly worthy cause).
```

I decided they didn't need to have an extra e-mail seminar after all.

Protect Yourself

Create a company policy for using e-mail. Emphasize clarity and professionalism. Help employees understand how the casual nature of e-mail can be misleading. Apply the same rules to the company's e-mail capability as you do to the phone, the fax, and the copy machine. If an employee cannot live without daily postings about bicycle racing, make it clear that he or she should get a private e-mail address. The office account, especially with @company.com attached to the user's name, should be used for business only.

Besides protecting the company from embarrassment and deeply unhappy customers, an e-mail policy can protect the company from litigious ones as well. An e-mail is a legal document. It is words on paper. If somebody is going to send the wrong thing to a customer, it's much better to be able to say it was the individual's failing. They were going against policy.

USING NEWSGROUPS FOR CUSTOMER SERVICE

Customers have created electronic bulletin boards where they can publicly discuss their likes and dislikes regarding a particular product. In the area of computer databases alone, there are 14 newsgroups about specific database products and 1 about database theory. Notice there are four about Oracle alone:

comp.databases.gupta

comp.databases.ibm-db2

comp.databases.informix

comp.databases.ingres

comp.databases.ms-access

comp.databases.ms-sqlserver

comp.databases.olap

comp.databases.oracle

comp.databases.oracle.marketplace

comp.databases.oracle.misc

comp.databases.oracle.server

comp.databases.oracle.tools

comp.databases.paradox

comp.databases.pick

comp.databases.progress

comp.databases.rdb

comp.databases.sybase

comp.databases.theory

comp.databases.visual-dbase

comp.databases.xbase.fox

comp.databases.xbase.misc

These newsgroups are a boon to customers and a mixed blessing to vendors. Customers may rant, rave, commiserate, and make suggestions. Customers may ask questions the vendor isn't able to answer.

In the computer world, it is very common to have problems getting one piece of equipment or software to work with another. Vendors don't have the resources to check every possible combination of equipment and code from other vendors. On a newsgroup, however, with participants from all over the world, a vendor is likely to get answers to such questions. The answers will come from individuals with firsthand knowledge about the products up for discussion. They'll offer suggestions and recommendations—including recommending a competitor's product.

You don't have a database product? You don't think people are talking about you out there? There's a newsgroup called alt.mcdonalds; a quick search across the board found more than 2500 mentions of Burger King. Burger King showed up in such diverse groups as these:

soc.culture.filipino

rec.arts.disney.merch

rec.collecting.sport

rec.autos.sport.nasca

soc.penpals

This type of activity makes monitoring and participating in newsgroups imperative. Both of these assignments can be considered part of the public relations responsibility. Select those individuals in an organization who are best able to write informative, articulate posts. Allow only them to respond to the confused, churlish, angry, spiteful, or merely curious.

Fortunately, there's help. Dejanews (www.dejanews.com) keeps track of the more than 50,000 newsgroups for you. It even keeps an archive. You can do a search for your company (Charles Schwab had 210 mentions in the past 30 days), your product (203 for Altoids—mostly in alt.support .stop-smoking), or even your boss (14,320 for Bill Gates).

USING THE WORLD WIDE WEB FOR CUSTOMER SERVICE

Quality customer service is critical to happy customers, repeat customers, and word-of-mouth referrals. Having the right answers to customers' questions and solutions to customers' problems is central to excellent service. Getting those answers and solutions to customers in a timely fashion is the deciding factor; a Web site can automate this function and improve satisfaction significantly.

The Frequently Asked Questions (FAQ) Solution

Your customer service people hear most of these questions daily:

- How much will it shrink if I wash it in hot water?
- How long is the warranty?

- How long does it take to paint and ship a custom-colored version?
- Where can I get it fixed?
- Has it been reviewed by *Consumer Reports?*
- Can I read version 6.0 files in Office 98?

The answers to these questions are ingrained in their thought process and have become part of their speech pattern. These are the questions and answers taught to new employees on the first day. Each time a customer learns one of those answers without calling your toll-free 800 number, you save the price of a call and the service representative's time.

The most helpful resource on a Web site is often the Frequently Asked Questions (FAQ) page. This is a practice borrowed from newsgroups and FTP sites. The most common questions and their answers are collected and made available for electronic retrieval. At any time of the day or night, from anywhere around the world, customers and would-be customers can find solutions to the problems they face at that very moment.

If the answers are plentiful and cogent, you have reduced the customer frustration factor. You have electronically turned an annoying problem into a pleasant experience. Compare that to a customer waiting for the proper time of day, waiting on hold, explaining the problem two or three times to two or three different people, and then waiting for an answer.

And don't forget to post Frequently Asked Questions for prospects as well. There's no better way to hasten the education portion of the sales cycle. But there's an even bigger upside. If you track which questions people are reading, you might learn that you need to change your marketing materials to better describe your products in the first place. At the very least, you'll find out what's important to people—and that is the first step to decent marketing.

The Special Question Opportunity

When a solution or answer isn't immediately apparent, the customer is invited to contact the company via a fill-in form on the Web page or to send an e-mail. This option doesn't provide the same immediate gratification as finding the answer, but it offers two aspects that may make the transaction an even more positive experience for the customer.

Asking a difficult question may provide its own source of pleasure. This customer may feel that he or she knows more than the others, has more insight than the others, and therefore is able to ask better questions than the others. This is the pride found in knowing that your question isn't frequently asked. A special question posed to an automated Web page also may receive a really good answer. This is the second opportunity to turn this problem into a positive experience for the customer.

In a typical telephone interaction, beyond the aggravation of being on hold forever, the customer is subjected to the rigors of explaining the problem to an operator, clerk, or help desk representative. This is a trepidatious task. Explaining a complex problem to somebody who is armed only with the standard answers to the typical questions can be difficult. Further, it may take hours or days to get an answer.

On the other side of the phone, the helpful telephone jockey is using everything in his or her arsenal to find an answer: look it up in the database, ask the coworker at the next desk, leave a voice mail for the product manager or the chief engineer in hopes of getting a reasonably understandable answer in a timely way. All the while, this brave soul is logging more problems, questions, and complaints, and he or she may not make it to lunch today.

By contrast, questions received via e-mail, as typed into the Web page form, appear one at a time in an orderly fashion. Questions with readily available answers can be dealt with instantly. Special questions are logged and forwarded to the proper authorities in the company.

The proper authorities provide the quintessential answer to be stored in the customer service database for all time. If they don't have the answer at the tip of their fingers, they are sure to know who does and can pass the question along. The person with the proper response writes it up and e-mails it out to the customer with a copy to customer service. Case closed, customer satisfied, customer service updated. As a result, the customer receives a considered, rather than a canned, answer. It is an answer from the corporate expert on the subject. Due to the electronic means of communication, the question was answered in a fraction of the time it would otherwise have taken.

The Right Customer Service Information

If you sell computer systems, chances are your customers are going to want to see product specifications, compatibility charts, product release schedules, and pricing. If you sell tickets to local events, your customers are going to want to see performance schedules, ticket pricing, theater seating charts, and driving directions. What goes up on your customer service Web site depends on your product.

Federal Express offers package tracking on its Web site. Type in your tracking number, and you receive a listing of your package's trip across the country. When it was picked up, when it made it to the airport, when it was delivered, and who signed for it appear on your screen in less time than it takes to dial the 800 telephone number.

The entire Web site at Silicon Graphics (www.sgi.com) was born of its customer service department. Anita Schiller, Director of Electronic Marketing, explained why in 1995:

> Back in the late 80s the customer base grew very fast, and we wanted to use brains instead of brute force to meet their needs. We didn't want to have to grow our support and engineering force as fast as our installed base was growing. We wanted to find better ways to deal with high volume and still provide high quality and highly responsive support.
>
> We had implemented knowledge bases for our customers to access. Originally that was through dial-up or cutting tapes and eventually with quarterly distributions of compact disks. But information changes so quickly, and even though the cost of cutting a CD is so much lower than hiring and training engineers, it was still a growing cost. So many of our customers were on the Internet that it seemed like a reasonable approach.
>
> When the Web first appeared on the horizon, the customer service people just jumped right on it and said, "Hey, let's try this and see what happens." So it started as a grass roots effort. There wasn't a special team called together or any new people hired. The first three to six months were proof of [the] concept, and management realized the value pretty quickly and let us hire some graphics people and managing editors. Then it was time to bring it under the wing of the marketing side of the house.

Customer service remains one of Silicon Graphics' central reasons for having a Web site (Figure 5.1) (www.sgi.com/support).

A customer service Web site can answer technical questions before they are asked and solve technical problems before they occur. Hours of telephone time can be saved simply by posting known problems, solutions, and suggestions.

Instead of arming an 800 operator with a database of solutions, the company makes the database available to the customer. The savings in personnel costs can be dramatic. Federal Express (yes, it's the law—if you write about the Internet you have to talk about www.fedex.com somewhere) learned the value of having customer information available online.

When FedEx started giving customers access to its package tracking system over the Internet (Figure 5.2) the press and the public were very

Figure 5.1   The SGI customer service department initiated its Web site and continues to support its customers there.

pleased. But what about upper management? When they heard that hundreds of people a day were tracking packages online, they said, "So what?"

Several months later, thousands of people were tracking their packages online. Upper management said, "So what?"

"So," said the Web team, "It costs us $7 every time a customer calls 1-800-GoFedEx, and it costs .07¢ every time a customer does it on the Web, and we've put a big dent in the number of calls we're getting."

"Cool!"

For a very serious look at a very serious customer service Web site, check out how Cisco (www.cisco.com) uses the Web on its support site (Figure 5.3).

Cisco is automating as much of the process as it can: the shopping process, the buying process, the support process, all of it. It has implemented Configuration Agents that allow you to search for and create a product

Figure 5.2   Federal Express is often credited for being the first to give customers access to live data, in this cae package tracking.

configuration: Pricing Agent allows you to access Cisco's online price list, Status Agent provides status reports on open orders, and RMA/Service Order Agent lets you get status on a service order.

The Software Image Library provides downloadable software updates for all Cisco products, with interactive upgrade planners to help you choose the right software for your environment. The Bug Toolkit contains a variety of popular bug searching tools. You can also set up a network profile so that Cisco can alert you to new bugs via e-mail or fax. The Open Forum provides database searches for quick answers to technical questions. The Troubleshooting Engine helps customers resolve a variety of common internetworking problems using an intuitive Web interface.

If that's not enough, Cisco also has both customer service engineers who wear beepers that notify them of high-level e-mails and online training to become a Cisco Certified Internetwork Expert.

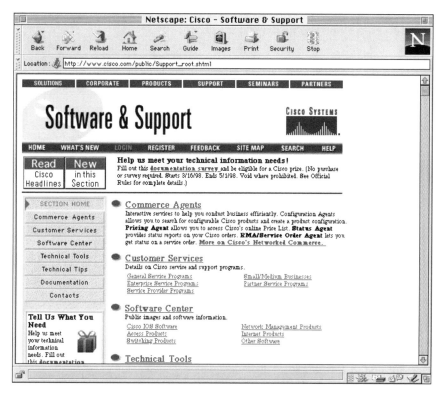

Figure 5.3   All of Cisco's customers are online, and Cisco spends a lot of effort supporting them there.

There's a lot more to learn about Cisco's customer service efforts in Chapter 8 "Cisco Systems—A Case Study," of *Customer Service on the Internet.*

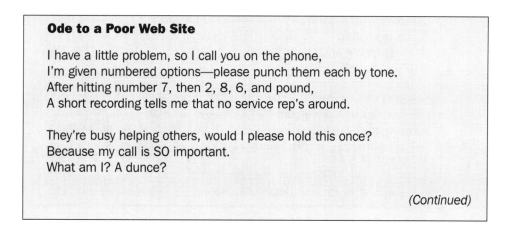

Ode to a Poor Web Site

I have a little problem, so I call you on the phone,
I'm given numbered options—please punch them each by tone.
After hitting number 7, then 2, 8, 6, and pound,
A short recording tells me that no service rep's around.

They're busy helping others, would I please hold this once?
Because my call is SO important.
What am I? A dunce?

(Continued)

Ode to a Poor Web Site *(Continued)*

My call's not so important that I'll spend an hour on hold,
While my shoulder aches, my patience bakes,
And my coffee grows green mold.
Nothing your recording says can cause me to believe
That my call will be taken in the order it was received.

So down I put the telephone and up I pick the modem
To find solutions on the Web, and once found, download 'em.
I calmly wait while DNS looks up your URL.
I wait until your server answers your home page front door bell.

I wait for frames to paint themselves, my problem to resolve.
And then I wait for plug-ins for your logo to revolve.
I wait to get an audio file—greetings from your CEO.
He doesn't get the Internet, but he loves the radio.

I wait until a picture of your building is on my screen,
And I realize that some things should not be heard or seen.
Finally, there's a menu, and I poise my mouse to click.
But first, a Java applet! "Starting Java."
You know that won't be quick.

The menu choices indicate you know yourselves full well.
You know all about your company, and that's what you want to tell.
But where's the button I can push, that takes me to the page
That solves my problem? Feels my pain? Soothes my mounting rage?

There, in the lower corner, down by the copyright,
There's a little tiny icon that looks as if it might
Link to customer service, my troubles soon will quit!
I click upon it and I get—a 404.
Ohhhh, sugar.

And when I finally reach that page that promises relief,
I'm staring at a document that's far beyond belief.
For where there should be answers to frequently asked questions,
And online help, and knowledge bases, is only indigestion.

There in type italic, underlined, and bold,
Is the number for your help desk phone.

I should have stayed on hold.

CHAPTER 6

The Usable Web—
Be Kind to Your Users

With your goals firmly prioritized, it's time to create the virtual version of a visit to your office. Designing a World Wide Web site is as simple as creating a combination magazine ad, brochure, trade show exhibit, demo diskette, and CD-ROM. A child can do it.

In fact, with the tools available, it barely takes a child. After all, how hard can it to be "Save As HTML"? The problem is that it's so easy, everybody can and everybody does—and not everybody is good at it.

The single most important consideration is your intended audience. Take care to strike a balance between what you want them to see, hear, read, learn, and do, and what they want to see, hear, read, learn, and do. If your site is not easy to access, interesting, and valuable, they won't give you a second thought.

You have to experience your Web site through customer-colored glasses.

You must take three elements of Web site design into account every step of the way: navigation, interaction, and feedback. If it is difficult to maneuver through your site, if you don't offer audience participation, if you don't collect your prospects' opinions, you have made it hard for people to learn about your products, you have created a boring experience, and you haven't taken advantage of the most elemental truth about the Internet—it is a multidirectional communication medium.

Coming up out of a subway station is horribly disorienting. You can spot the street signs, so you know what corner you're on, but what direction are you facing? Which way is your destination? Why aren't there arrows pointing north at subway station exits all over the world? And while we're at it, why isn't there a standard approach to Web site navigation?

Navigating in a virtual world is an acquired skill. Navigating a ski slope, a crowded freeway system, or through a computer game filled with danger and surprise all require agility. Practice can help a lot. When people come to your Web site for the first time, they will react like novice skiers and student drivers. Be considerate of them. Give them lots of visual clues, and make your site as intuitive as possible.

When I arrive on your electronic doorstep, I have a fairly good idea of where I am. Your corporate logo is prominent, and there's a short description of what your company does for a living. But as soon as I step off the home page and into the traffic of your pages, it's easy to get lost. The challenge for Web site designers, therefore, is to make navigation information as comprehensible as possible.

Think about the first time you installed a new piece of software on your computer. Aside from the commands we've all grown to know and love (File: New, Open, Close, Save), the different features of a new program are hard to pick up. Once they're explained, they seem obvious. But if the documentation or Help screens aren't in place or are so full of help you can't find what you're looking for, you struggle to find your way around. It seems hard to fathom that this software will make you more productive in the long run.

Consider first-time Web site users and reach out to them. Give them guidance without being overly protective. Give them encouragement without hindering their progress. At the same time, consider users who may be coming back again and again. Give them shortcuts to the information they want. Make it easy for them to use your site as a resource.

To design a better Web site, go visit lots and lots of others. Copy what seems worthwhile. Be inspired by new ideas and examples of people thinking outside of the box. Above all, look at the ways in which Web site builders are making it easier for people to get around. Navigation is a serious matter in this electronic environment. You don't want to lose your audience in a maze of entertainment. You don't want them to get turned around and give up because they can't find what they're after. The Webmaster must provide some sort of an electronic map so they know where they are at all times.

We'll spend a good deal of time on navigation because it's critical. First, we pause for a word about graphics.

LARGE GRAPHICS

When I started admonishing Web developers back in 1994, the first thing I begged them to do was to take pity on all of us who dialed up with 14.4 kbps modems.

"Stop the insanity!" I cried. "We don't want to wait forever for a picture of your CEO and a picture of the new corporate headquarters. We don't care!"

I knew that, in time, technology would give us faster connections. We went from 14.4 to 28.8 in a matter of months. At the moment, I can get a 56 modem for $50. You may be hooked up through ISDN, or a cable modem, or a satellite dish, or an ADSL hook-up. That's great, but the rest of us aren't.

The rest of us are still hovering at slightly better than 28.8. Why? Because we got tired of constant upgrading, especially when the tech press is filled with silver bullets right over the horizon.

And should you hear others say that *your* customers are more sophisticated than the rest, that *your* customers are connecting at the office over high-speed T1 lines, don't fall for it. Are you connected at the office over a T1 line? It's great at 7:00 in the morning before anybody else is there, isn't it? But as soon as the other 200 people you share it with start checking stock prices, football scores, competitors' Web sites, and the latest industry gossip, things tend to slow down, don't they?

The Web allows for multimedia. Multimedia is good. A picture is worth a thousand words. But a picture takes a thousand times more data than a word.

Netiquette calls for FTPing from the site geographically closest to you—not just because it's faster, but because you're not wasting bandwidth. The amount of backbone is finite, so download something once and keep a copy. In the same vein, it is simply good netiquette to keep your Web site offerings to a minimum. We all share this precious Internet resource. It is incumbent on us to use it sparingly.

The more data you put on your Web site, the longer people have to wait to receive it. The longer people have to wait, the more likely they are to leave the store, hang up the phone, or go look at some other Web site that's more responsive. Many Web sites use large pictures to offer a pleasant visual experience. The drawback to this approach is the time it takes a picture to reach the user's computer.

If graphics are critical to your customers and prospects, or if all your customers and prospects have superior Internet connections, then you might think a graphics-heavy approach is a requirement. But not all your customers are logged in from the office.

Your customers may have high-speed connections at work but 14.4 modems at home. Your home page comes screaming out of your high-powered computers and flashes through the giant backbone running down the California coast. It blasts into town on a supercharged connection and then trudges slowly up a forty-year-old pair of copper wires that gently wend their way down the street and up the hill to my house. The result of that trip is a five minute wait for the pictures to paint themselves on the screen.

Bad

A quick look at the Apple home page (www.apple.com) (Figure 6.1) reveals a minute and a half of download time just to show everybody they're not afraid of Intel. Why that long? Because this isn't just a 32k picture—it's *two* 32k pictures. One has the figure looking at a flaming foot, and the other looks just like the smaller version at the bottom of the screen.

You remember the Intel "Bunnypeople" ads with dancing figures in cleanroom suits. As I write this, a Beanie Baby version sits atop my 17" monitor, attached to a Macintosh. So, am I a Mac fan? Sure. Am I pleased that Apple took so much time to take a pot-shot at Intel? No.

When people come to your Web site (assuming you're selling some-thing and you're not on the Web just to entertain the world) they are look-ing for something. They are hungry for information and they want it as fast as possible.

Turning to the telecommunications world, we find a surprising slap in the monitor dished up by BellSouth (www.bellsouth.com) (Figure 6.2). This page took three minutes to reach me in full, using a 28.8 modem, on a weekend when overall network traffic was low.

This is an unbelievable example of what happens when the artist plays too long in the technology toy box. To begin, the page is made up of 30 or so little graphics. "Oh good, little ones." Not so good. They all have to load one by one, and the entire home page takes more than three minutes to show up in full.

One of the reasons for this is the head-and-shoulders picture of the guy in the middle. This is actually four pictures: He talks, he gestures, he smiles.

Figure 6.1   Apple takes up my time to poke Intel in the eye.

In the upper right corner, there is a series of rotating banners. As shown in Figure 6.2, BellSouth invites you to tour its exhibit of award-winning artists, but others pop in and out as well. Now that wouldn't be so bad if it were an animated picture (that is, a picture with several parts that are downloaded together and then displayed in sequence). Instead, BellSouth created a page that goes back to the BellSouth server for the next one—over and over again. This page *never* finishes!

What's more, the menu along the left side consists of roll-overs, pictures that change when the mouse rolls over the top of them. Roll-overs are a nice way to indicate which button will be activated when you click. In this case, the "other" button, the rolled-over version, isn't waiting in your cache file. The browser has to go back to the BellSouth server to fetch it. You want to click, but the browser is still busy getting the cute little graphic and the next banner for the upper right corner.

**Figure 6.2   BellSouth uses up lots of telephone time to send you
its home page.**

This is a home page that resembles a giant steel door with a sign on it
that says "Your Modem Is Too Slow To Buy Anything From Us. Go Away!"

There are only three reasons for graphics on your Web site: decoration,
navigation, and information. Decoration is what gets everybody in trouble.
Web developers create these pages on fast machines with big monitors and
when they demo the results to their peers, the pages pop right up. They're
not wearing their customer-colored glasses.

Better

Another telecommunications company seems to have gone a bit too far
in the other direction. Southwestern Bell Wireless has a page (www
.swbellwireless.com) that loads so fast you only need two hands to count
the seconds (Figure 6.3).

Unfortunately, the company sacrificed attractiveness to garner speed.
It's blindingly fast, but it isn't pretty. What's needed is a compromise.

Best

Staying with our telecommunications theme as an example, take a look at the GTE home page (www.gte.com), shown in Figure 6.4. This Web site is simple, graphic, and even has animation. But it loads in less than 30 seconds.

The overall best solution to the big-picture dilemma is increased bandwidth. When everybody on the planet has T1 speed, roaming, cellular connections to the Internet, we will all enjoy real-time, two-way video communications. All of the AT&T "You Will" commercials will look like Jules Verne's *Trip to the Moon*. Until then, we must take the lowest common denominator into account.

Offer a Choice

When Silicon Graphics first put up its Web site (www.sgi.com), it was full of deeply colored, highest-resolution, ultra-fancy, computer-generated graph-

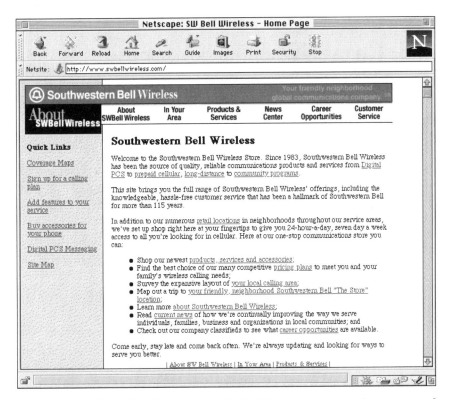

Figure 6.3   The Southwestern Bell Wireless page is a speed demon.

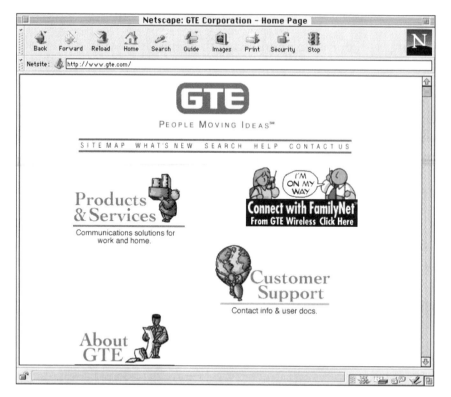

Figure 6.4   GTE's page is not too hot, not too cold . . . just right.

ics. When I saw it I fired off an e-mail message to webmaster@sgi.com, thanking SGI for the "text only" button at the bottom of the screen, but would they please be so kind as to put it at the top? Otherwise, those of us with slow modems must wait *forever* before we even see the option!

The page was changed the next day. And they've kept that "text only" button at the upper left corner. Now, instead of waiting for the rest of the page to paint, you can click on it right off the bat (Figure 6.5).

One click, and your screen instantly fills with the text-only version (Figure 6.6).

Another way to offer a choice is to show a small version of pictures first. Indicate the size of the larger version, and allow the user to make the decision. The user may then opt for the larger picture, to see some detail. This also works well for video clips. Video can use a megabyte for 10 or 15 seconds. Streaming videos require plug-ins that stop surfers in mid-surf and force them to reconfigure their browsers. It's best to warn people that you are going to tie up their modems.

Figure 6.5   Silicon Graphics offers a quick exit from the download dilemma.

Multimedia Must Add Value

As compression techniques improve and bandwidth grows, this issue will fade. For now, be aware that many people on slower connections might be interested in your products and services. Don't create hurdles that will keep them out. Regardless of bandwidth, remember the three reasons to use multimedia: decoration, navigation, and information.

Decorative pictures and interesting videos make the site look nice.

Navigational elements keep the user from getting lost.

Informative components communicate information that the user otherwise could not glean or could not glean as fast as from text.

Pictures that belong to the decorative category should be kept as small as possible, without losing their artistic appeal. Larger graphics for aes-

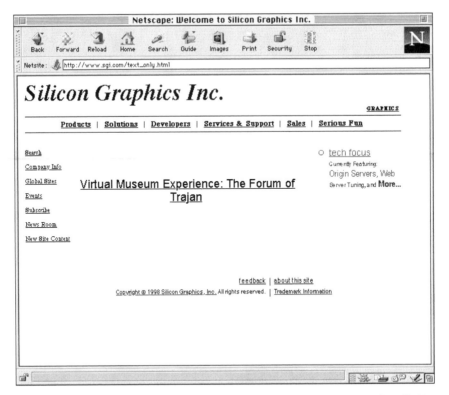

Figure 6.6   SGI's text-only version of the home page is simplicity itself.

thetic use are likely to offend, due to the time it takes to download them. Once downloaded, these images do nothing to help users locate, retrieve, or understand the information they're after.

In a magazine ad, the reader sees the whole page at a time. A giant logo with a few words can work here because the mind will register the corporate identity, accomplishing the exposure goal. On a Web site, people are looking for information, not exposures. They won't appreciate your using their reading time, no matter how fast their connection.

If users are required to wait for full-screen graphics at each of three levels of browsing, they may decide the information they want is not worth the price—their time. They will assume that all other levels of information contain the same signal-to-noise (information-to-graphic) ratio and discontinue browsing.

If what you are offering has intellectual value, then by all means let people have it. Such is the case with the Nokia 9000 Communicator. This is the mobile phone with a keyboard inside that lets you get your e-mail, send faxes, and even surf the Web. Nokia put up a wonderful Shockwave demo of this phone that's well worth the wait, even at a hefty 350k (Figure 6.7).

NAVIGATION IN ALL THINGS

A Web site designer's job is to help people find their way around. If users have trouble finding anything of interest or get lost within your Web site, they will become frustrated and disinterested. Strong visual clues can help users access desired information—including the information you want them to see.

Take several factors into account when you give navigational clues. People respond to the computer screen differently than they do to paper, but we continue to create Web sites as if they were going to be printed. Learning to shift gears is not simple.

Computer design has traditionally been in the hands of engineers, with some help from human factors researchers. Engineering frequently comes first in design due to economic constraints. When Xerox rolled out its 860 word processor, it had an $8\frac{1}{2} \times 11$-inch screen to mimic paper and used dark letters on a white background. These were very unusual features at the time. But the marketplace voted with its feet and demanded less expensive machines, which meant smaller screens—something we've lived with ever since. Now that laptops are ubiquitous, the small screen is here to stay. Therefore, we must design with this format in mind.

There are an infinite number of ways to navigate through electronic space. We've seen enough good and bad examples to get a handle on what works and what doesn't.

Page Size

The majority of users, whether at work or at home, view the Web from a PC or Macintosh platform with screens smaller than those found on the majority of UNIX workstations. Although it is impossible to gauge the size of a browser window (it's user selectable), it is better to err on the assumption that the window is small. This creates an uncoupling between Web developers (usually on UNIX workstations or graphically configured PCs and Macs with 19" screens) and users (usually on screens 14" or smaller).

Navigational tools should be organized to accommodate smaller screens by allowing quick traversing without scrolling. People look at a

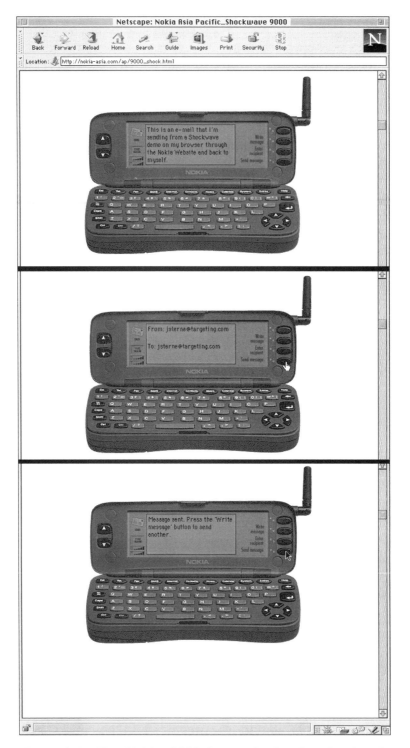

Figure 6.7 The Nokia 9000 is worth the download wait because it's packed with information.

FROM *WHAT MAKES PEOPLE CLICK:*

At the International Design Festival 1996 in Glasgow, Peter Gillespie from VOICE Creative Engineering got up and told the highbrow audience of artists and engineers that he felt certain the World Wide Web would be the engine of the return of style. Pure style.

I had seen enough of the Web to wonder what on earth he'd been drinking so early in the morning. Most Web sites circa 1996 were dreadful affairs created by members of the MIS department in their spare time. Only a handful of marketing people were on the ball and creating anything that could even remotely be thought of as stylish. "I rest my hopes on the fact that the Web is one of the most restrictive canvases ever offered to an artist," said Gillespie.

I cocked my head in attention.

"The Web's usable area for presentation is not much bigger than the span of your hand."

I sat up in my chair.

"The color palette is actually less than 256 colors if you want your work to be the same on all monitors."

He was speaking from experience.

"There are limitations to the nifty computer images you can create due to the need for the smallest file size you can manage."

He got it! He understood what Madison Avenue had missed by a mile.

"When you only have black ink and a twig to draw with, you tend to sharpen your sense of style. So it is my hope that, as this medium grows in popularity and attracts more and better designers, they will recognize these limitations and work within them. Doing so can only result in a return to pure style."

He had convinced me. I'm now hopeful, too.

---

paper page of text and assume an unfinished article will continue on the following pages. People consider computer screens differently. A word processing document is scrolled as it is created and scrolled as it is read. But most computer software has trained us to view a page at a time. You would never expect to scroll horizontally to read a document. This aversion to "thinking outside the box" should be recognized and considered in respect to vertical scrolling as well.

Using the Title Bar as Placeholder

A common approach uses the title bar as a placeholder, allowing the user to move back "up" the hierarchy. It's implemented by having a solid icon across the top for the home page and smaller icons designating layers. The user can see the depth of the current level by glancing at the bar.

One of my favorite examples of good navigation is found on the Epson site (www.epson.com) in its section on imaging products (Figure 6.8). There is such a simplicity of design that it's worth a quick look.

The menu bar across the top uses color coding. The first four buttons are blue, which groups them as product categories. The next, "Epson Connection," is yellow and "What's New" is red, setting them apart as separate types of content.

The next horizontal section identifies the current page as being Home/Office Products (on the left) and presents an internal advertisement (on the right). Between the two is a submenu with next-level navigation. The submenu identifies this page as the Product Information page by showing the button next to the menu choice as being pushed in. It's also colored red, while the rest are gray.

The bottom of the screen has the Web-site-wide, corporate button bar, which cuts across all products and ties the whole piece together. Those choices appear on every page. But it's the top two menus that hold your attention as you move from one subcategory to the next and from one product type to the next.

Figure 6.9 shows product information for the Graphic Arts products. What you notice right away is that the second horizontal section identifies the current page as being Graphic Arts Products (on the left) and presents an internal advertisement (on the right). Between the two is a submenu with next-level navigation.

By looking at only two screens, you know exactly how the rest of this Web site is laid out. You'll never get lost, and you know right where to look to determine where you are and where you want to go.

Using an Index

When designing a navigational metaphor, remember that you are dealing with conflicting goals. On one hand, you want to make it as easy to get around as possible. On the other hand, you want to engage and entertain your audience.

John December was offering Internet advice and information through his company, CMC Information Sources (www.december.com), long before the Web's existence. John sits at the opposite end of the interface spectrum from the Big Graphic approach.

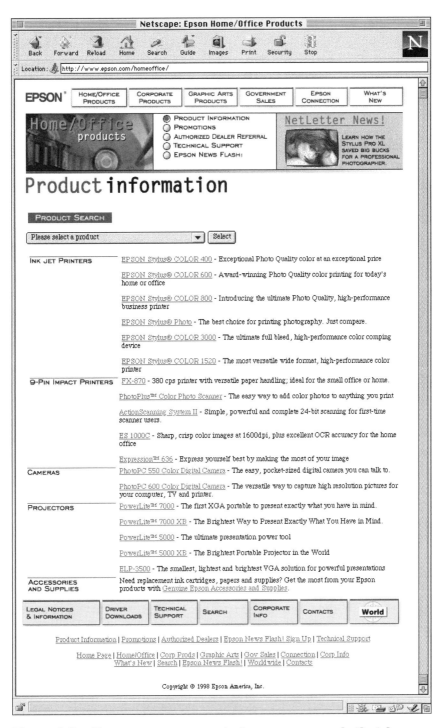

Figure 6.8   Epson uses a menu/submenu approach that is very straightforward.

Figure 6.9   Espon makes a point of staying consistent.

CMC Information Sources offers an Internet guide (Figures 6.10 through 6.12) with an indentable index. The user may select from three levels of indentation to find a general topic or a specific item. Although not very entertaining, this menu system is extremely efficient. It uses a table of contents metaphor that is instantly familiar to all. Being able to dig deeper into the index from the topmost level lets users see the whole document at once. At the same time, there is no need to scroll through an interminable alphabetical list or click over and over again to reach down into the depths of a Web site.

If a user has to select subgroup after subgroup, the opportunities for frustration and disappointment run high. Help for most software packages used to be found in manuals only. Then software manufacturers put their documentation online. After they received sufficient user complaints, companies added search tools to online Help. As a result, somebody looking for advice on a specific feature could ask for the section instead of having to hunt for it.

Using a Map

GTE (www.gte.com) uses a simple screen full of text as a site map (Figure 6.13) and makes use of information clumping to separate the different categories.

Sears (www.sears.com) takes a more graphical approach (Figure 6.14), although they are also kind enough to provide a text-only version called the Site Index. They give you the choice.

Cisco Systems has such a large site that they offer a bit of mapping right up front on their home page (Figure 6.15). They use the mouse roll-over

Figure 6.10   CMCs Internet Guide Index 1 shows chapter headings only.

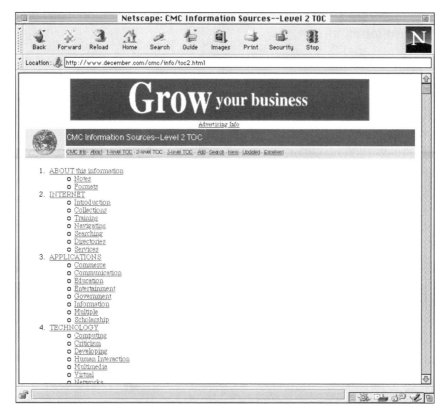

Figure 6.11   CMCs Internet Guide Index 2 displays the sub-headings in each chapter.

technique to help you see what you will find in each category. Its real site map is one of the most complex you're likely to find (Figure 6.16).

Using a Picture as a Map

The folks at Nabisco (www.nabisco.com) know who their audience is—kids! That's why they chose to fill their home page with lots of colorful and animated Stuff, with a capital S (Figure 6.17). They must think kids are gluttons for Web punishment. They may be right; most kids have more patience than I do.

The Arcade, the Cinema, the Promos building, the Town Hall, and the Kitchen are joined in a click of the Uptown/Downtown buttons (and several long moments of waiting) by the Store, the Museum, the Health Club, and the School (Figure 6.18).

Figure 6.12   CMCs Internet Guide Index 3 reveals the subsub-headings to give the user a clear picture of the contents.

Do you suppose the design team had really wide monitors and it worked fine for them? My guess is that they went for the navigation-as-game model, which may work. All I ask is that you know exactly who your target audience is and that you test the heck out of any design that gets between your audience and the content.

These days there are too many games to play and too many Web sites to see to let yourself be pushed around by the graphic artists. This home page looks great on paper, but I'll bet it appeals only to kids from three to seven. I actually want to know what new Snackwell products they've got because it is the brand that entices my tastebuds and satisfies my need for low-cal snacks. But the home page is just too much of a barrier.

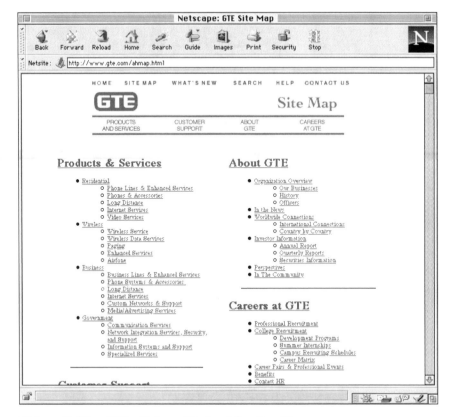

Figure 6.13   GTE sticks with text for its site map.

Using Search Tools for Navigation

The first time users call up your Web site, you should provide plenty of visual clues. They're going to need a hand understanding the metaphor you've selected, how you've laid out the site, and how to find their way around.

The first time they come to your site, they know they'll have to spend some time looking around, surfing, just to get the hang of the place. The second time users come to your site, they are usually looking for something in particular. Give them the tools to find what they're after.

Computer search tools have been the realm of the technician from the beginning. The tools created to find information have become quite efficient. Unfortunately, there is a trade-off between ease of use and value of

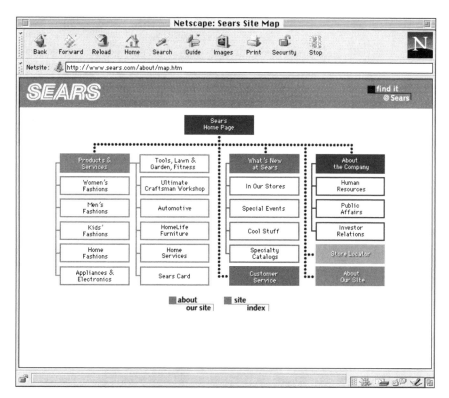

Figure 6.14   Sears uses an organizational chart to help you locate things on their site.

the output. On some sites, putting in a search word and clicking the Submit button is simple, but the value of the reply may be low.

A quick search on the Mercedes-Benz site (www.mercedes.com) for a CD player turns up some startling results (Figure 6.19).

You have to love the first couple of responses:

Just a quick aside: I'd like to entreat you all to find something other than "Submit" to put on those search buttons and survey forms. I mean, really. Somebody says "Submit!" to me and I figure I'm supposed to fall to the floor and put my paws in the air. "Surrender, Dorothy!"

How about "Search"? That's not so hard. And on forms and surveys, how about "Send" or "Transmit"? Come on, let's show a little originality. Anybody for "Vouchsafe"?

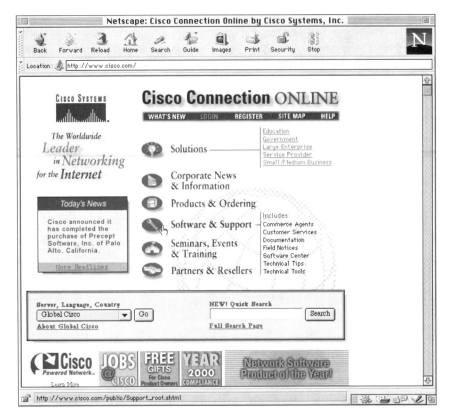

Figure 6.15 **Cisco lets you take a peek into each of the subcategories available from their home page.**

```
Summary: 10 && to_url. indexOf("//") > 0) { to_url =
to_url.
substring (ns3pos, to_url. length); to_ns3url += to_url;
} else {
to_ns3url = to_url; } self. location = to_ns3url +
"?_back=" + _url.
```

The first two are merely incomprehensible and can be ignored. The problem comes when trying to figure out which of the next choices will have any real information on CD players.

There's something about a digital road map stored on a CD-ROM from the Engineering Glossary. And there's the Owner's Manual and something

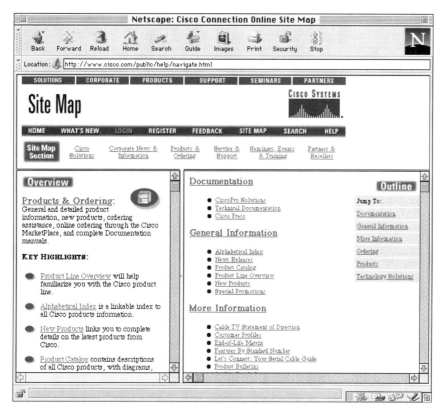

**Figure 6.16   The complexity of the Cisco Site Map exhibits the
depth of the site.**

about Mercedes sponsoring the ATP Tennis Tour. Ah! Here we go, ninth
one down says "Standard Equipment on the G 500 V8; Interior Air condi-
tioning, 'Audio 10' radio (representing a new generation of radios) with
cassette-tape player, steering wheel and shift lever in burled walnut/
leather, shift lever knob emblazoned with star and . . ." I read all the way
down to, "Chrome-effect radiator crossbars and white blinkers in front
and on the side," and I figure I'm in the wrong place. And the rest of the
entries are like the first two. About as useful as a CL600 Coupe with no
wheels.

I don't mean to blast Mercedes as being the only navigationally
impaired Web site out there. Search tools are very hard to implement well.

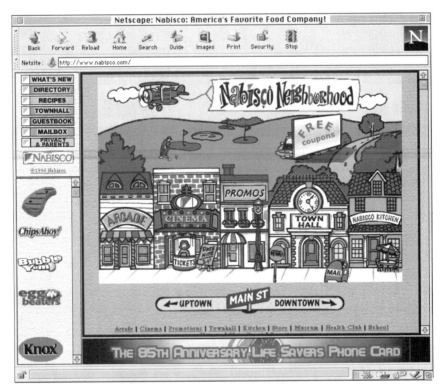

Figure 6.17   **Nabisco gives us the chance to take a scroll down-town.**

User Interface Engineering (www.uie.com) ran an article about it in its Fall 1997 newsletter entitled, "Why On-Site Searching Sucks." The conclusions?

First of all, typos. You don't really think of it as much of a problem until you see the newsletter's list of 16 different ways to misspell "JavaScript." Next: meaningless results. Not just the meaningless jabber that Mercedes is guilty of, but questions of relevancy, results with too little information to be useful, and the fact that the word "dinosaur" shows up prominently in a *Smithsonian Magazine* article about the steel industry. The bottom line, it concluded, "showed that today's on-site search engines are worse than nothing—significantly worse. Searching is a difficult problem with no solution visible on the horizon. Until the technology is equal to the challenge, we suggest that designers seriously consider not including a search engine on their sites until the technology is equal to the challenge (sic)." Please take that with the appropriate grain of salt.

As a group, the search engines of computer software companies received the highest mark overall (3.8 average out of 5). One of the smartest search engines we found was at IBM's site. When reviewers searched for Lotus Development Corp.'s somewhat obscure word processing program, AmiPro, the engine returned links to WordPro, the program that replaced AmiPro. But even more impressive, it didn't bring back numerous links that had nothing to do with the subject. IBM's summaries were refreshingly direct, devoid of any mysterious characters and presented in plain English.

But there is some good out there. When *Computerworld* (March 9, 1998, page 83) reviewed search engines on various Web sites, it gave the highest rating to IBM.

A search tool that can find things on your site quickly and elegantly might also be able to find things on the Web quickly and elegantly. The cre-

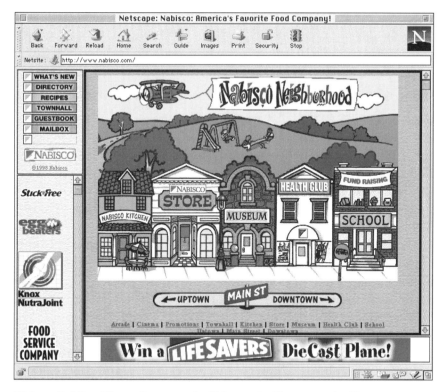

Figure 6.18   There is more to this page than meets the eye.

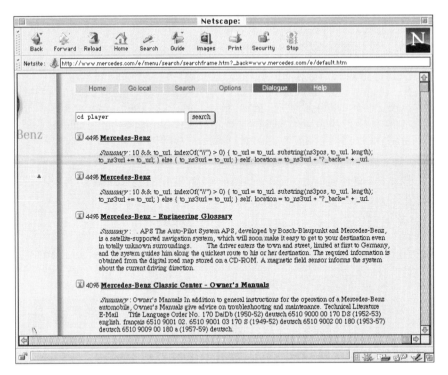

Figure 6.19   Mercedes doesn't pass the smog inspection for searchability.

ator of such a tool will eventually be able to compare houses with Bill Gates. It's a monster problem, and millions of us are anxious for a solution.

Interesting efforts are underway as we speak. Inxight (www.inxight .com) has come up with several alternatives including the hyperbolic tree (Figure 6.20) and the cone tree (Figure 6.21).

For locating more complex information, more sophisticated tools are required. The Web builders at Sears, Roebuck and Co. knew they faced an uphill battle trying to point the way to more than 2000 products in the Sears' Craftsman line. Their solution, called The Craftsman Tool Search, puts technology to good use (Figure 6.22).

Five different tool categories are represented on the left. They stay there—they're static. Click on a category, and its contents appear in the list in the middle column. Click on another category, and the list in the center column changes. This arrangement allows you to move quickly through "Bench/Stationary Tools" to "Hand Tools" to "Portable Power Tools" without leaving the page. The middle column lets you scroll through Cord-

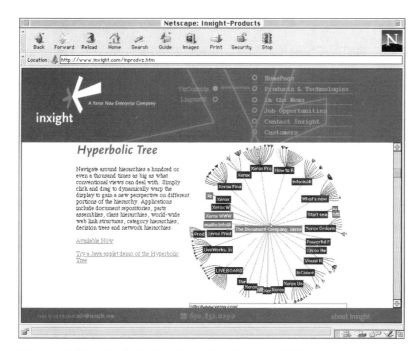

Figure 6.20   Inxight has imagined your Web site as a multi-dimensional globe . . .

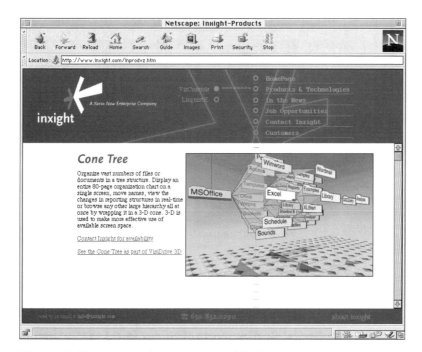

Figure 6.21   . . . and as a cone of links.

less Tools, Drills, Planers/Plate Joiners, Rotary Tools, Routers and Saws, and their subcategories. One more click shows you the 3½-Hp Plunge Router of your dreams. This page lets the home improvement maven sort through all those lovely tools without learning about Bayesian logic.

The goal is to get the computer to think like a human instead of making the human think like a machine.

Think Like a Customer

You have to forget that you know everything there is to know about your products and services. You have to try to understand what it's like being a customer who tries to slog through your massive Web site in search of that one bit of information that will help them decide which of your offerings is right for them.

Everybody with a computer needs a printer. But have you seen how many choices there are in the wonderful world of computer printers?

Figure 6.22   The Sears' Craftsman tool finder is a great example of using a specific tool to solve a specific problem.

Where's the aspirin? A quick look at two manufacturers' sites, HP and Xerox, gives an eye-opening look at the fact that a Web site is a software application, not a brochure.

HP Printers

Time was, if you went looking for a printer on the Hewlett-Packard site (www.hp.com), you would begin by scanning the home page for the "Products" button. The Products page (Figure 6.23) was a test to see how much of a nerd you were. Did you know enough to click on "Peripherals," as opposed to "Computing" or "Components"? "Peripherals" led to a page that included the "Printers" button, in all its glory. Not exactly the shortest distance between two points.

HP took a look at its logs and discovered that quite a few people were interested in printers. In fact, almost half of those who came to the home page were seeking printer information. So, HP took a bold step: It changed its home page. Now the very first button on the home page is "Printing & Imaging."

When I searched the HP Web site for "printer," I got 11,177 documents that HP thought I should take a look at. The first one is "Printer Compatibility Guide for Network and Spectrum Analyzers." Not quite what I was looking for.

At this point I clicked the "Search Help" button on the side and got a big surprise. In an earlier rendition, HP offered search instructions that went on for pages and pages. It was remarkable. Even computer scientists would need to read the instructions to understand the difference between a concept search and a Boolean search and study the "Keyword Advisor," the "Dictionary Advisor," the "Relate Advisor," and the "Fuzzy Match Advisor." There were also choices for a UNIX search screen and a Windows search screen. But that was before.

This time, the Search Help page is short and sweet. And to my amazement, exactly what I was looking for (Figure 6.24).

It sure looked as if HP knew I was looking for printers and showed me examples of how to find the printer of my dreams. But it was not to be. A quick search for "blood-gas analyzers" turned up a very manageable 13 documents for my inspection. A subsequent click on Search Help revealed that the "LaserJet OR printer-LaserJet AND printer-LaserJet NOT driver" suggestions are static and not context-sensitive at all. Shoot. I *so* wanted HP to be way out in front.

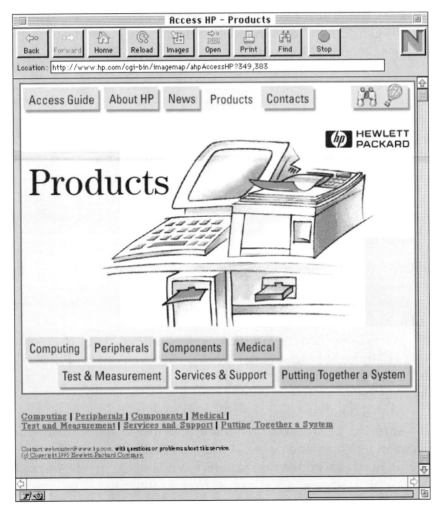

Figure 6.23   Quick! What do you click on for printers?

Knowing HP, I recommend that you head back over to its site and look for yourself. Things change fast on the Internet.

Think Like a Customer—Xerox

I've been following a technology company called Saqqara for several years now. It makes a database/search engine called Step Search, and it's a winner. I've seen great demos with laptops, and I've seen customer implementations like integrated circuits and electronic components—they are all top notch. When I saw what Xerox had done with it, I realized I had found an application everybody could appreciate.

At first glance, the Product Selector (www.xerox.com/cgi-bin/selector?RT=SS&FAM=Printers) (Figure 6.25) looks a bit intimidating. There's a lot to choose from, but that's deceptive. Instead of trying to build a printer from scratch, Xerox asks you to select the single most important thing to you:

> START YOUR SEARCH by finding your key feature on the left.
>   Then select ONE of its options on the right that best meets your needs.
>   Each time you select an option, a new screen with your remaining choices will appear.
>   You can UNDO a selection at any time by clicking again on that selection.

Let's say the most important thing to you is that the printer is capable of putting out documents with a resolution of 600×600 dots per inch. You

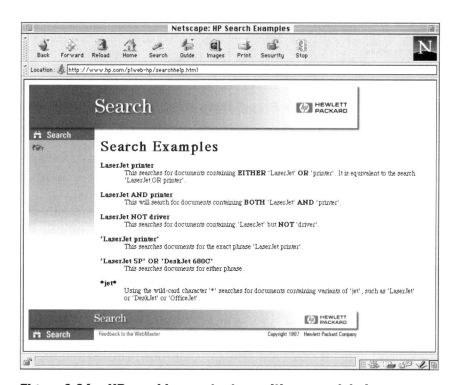

Figure 6.24   HP provides context-sensitive search help.

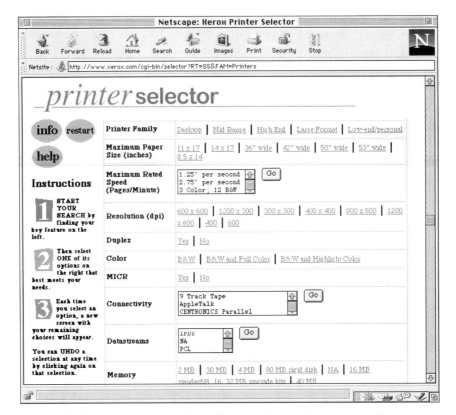

Figure 6.25   Xerox uses Step Search from Saqqara to "help you choose."

click on that one option for that one feature, and the rest of the noise fades away. The very next screen lets you know that there are 11 Xerox printers to choose from (Figure 6.26) and awaits your next criterion.

Looking over the choices, you see that you realize you only need 8½ × 14-inch paper so you click on that. On the next page you indicate you don't need color printing. Now you're down to four printers, and things are about to get interesting (Figure 6.27).

Notice that this screen has sprouted a new button: Compare. It wasn't there a moment ago. Xerox selected a threshold number at which the compare button pops up and gives you a chance to really inspect the products that fit so that you can find the product that's best.

When HP felt it had found the three or four printers that fit, it showed pictures of them, offered a brief description, and added a link for each one to take you to the detailed account. Step Search lets Xerox do a little more leg work for you, and the result is shopping-made-easier (Figure 6.28).

Take a look at the bottom of the screen in Figure 6.25. That's what all four printers have in common—not just the things you selected, but also some things you didn't know about. In this case, none of the printers has MICR (Magnetic Ink Character Recognition). You weren't going to print checks anyway, were you?

The top part of the screen lets you ponder the differences. You might lean toward 12 pages per minute rather than 8, but 135 is completely unnecessary. The printer you want will be attached to an Ethernet. The big question then is whether you need 2 or 4 megabytes of memory. Oh—and the price, of course. Unfortunately, we run up against one of those thorny

Figure 6.26   With 11 printers that meet your needs, it's time to define your needs a little better.

Figure 6.27   In just a few clicks, you've considerably narrowed the field.

issues you'll find discussed in Chapter 12, "A Few Thorny Issues." HP is a manufacturer, and the distribution chain gets a little kinked when the manufacturer publishes pricing.

Think Like a Customer—Yourself

No matter what you sell, people want access to information about your product. Your job is twofold. On one hand, give them so much information that they will not go wanting. Everybody will be able to find that scrap of information he or she is after. On the other hand, use all the tools, techniques, tricks, and ingenuity you can muster to help users find that information as quickly and painlessly as possible. Make sure they can get to it and make a buying decision before they click away to the next vendor down on the Yahoo-list.

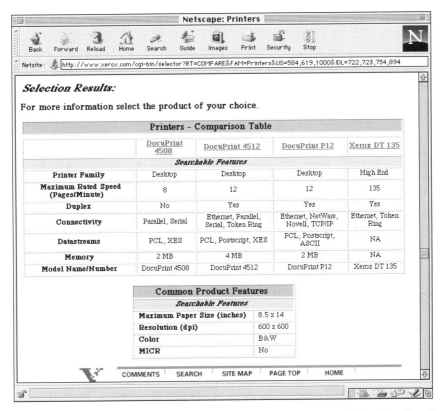

Figure 6.28   A quick compare lets you quickly pick the best printer.

Don't Lose Them to Another Site

Many are the times it makes sense to offer a promotional plug to a business ally. A Web site should be a resource to your customers. That may mean telling them where to get additional information on specific subjects. These types of links are valuable to people, and they will come back to your Web site again and again if they see it as a useful source of pointers to other information. But first, consider a couple of ideas to ensure that you haven't spent a lot of time encouraging your users to see P. T. Barnum's Grand Egress.

You want to be sure that the links to the outside world are properly positioned so that it is abundantly clear that the user is now leaving your site. The underground interconnections between the buildings around New York's World Trade Center are very useful all year round, but it's quite easy for visitors to lose track of which building they're under at any given time.

Tell users that they may find more information at these sites, but be sure to let them know why they need to come back after they've been here. You might even offer an incentive if they come back with proof of their visit, like getting a game card stamped at a trade show.

"We're Not Liable"

Some company lawyers feel it's necessary to tell people that the company is no longer responsible for anything found beyond the next click.

The folks at Staples didn't want to be burdened with managing their own press-release clippings page, but they did want to let people read about their achievements. On the About Staples, Inc. page (www.staples.com) (Figure 6.29), they offer press releases, stock quotes, and SEC filings—but not directly.

Right there, next to the link, Staples invites you to "Access these topics and more via the Business Wire news distribution service." But they don't let you get away easily. A clerk at the door stops you and says, "Are you sure there isn't something else you'd like to buy?" (Figure 6.30).

It's not exactly a disclaimer, and it's not a warning; it's a heads-up. If you've ever watched people who are relatively new to the Web as they navigate around, it's surprising how quickly they can get lost. This is Staples' way of adding that software application function that says, "Are you suuuuuuure?".

Sidetracked

Because HP doesn't quote prices and doesn't sell direct, it wants you to find a dealer or a reseller in your neighborhood. Put in your Zip code and up comes a map with stars on it indicating the locations nearest you. Each location is listed in a table with addresses and phone numbers—and links.

But HP doesn't really want you to go. Good netiquette says it should provide a link, but time-honored business sense says don't let them out the front door! So HP created an alternative universe.

You click on a link to a dealer and up pops a brand new window with the dealer's Web site in it while the window with the HP site sticks around for further surfing. Good strategy? Could be. Potential problems? Yes.

I'm the kind of guy who surfs multiple windows at a time. I'll go to Yahoo! to search for something, and then "Open new window with this link" on the first thing I think might have what I want. As soon as the new window is open, I click on the Yahoo! window to bring it to the front. Then

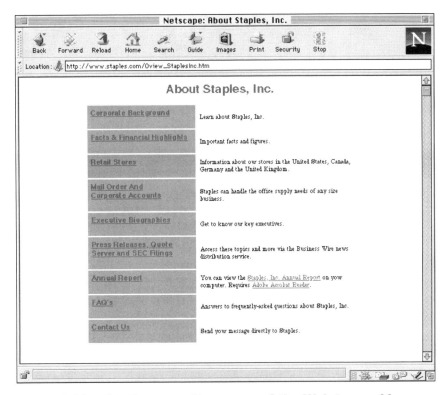

Figure 6.29   Staples uses the power of the Web to provide more content to visitors.

I can "Open new window with this link" on the next item that catches my eye. This way, data is being downloaded from three or four sites at the same time. I can go back to window 2 and read it while windows 3, 4, and 5 are still drawing down data.

If one of those windows is running Java and I open another one with

---

JAVA

Briefly put, Java is a programming language that's wonderful for the Web. It lets programmers write very short pieces of software that download and run on your computer. The advantage is that you can do calculations, paint pictures, fill in spreadsheets, all on your local machine, without having to go back to the Web site server for the results.

Java offers lots of power on your Web pages, but it must be used with caution because downloading programs is much slower than downloading pages. Plus, there's the "conflicting pages" problem I've just described.

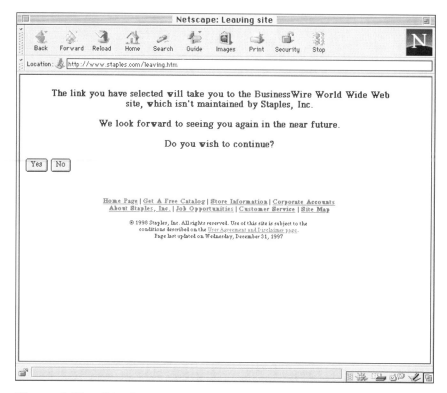

Figure 6.30   Staples stops you before you surf away.

Java, they can conflict and hose my machine. A Java conflict will make a Windows machine browser disappear in the blink of an eye. On a Mac, it will freeze the whole system and force you to restart.

So, if you choose to pop open a new screen without the visitor's consent, you might use up system resources that user doesn't have available. Too many open windows can thrash memory. That's not a nice way to treat people.

The Distributor Dilemma

A distributor makes a living by promoting and selling other companies' products. Retailers that create Web pages with links to all of their vendors' Web sites will never make a sale. "Welcome to Jim's Ski Shop—Click here to go to any of our fine manufacturers: Atomic Skis, Fischer Skis, Ghost Snowboards, and Rossignol. Oh, and thanks for dropping by. Have a nice day!" Distributors have the same problem.

Marshall Industries (www.marshall.com) is a distributor of electronic components. On their Search By Manufacturer page, they list 271 different manufacturers. If they let you go to those manufacturers' sites, Marshall would never make a sale. So what do they do?

Marshall solved this problem by creating a separate set of Web pages for each of its vendors. Users at the Marshall site are treated to a site within a site, in this example, Fujitsu (Figure 6.31). Marshall has hosted the vendor's information on their own Web site to make sure the user won't wander off and miss all the other products Marshall sells. This requires a good bit of extra work, but it is a safe and sane solution.

Knowing that their customers will not be satisfied with the limited information Marshall can post compared to what the manufacturer offers, Marshall implemented something not too distant from the HP approach, but much more palatable and less confusing to the surfer: closed captions for the surfing impaired.

You'll notice in Figure 6.32 that there's a section called Smart Links. Marshall has identified the best pages on its manufacturers' Web sites and offered links to those pages, but without letting the site visitor leave completely.

No matter where you go in the Fujitsu site, the Marshall header goes along with you. One click, and you're back to Marshall's Fujitsu page. Clever.

CONTROLLING THE ACTION

A brochure is a linear medium. You expect people to read it from front to back. People expect you to have written it to be read from front to back. Knowing that some people will want to jump right to the information that's important to them, you can offer an index or table of contents. A Web site is not a linear medium. By its nature, people are free to hyperjump wherever they choose. It is incumbent upon the Web designer to create a site that encourages people to select the right links.

Many dollars are spent studying what people look at when they see an ad, a store shelf, or the inside of a department store. The graphic artist spends hours arriving at just the right layout to draw the prospect's attention to the salient components. The department store designer works feverishly to ensure that the sight lines from every entrance lead shoppers to the most profitable departments, aisles, and shelves. Consumer goods packaging is a science. Shelf positioning is a hard-fought contest steeped in the

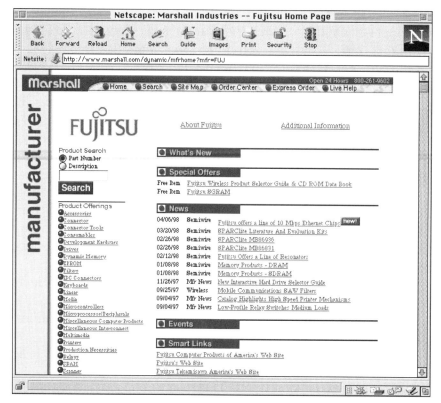

Figure 6.31 Marshall Industries creates micro-sites for their vendors, to keep customers from leaving the Marshall site.

knowledge of how the eye roves over competing brands. These activities are a mere game of checkers when compared to the three-dimensional chess of an interactive Web site. CD-ROM designers have been sweating the details over the management of game players, and now you are tasked with helping the online shopper.

You are going to create an electronic environment for people to explore. What do you want them to find? Where do you want them to look first? What do you want them to learn? And, most of all, what do you want them to do? Whether you're selling a toy, a car, a service, or a political perspective, you must determine what outcome you want. In fact, you have competing desires: You must support multiple products.

You must also cater to the casually curious, the seriously prospective, and the current customer with a problem to solve. Therefore, with your

Figure 6.32   Marshall encased Fujitsu's site with a header that will bring you back when you're done.

goals firmly in mind, look to your home page (the first thing a user sees when visiting your site) to set the standard style and begin the process of moving the user toward your objective.

The Home Page

There are as many choices for the look and feel of a home page as there are artists, programmers, and marketing managers. No matter what corporate personality you are trying to project, some basics apply. The first is to make it a nice place to visit.

Learning from the Past

The Microsoft home page (Figure 6.33) used to be hideous. There. Now I've done it. Somewhere in the world is a programmer who created this vision of a home page in 1994, and I have offended him or her deeply. Maybe some of you reading this book like this graphic. Maybe I've offended more than just one.

You may or may not like the picture, but it's devoid of meaning. Is it a landscape? Half a nova exploding? A diskette partially eaten by screensavers? It doesn't communicate Microsoft at all. The only brand awareness on this page was the Microsoft typeface. Where's the Windows logo? Is this really Microsoft? This flat, low-resolution image did nothing to instill confidence in the company.

Keep It Simple   The basic rule Microsoft seems to have ignored is the KISS principle (keep it simple, stupid). Keep it crystal clear. The KISS principle is in effect on the Web like nowhere else. People want instant gratification from their computers and from you. They want to get where they're going. If you don't offer supercool visuals, then let me at the information.

Unfortunately, this home page was cumbersome. Too many choices were scattered across the sky. It took a few minutes to determine which category to select to find out about a bug.

A handful of usual suspects is found on most home pages:

```
What's New
      What's been added since (date)
      Press releases
Company and Industry Events
About the Company
      History
      Current accomplishments
      Financials (for public companies)
      Upper management Who's Who
About the Industry
      White papers
      Special knowledge we have that you want
About Our Products
      Product line A
      Product line B
      Product line C
Customer Service
      Frequently asked questions
      Order processing support
      Product support
      How to contact us
Employment Opportunities
```

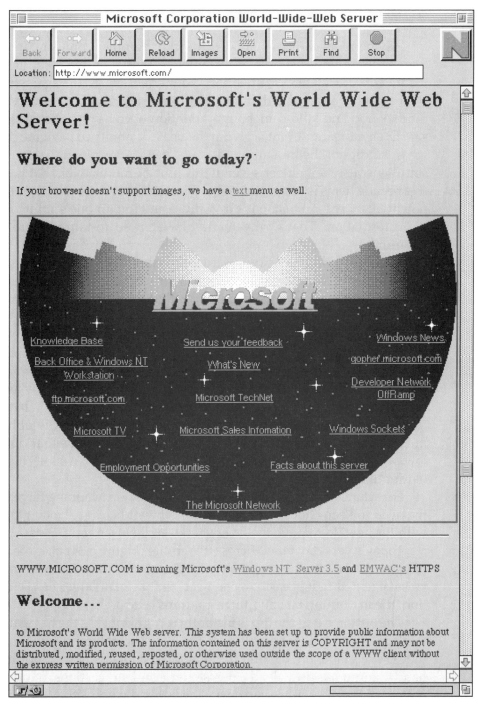

Figure 6.33   The Microsoft home page of old—ugly and disorganized.

Having more choices than these quickly becomes confusing in any setting. Keeping things simple is absolutely essential on the Web. In the first place, you are vying for attention. Your Web site is up against 250,000 choices today and twice that by noon tomorrow. You have a very limited time to grab and hold somebody's attention once he or she comes to your site. Even more important is giving the user the ability to navigate properly.

In studies of the human mind, it has been determined that people can simultaneously remember seven items plus or minus two. That is, a list of five to nine items is just about right. Less than that doesn't make use of the potential; more than that tends to confuse and impair one's ability to retain the information. That's why menus in Chinese restaurants are always daunting.

Information Mapping (www.infomap.com) has made it its business to help companies put their information, instructions, and procedures online. It started years ago on mainframes. At that time it was determined that, on a computer screen, people can remember only five items, plus or minus one.

The reasons for this are still being argued. Perhaps because the page is smaller, there are fewer spatial clues than on paper. Perhaps people expect the screen to scroll away or present new data any second, so they are speed reading instead of concentrating for retention. Maybe they have been trained by television to believe something on the screen is ephemeral, momentary, and of dubious authenticity. Mostly, it seems that due to the lower resolution on a screen (72 dots per inch, rather than 600+), it's simply harder to read.

For whatever reason, the people at Information Mapping have verified the need to keep choices to a minimum. The art lies in balancing that limit with the need to remove the layers between the user and the data.

Today's version of the Microsoft Web site (Figure 6.34) uses the concept of information chunking quite well. What looks to be an overwhelming mass of text at first is easily recognized as four main areas of visual attention, the top button bar, and three columns of text.

The button bar at the top is instantly recognizable as the navigation tool that's going to follow you all over the site. The column on the left is the index/site guide, the column in the middle contains news, and the right-hand column has downloads, newsletters, and suggestions. (Notice at the bottom of the right side, even on a page as text-heavy as this, there is a text-only option. Unlike many others on the Web, this option really is text only.)

After four years of Web site development, the de facto standard seems to have fallen to the left side for the site guide and, in keeping with the times, Microsoft chunks this menu once again. There are seven choices, none of which contains more than six options:

Recommended For You
    Free Newsletters
    Visitor Guide
Products & Services
    Free Downloads
    Product Catalog
    Technical Support
    Events & Seminars
    Training & Certification
    3rd Party Referrals
Business Solutions
    Digital Nervous System
    IT Executive/SystemPro
    Industries
    Small Businesses
Developer & Partner Resources
    Software Developers
    Web Site Builders
    Solution Providers
    Resellers & Consultants
    Becoming a Partner
Personal Computing
    Magazine
    Games
    Kids
    Online Services
Education Computing
    Education Resources
    Higher Education
    K–12 Education
About Microsoft
    Your Privacy
    About the Site
    Company Overview
    Jobs
    News for the Press
    Stockholder Info

Figure 6.34   Microsoft counts on "chunking" to help the neophyte visitor decipher this home page.

I'll be the first to admit that I am over 40, wear glasses, and refuse to buy a monitor that costs more than a decent hotel room for a night in New York. Nevertheless, I can't help but believe the majority of people surfing the Web these days finds that left-hand column just a tad too small to make out.

Aside from that, Microsoft has found a way to cram a lot of information on a page without making it a giant muddle.

Keep It Flat Looking for information is hard enough if you don't know where to look. Pursuing data requires patience and fortitude. Using a Web browser means honing your skills at following a train of thought.

If you are offering a service to the user, make it easy to use. If you are providing valuable data to the user, make it easy to find. You must not give too many choices on each menu, but you must not require too many clicks to get to the information. So, you're damned if you do and damned if you don't. After all, each click is an opportunity for users to choose the wrong path, forget what they wanted in the first place, and become frustrated that this marvelous medium (and therefore your company) isn't delivering on its promise.

Federal Express seems to have taken a giant step backward in this regard. When the Web was young, the FedEx home page was, well, boring (Figure 6.35). But that was OK because you could find the one thing you were looking for.

Federal Express got it right the first time for two reasons: technical limitations and lack of imagination. Back in the dark ages, the background of your Web site could be any color you wanted as long as it was gray. Everybody's Web site was gray; that's what there was. For navigation, it was a breeze. The third item got all the attention: Track a FedEx package. That's what we all wanted to do.

Over the course of time, Federal Express has altered its design. It has more technical choices in how its pages look. It has more graphic artists designing the site, instead of the task being left to the engineers who built it. The result is absolutely frustrating (Figure 6.36).

How long does it take to track a package now? Consider the steps required. From the home page (which does not load in a jiffy), you have to identify which country you're in. Or is that which country you're shipping to? If you're visiting Mexico, do you pick Mexico or "your" country?

Then, there is an interminable wait for the next page to show up (Figure 6.37). Even if you know where the "Tracking" button is going to pop up, it takes a lifetime to do so.

Maybe FedEx did a study, reviewed its server logs, and stopped people on the street for interviews. Maybe it discovered that most of the people who come to www.fedex.com are there for the Employment Opportunities. But even if the vast majority are *not* there to track a package, the people who are tend to be a bit anxious. Why put them through the torture of multiple pages? Why not let people enter their airbill numbers on the home page?

Study How the User Uses—The Sun Story In their paper "SunWeb: User Interface Design for Sun Microsystems' Internal Web" (www.sun.com/sun-on-net/uidesign/usabilitytest.html), Jakob Nielsen and Darrell Sano described four different usability studies to help them determine the navigational tools for the Sun Microsystems internal Web site:

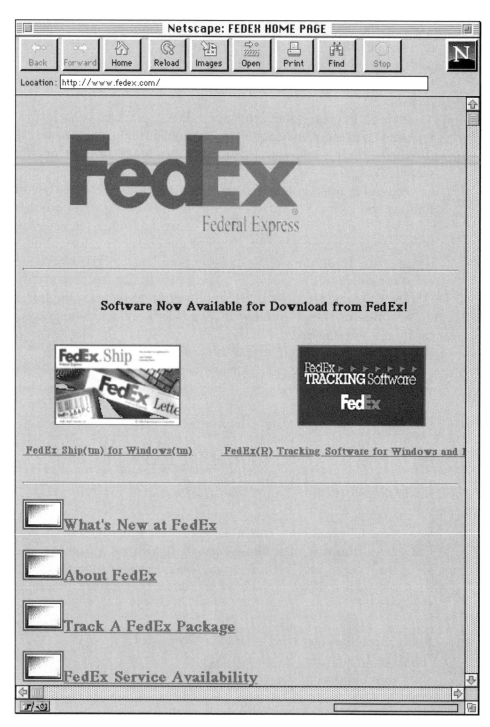

Figure 6.35   FedEx also started Web life as an ugly duckling.

1. Card sorting to discover categories
2. Icon intuitiveness testing
3. Card distribution to icons
4. Thinking aloud walkthrough of page mock-up

The team wrote up 51 types of information that might be found on the internal Web site. They wrote each on note cards and scattered them across a table. The experiment subjects were asked to sort these cards into piles based on similarity. As a result, they created proper groupings for information categories for the home page.

The resulting categories required icons or pictograms to represent them on the home page. Once the first draft of these icons was created, they were submitted to the icon intuitiveness test. Subjects were asked to interpret each unlabeled icon to see how understandable it was. Most were good or excellent, but several had to be substantially altered.

Figure 6.36   FedEx takes one step forward and three back with its new design.

The two tests were then combined. The new icons were printed and handed to subjects, who then had to place them in the proper categories on the table. This test ensured that users would associate the correct concepts with each of the general groups previously defined. The "thinking aloud" study simply asked subjects what sort of information they would expect to find behind each of the icons.

> The conclusions from this project are that a uniform user interface structure can make a Web significantly easier to use and that "discount usability engineering" can be employed to base the design on user studies even when project schedules are very tight.

Today, the Sun Web site is the starting point for more than a thousand internal Web servers.

Study How the User Uses—In Real Time It's one thing to think about how you would use your Web site if you were a customer or a prospect. It's quite another to watch users in action. You can learn a huge amount from simply looking over a user's shoulder. Paul Youngworth, a programmer/analyst at a Midwest-based manufacturing company, learned by simply watching people use a software package he had just written. Youngworth offers some observational advice in an article titled "Being There" in *Computerworld* (April 10, 1995, p. 99).

> You are likely to get the most information about your subjects' natural working habits if you keep a low profile. Here are some tips for observing users in action:
> When you talk to users about your visit, make it clear that you will be judging the (software) application you've just installed—not their proficiency.
> Place yourself out of the way.
> Fight the temptation to offer unsolicited advice about their use of the application during the session. Be a silent observer as much as possible.
> If users seem distracted by other priorities, offer to come back at a more convenient time.
> If users seem unusually self-conscious because of your presence, try getting up for a drink of water or some other excuse and then quietly returning when they are concentrating on their work.

More Modern Methods For a slide show on how to do usability testing of your Web site, visit Usable Products Company (www.usableproducts .com). Many companies are springing up to lend you a hand. See what Two

Figure 6.37   FedEx, take two. You're getting closer . . .

Figure 6.38   . . . to entering your airbill number.

Rivers Consulting is up to at www.tworivers.com, and subscribe to *User Interface Engineering*'s newsletter at www.uie.com.

Like other areas in this book, this section has just covered the tips of the icebergs. For more in-depth information, I recommend *Information Architecture for the World Wide Web* by Louis Rosenfeld and Peter Moreville (O'Reilly, 1998) and *Designing Large-Scale Web Sites: A Visual Design Methodology* by Darrell Sano (John Wiley & Sons, 1996).

WATCH YOUR LANGUAGE

Ron Richards of ResultsLab (www.resultslab.com) has a great deal of experience fine-tuning new-media materials for his clients. He points out ways you can multiply response severalfold by making even the slightest changes in copy:

> To get big gains for a Web advertiser, the first task is to rewrite the words you want people to click on (the jump points)—turning them into compelling grabbers, with lots of genuine curiosity. For example, one of an Internet bookseller's jump points reads, "Different Trips, Different Styles," which is an attempt at creating blind curiosity, which usually fails to get users to jump because it only makes sense after the jump. By rewriting it to read "Which Guides Are Best For Which Interests, Destinations, and Budgets?", the grabber becomes a clear offer of valuable learning and creates benefit-oriented curiosity.
>
> The key is to realize that about 95 percent of all persuasion tools are riddled with poison language and poison graphics—often dozens of hidden elements, any one of which can kill the response. Even the best sites could multiply their response if they found their missed bets. The trick is to look for the subtle ways in which you've built in confusion, triggered a qualm, suboptimized the argument sequence, lost eye-control, or failed to find language psychologically grabbing enough to stop and fascinate the fast-browsing mind.
>
> In the most powerful sites, a "gift of learning"—a "How to . . ." approach is used to "de-commercialize" the message and make it appreciated. And the advertiser's message isn't kept separated under a "click-here-for-commercial-message" icon. Instead, the advertiser's message can often be intimately bundled with the learning gift. That allows stronger, undefended persuasion. In fact, it's amazing how often this approach can virtually reset the product/service standard and disqualify all competitors.

JUST MAKE IT AS EASY AS POSSIBLE

As strangers in a strange land, your Web users need all the help they can get. As more and more sites populate the Web, more and more navigational methods, models, and tools will be created and tested on the public. Over time, some will win favor and some will be looked on as old-fashioned and clumsy. Some will appeal to different market segments, and some will be rendered useless by the changes in technology. Insist that the goals for your Web site be well established before heading out to create road signs, maps, and online suggestion-toting databases.

In April 1998, Shelley Taylor & Associates announced the results of a study of the world's 100 largest companies. The results included the fact that only 42 percent of the sites incorporated global navigation, only 22 percent used subsection navigation, and only 38 percent had site maps.

If you keep your customers' needs and desires clearly in mind at all times, it will be much easier to help users find what they're looking for.

Congratulations. You've managed to put together a Web site that offers people what they want, and they can get at it without waiting a lifetime or getting lost along the way. Now you have to find a way to hold their attention.

CHAPTER 7

Interactivity Goes
with the Flow

A Web site is not something people read, it's something people do.

A brochure is a linear, passive medium. As the reader peruses your prose she lets the information wash over her. Television is a linear, passive, time-constrained medium. While the viewer is glued to your wildly expensive 30 seconds he lets the images and sounds wash over him. A brochure is not time-constrained. The reader can pick it up and put it down any time. The television is time-constrained, unless your viewer has carefully videotaped your commercials for playback at a more convenient time. Accessing the World Wide Web can be done at any time, but it is time-constrained nonetheless.

Your Web site is always available for "picking up." Once ensconced in a Bookmark file, your home page can be retrieved as easily as if it were stored on a local disk. But people don't usually treat it that way. Usually, they set aside a period of time for an online session. During that session, they are looking for something that provides value. You can create value by offering in-depth knowledge. You'll see examples of that in Chapter 9, "Value Added Marketing—It's Personal." That chapter is about providing the perception of value. This chapter is about holding their attention.

On television you can provide the impression of authority by placing an older actor in an expensive suit behind a large desk and shooting from a lower angle. You create the impression of value with classical music, rich colors, and repetition, repetition, repetition. (If they can afford to buy all this TV time, they must be doing well!) On the Web, graphics are important, but the central mechanism to improve the impression of value is interaction.

Interaction means convincing users they are getting information instead of its being given to them. It means users feel they are actively pulling instead of having data pushed at them. To do this, you need to make them work for it.

> Wait a minute, Jim. You just got finished telling me that I have to put up as much information as possible and make it as easy as possible and now you say I should make them "work for it." Which is it?

There is a fine balance between effort and reward that will make a major difference in the perceived value of your Web site. Make it too easy, and you give the impression that it's not that important. Make it too hard, and you give the impression that it's not worth the effort. Let's try an example.

Robin, a student, picks up a book from a classmate, looks at the marked page, and copies out the paragraph into her report in progress. John, her classmate, spent two hours looking through the library to find that book and that paragraph in that book. John perceives the information to be of higher value due to the ratio of content to effort.

Robin takes John's word that the information is good. John knows that this is the right information and that it's the best information because he made the determination himself.

THE FLOW CONSTRUCT

This balance of effort and reward as it pertains to the World Wide Web is explored in "Marketing in Hypermedia Computer-Mediated Environments: Conceptual Foundations" (www2000.ogsm.vanderbilt.edu, December 15, 1994), by Donna L. Hoffman and Thomas P. Novak of the Owen Graduate School of Management at Vanderbilt University. They first define the psychological term "flow":

> Flow has been characterized as a "peculiar dynamic state—the holistic sensation that people feel when they act with total involvement." Flow involves a merging of actions and awareness, with concentration so intense there is little attention left over to consider anything else. A consumer's action in the flow state is experienced "as a unified flowing from one moment to the next, in which he or she is in control of his or her actions, and in which there is little distinction between self and environment, between stimulus and response, or

between past, present, and future" (*Beyond Boredom and Anxiety,* Csikszent-mihalyi, Jossey Bass, 1977, p. 36). Self-consciousness disappears, the consumer's sense of time becomes distorted, and the resulting state of mind is extremely gratifying.

This conjures up pictures of small children at play, athletes in the heat of competition, and any teenager glued to a video game. It also conjures up a picture of the Internet junkie at 2:00 in the morning, unable to extricate himself or herself from the screen. Hoffman and Novak explain why the experience is so addicting:

> Only when consumers perceive that the hypermedia CME [Computer-Mediated Environments] contains high enough opportunities for action (or challenges), which are matched with their own capacities for action (or skills), will flow potentially occur. This congruence between the control characteristics of the consumer's skills and the challenges of network navigation enables the consumer in flow to feel "in control of his actions and of the environment. He has no active awareness of control but is simply not worried by the possibility of lack of control" (Csikszentmihalyi, 1977, p. 44). In such cases, consumers have a sense that their skills are adequate to cope with the challenges presented by navigating the environment. When flow occurs, the moment itself is enjoyed and consumers' capabilities are stretched with the likelihood of learning new skills and increasing self-esteem and personal complexity. However, . . . if network navigation does not provide for this, then consumers will become either bored (skills exceed challenges) or anxious (challenges exceed skills) and either exit the CME or select a more or less challenging activity within the CME.

Why is a hypertext environment like the World Wide Web absolutely captivating to newcomers? Because they come to the Web with some skills in place: computer keyboard familiarity and mouse control, and a desire to see what's out there on the Net. The first thrill of astonishment comes when they grasp the portent of being able to view files from a computer in Spain one moment and from one in Finland the next. The second rush comes as they find Web sites with information of personal interest. "Gee— I could use this Web thing for school or work!" Now the new Internaut is off on the never-ending surf, clicking freely to see what else there might be.

The Web as Time Sink

It's no wonder corporate executives dread giving Web access to employees. Once hooked, the new Web surfer can spend hours and hours online. The fascination comes from the balance between skills and challenges.

In the past managers were terrified of the telephone. "Give one to each employee? What on earth for? Do you know what that would cost? Do you know how much time would be wasted? People would spend all day talking to each other instead of getting their work done!"

When Microsoft decided to put a solitaire card game in their Windows, managers were aghast. "I'll have hundreds of people playing games all day long!" In fact, it was an excellent way to train users on the hand-eye coordination required to use point-and-click functionality.

Over time, the novelty wore off. People stopped making calls just because they could and used the phone to help them do their jobs. (Except for a brief relapse a few years back. Remember those calls? "Hey! I'm on a cell-phone! That's right—I'm calling from my car!") Solitaire quickly lost its excitement, and the computer once again became a tool for efficiency.

Yes, people will spend an inordinate amount of time on the Web looking at insignificant rubbish—at first. In doing so, they will hone the skills they need to make it a truly useful tool.

Putting Flow to Work

You don't send the owner's manual to everybody who calls for a brochure. You don't offer a tour of the factory to somebody who circles an item and returns a bingo card found in a trade journal. You don't fly the president of the company out to meet somebody who just bought a box of your breakfast cereal.

You want prospects to learn about your products at a speed appropriate to the product and appropriate for them. You want them to understand each step. You don't want to overwhelm them with information. Instead, you want to calibrate their reaction at every turn so you can determine what the proper next step might be. Now you can let your computer participate in that decision-making process and let it "distribute product literature" for you.

You're selling yo-yos? Show a picture or two and a video clip. Explain how consumers can amaze their friends with the skills they'll learn on your Web site. Only then should you announce the price. Selling sophisticated network management and security software? Walk prospects through the learning process slowly. Make sure users feel they are getting the information they want, rather than the information you want them to get. Be sure to engage the users in the activity of learning about your products. Make them participate instead of being passive spectators. Demand action from them. Force them to make decisions. Keep them actively involved.

Knowing that *flow* increases the learning experience, knowing that people can be captivated at their computer screens, and knowing that your company has or knows something that can be useful to your prospects and customers—how do you tie these ideas together to sell your wristwatch, vacation package, software, company image, or political beliefs?

It is up to you to provide an interesting, engaging activity. Your Web site should be fun, interesting, or useful—or all three. Picture a trade show with no marketing or salespeople and nobody staffing the booths. Your task is to create a booth that is attractive in the purest sense: It must attract people. It must hold their attention sufficiently for them to step inside the booth, pick up the brochure, and touch the samples. We'll address getting them to your booth in Chapter 8, "Feedback." For now, let's focus on holding their interest.

Interacting on a Web site can be a rhythmic process:

Make a selection; get an answer . . .

Make a selection; get an answer . . .

Make a selection; get an answer . . .

Use that rhythm to your advantage. Don't force your users to stop what they're doing in order to read instructions, directions, or extraneous marketing pabulum. Give them choices, but not too many. Give them control, but not too much.

In *Computers as Theatre* (Addison-Wesley, 1993), Brenda Laurel describes the continuum of computer game interactivity as being composed of three variables:

> Frequency (how often you could interact), range (how many choices were available), and significance (how much the choices really affected matters). A not-so-interactive computer game judged by these standards would let you do something only once in a while, would give you only a few things to choose from, and the things you could choose wouldn't make much difference to the whole action. A very interactive computer game . . . would let you do something that really mattered at any time, and it could be anything you could think of—just like real life.

The World Wide Web as we know it is not a "very interactive" place by Laurel's standards. Too many choices too often will create confusion, and as marketers, we wish to maintain control over the significance of the outcome. After all, we are trying to sell something. If your goal is to attract foot traffic in order to sell advertising on your Web site, you might wish to model your design toward the high end of the interactivity scale. But if you are merely trying to promote your company, product, and/or service, you need to guide users instead of handing the controls over to them.

In designing your site, strive to keep visitors engaged. A long block of text will make their eyes glaze over. Too many clicks will frustrate them.

In determining the level of interaction that is best for your particular product and your particular sets of customers, you must remain conscious of the state of the technical art.

THE TECHNICAL LIMITATIONS

The World Wide Web is still in its infancy. New standards are being discussed in meetings and fought over in the marketplace. In 1995, secure transactions were not yet commonplace, and we'd only just seen words flowing freely around pictures. Today we have a cornucopia of animation options and streaming audio and video tools. The technical conditions of the Web are in flux and are changing rapidly.

Bear in mind that the majority of people on the Web use the most popular brand of browser. In the beginning it was the NCSA's Mosaic. Then it was Netscape Navigator. Today, Microsoft's Internet Explorer is just starting to tip the scales.

The majority of the people on the Web today are dialing in from home on 28.8 Kbps modems; by tomorrow afternoon they will be dialing in over dedicated fiber-optic lines to their desks at work.

On April 13, 1998, my local Santa Barbara newspaper ran a short article about GTE's plans to offer ADSL here. Because Santa Barbara isn't close to a major metropolitan area and has a population of less than 100,000, it's rare that phone or cable companies try out new technologies here. But these days, the competition is heating up. Everybody with a wire or a pipe to your house wants to sell Internet access. The latest reports show that electricity companies have figured out how to provide access over power lines.

Internet technology is moving so fast that you may want to allocate an engineer and a market researcher to the task of keeping abreast.

At the moment, the level of interactivity you can expect from a Web site is moderate. The speed at which the information travels is the single most limiting factor. A Nintendo-like computer game is unlikely until we all have fiber to our homes, but some inventive people are exploring the limits of this technology.

The discussion of technical limitations and advances will continue in Chapter 14, "Looking Toward the Future." For the moment, please do not look at a demo your Web techies have put together and take it at face value. They have large screens, fast pipes and lots of files cached on their hard drives. Go home, dial up, and see what it'll be like to the rest of the world.

INTERACTIVE EXAMPLES

Yahoo! (www.yahoo.com) is the most often visited site on the World Wide Web. Let's start there (Figure 7.1).

Knowing that people who visit are there to go somewhere else, the designers at Yahoo! have done everything they can to make the site as fast as possible. Notice the dearth of graphics. On the one page that is seen by more people than any other, they didn't even want to use color in the background. Why take the time? Keep it clean.

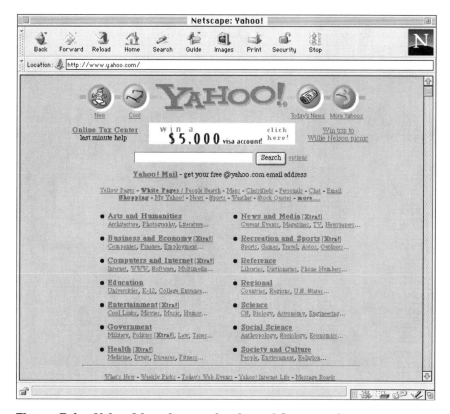

Figure 7.1   Yahoo! bends over backward for speed.

People who visit Yahoo! are on a mission, and they are able to have a flow-inducing dialogue with this site because it responds so quickly. It's a giant leap from static brochure to interactive, hyperlinked database. But it's a much larger leap to an immersive, online game environment.

With the arrival of Java and JavaScript, it became possible to get people to waste large tracts of time on games like WebTris, a Tetris knock-off (Figure 7.2). It's not much of a game, but it is a step beyond clicking a link. And it can be habit-forming.

That's where it started. You can now play chess online against computers or against other people. You can play Monopoly, poker, and slot machines. Yahoo! lists 13 versions of Minesweeper and several of my personal favorite, Whack-A-Mole. (My inside contact at Microsoft even e-mailed me a version in which you could throw pies at Bill Gates as he peeked up out of the holes.)

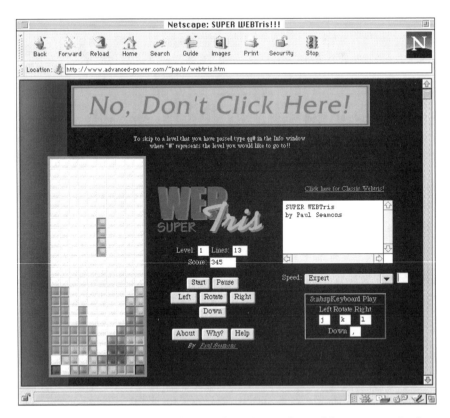

Figure 7.2 **Warning: WebTris will suck you in and keep you staring at the screen until your boss walks in.**

Fine. Games. So what? So think of your Web site as a place where people can have fun—if that's why they come to your site. If you are Disney, Warner Brothers, or Dilbert, then time-wasting, pure-entertainment activities are great. But chances are, you work for a company that sells products or services that solve problems or enhance the quality of life or improve productivity. People don't think about going to a Web site of a company that makes a dishwasher detergent to play games.

Instead, consider how this interactivity can be used to help people learn and decide and buy your products.

GIVE THEM THE REINS

The philosophy here is to put your customer in charge of the relationship.

When my dry-cleaning shop closed down, I had to find a new one. There were three nearby, and I went to the closest one first. "Your shirts will be ready by Friday," they said and gave me the ticket.

The next Monday I picked up my shirts and went to the next one to drop off the next load. "Your shirts will be ready on Friday. Is that OK?" I liked that. They were actually concerned about what *I* wanted.

The *next* Monday I went to get my shirts and dropped off the next batch at the third store. "When would you like your shirts back?" Bingo! I was in control; I was in charge. I was bringing my trade to them, and they knew it. Friday would have been fine, but Monday was just as good to me. Not only do I get my shirts when I want them, the laundry has an extra day to get them done. They are less stressed, and I am a happier customer.

There are three kinds of navigation on your site. The first is: Where the heck is the site? We'll cover that later in Chapter 10, "Attracting Attention." The second is: Where the heck is the information I'm looking for? The third type of navigation is different: Which of your products is right for me?

Remember, you don't want to hand the prospective customer the answer too quickly.

If you walk into a store and tell them what you want, a savvy clerk will ask a few more questions, even if there is only one model available that meets your needs. It's the difference between "You want a broom? Here," and "So, you need a broom that you can use in the kitchen but won't harm the finish on your hardwood floors? I think this one will be right for you." Customers feel they're getting the right thing.

If you have a large variety of items, choices, or configurations, asking site visitors to check the boxes and fill in the blanks is the only way to go.

If your back-end technology is sophisticated enough (and these days most Web servers are robust enough to handle it), the resulting "datasheet" can be assembled from content pieces stored in a database.

Just give me the opportunity to navigate your site by clicking on things about me. I'll feel like I'm getting closer and closer to the right answer. You'll amass a wealth of knowledge about the people who come to your site.

LEND THEM A HAND

Hewlett-Packard understands what it means to wear customer-colored glasses, and it understands how to involve the customer in the product discovery process. Nowhere is this more apparent than in the "Help Me Choose" section of HP's printer pages. This is a classic example of using the computer to help the person, instead of making the person help the computer.

The HP Personal Printer page contains products with names like these:

DeskJet 340 / 340CBi

DeskJet 400L

DeskJet 670C / 672C

DeskJet 670TV (Printer designed just for WebTV)

DeskJet 692C / 694C

DeskJet 720C / 722C

DeskJet 890Cse / 890Cxi

DeskJet 1000Cse / 1000Cxi

DeskJet 1100C

DeskJet 1120C / 1120Cse / 1120Cxi

DeskJet 1600C

LaserJet 6L / 6Lxi / 6Lse

LaserJet 6P / 6Pxi / 6Pse / 6MP

LaserJet 3100 / 3100xi / 3100se

LaserJet 4000 / 4000N / 4000TN / 4000T

LaserJet 5 / 5se

LaserJet 4V

These names give few clues to the poor shopper who simply wants to know if Hewlett-Packard has a printer that meets his or her needs.

Hewlett-Packard offers the "Help Me Choose" button. HP asks a few questions (Figure 7.3) and lets you click the "Next" button.

The next page has a few more questions:

You Selected: Solution for WORK Personal Printing
Based on your needs answer the following questions and we'll match you with the products that best fit your needs
What type of documents will you print? Choose two primary uses.
    Memos and Newsletters
    Business Letters and Proposals
    Spreadsheets and Graphs
    Presentations
    Photo Images
Do the documents you selected above need color?
    Not at all
    Nice to have
    A firm requirement

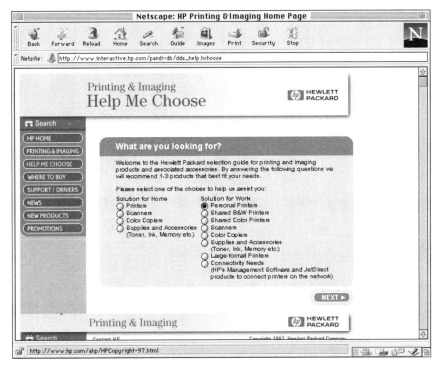

Figure 7.3   HP offers serious help with product identification.

In addition to letter and legal size paper what are your paper and paper handling needs?

Choose all that apply.

Envelopes

Duplex

Postcards or Index Cards

Transparencies

Glossy Media

Labels

Booklet and Brochure Printing/Tabloid (11 by 17)

Do you need a portable printer?

Do not need a portable printer

Interested in a portable printer

Definitely need a portable printer

How much do you expect to print?

Light—up to 35 pages a day

Moderate—35 to 45 pages a day

Heavy—45 to 130 pages a day

Workhorse—130 to 270 pages a day

Powerhouse—over 270 pages a day

What are your print speed requirements?

Speed is not that important to me

Speed is as important as any other feature

Speed is one of my most important requirements

Which of the following statements best applies to you?

The product's features are more important than price

Price is as important as the product's features

Price is one of my most important considerations

What type of computer will this be hooked to?

PC/DOS/Windows

Macintosh

Both

Do you need Adobe PostScript or PostScript emulation?

Yes

No

Based on the answers to these questions, the Web server sifts through the dozens of printers HP offers and selects a few for you to research further. This is like having an educated salesperson advise you on what fits and then leave you to decide what's best. This works.

This sort of search method is much closer to the popular Guide and Wizard features found in current software products. You want to create a graph? The Wizard walks you through the process. Looking for help? The

Guide asks a few questions to steer you in the right direction. You want a printer? Click "Help Me Choose."

This approach works because it engages the visitor in an electronic conversation about the visitor. This isn't about HP. It's not about HP products. As a potential customer, I want to click on the next button and tell the machine more about my needs.

USE CUSTOMER LANGUAGE

Or, in the case of AT&T Wireless, use any language at all. You want to buy a mobile phone? Fine. Here they are (Figure 7.4).

Oh yes, you can click on each one to read the details. In little, tiny print. (Please, folks, stay away from the little, tiny print. We're looking at this stuff on computer monitors, not in glossy magazines.)

Figure 7.4   AT&T feels you should be able to choose a phone based on how it looks.

But even worse is when text is confusing. Motorola was kind enough to offer a little description of each phone, but it leaves one a little less informed than without (Figure 7.5). Do you know the difference between a wearable cellular phone, a personal cellular phone, a transportable cellular phone, and a digital one? And Motorola didn't even stoop to techno-babble.

The secret is knowing your customers' vocabulary. For openers, ask your receptionist. If you have a machine answering your main telephone number, you're missing out on a wealth of information. What types of things do people ask for? What departmental designations do they use? Does the user need information about pricing from sales, product information from marketing, technical support from customer service, or shipment status from order processing? Have your receptionist keep a checklist next to the phone and keep track. You'll be surprised how informative it can be.

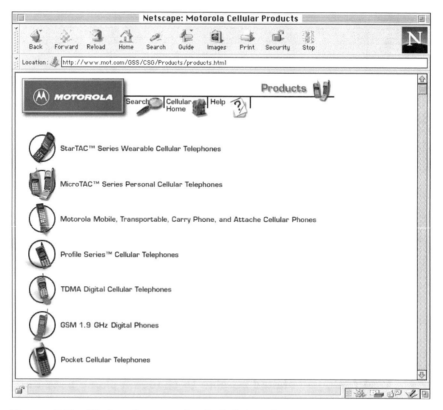

Figure 7.5   Motorola goes for helpful and ends up confusing.

The next source for learning which questions to ask is your sales force. They answer questions all day; it's their job. Have them keep track of the ways in which people ask about a product. Here's where you'll be reminded that people don't want to buy products or services, they want to buy solutions to their problems. As the saying goes, nobody wants a quarter-inch drill bit, they want a quarter-inch hole. Your sales team will tell you the important "search criteria" people use when they call and ask, "Do you have something in your product line that can . . . ?"

Your customer service people are intimately familiar with the right questions to ask new "visitors"—whether they're on the phone, in the lobby, or at your Web site. Customers and prospects will ask them questions they won't ask the salespeople. Why? It's a different relationship. A prospect wants to know about features and benefits and price and delivery from a sales representative, and about implementation and daily use from customer service.

Follow Hewlett-Packard's lead and keep the questions simple enough and few enough to make them painless to answer. Consider adding a second and even third layer of questions if necessary. Once you've established a pattern of query and response, you can toss in a few demographic and psychographic questions along the way.

USE THE POWER OF THE COMPUTER

The banking industry is dipping a toe in the shallow end. The multiple listing services are in the changing room deciding which bathing suits to wear. Lending institutions are waiting for somebody else to try the high dive first. Meanwhile, Financenter (www.financenter.com) (Figure 7.6) is creating a wake with a strong stroke and a clean kick.

Financenter President Sherri Neasham knew she was onto something from the get-go. "It's simple," she says. "People have tons of questions about borrowing money, whether it's for a home, a car, or even a credit card. Here's a place they can get answers and do some number crunching. It's casual, it's free, it's private, and there's zero pressure."

The number crunching itself is not simple at all. Amortization schedules may lack excitement, but they aren't written overnight. Rather than settle for mere payment schedules, Financenter created programs to answer critical questions such as:

How much can I borrow?

Should I pay discount points to get a lower rate?

How much will my closing costs be?

Figure 7.6   Financenter lets you calculate for yourself.

All free of charge.

Complex financial calculations for free? Yes, it's the Internet gift culture at work. Once you've figured out the perfect loan for you, Financenter invites you to apply for that loan online, with 48-hour response for approval.

Lending institutions are late to the game. Can they compete? Sure. All they have to do is put in a nauseatingly large number of hours finding the right talent and put a full year into raising awareness of their offerings—just as Financenter did.

They can also take the cooperative approach. Instead of competing with Financenter, people like the *Los Angeles Times,* America Online (AOL), Allstate Insurance, and Kiplinger Online became partners with Neasham. Some will lease the code from the Financenter server, paying a fee each time the server runs a calculation for them, and others will run their own offerings from the Financenter server. They understand that there is talent out there to be leveraged.

They also understand that these calculators add interactivity to their Web sites. They know, as Neasham will tell you, that this sort of interaction "enables a user to educate himself, better understand key financial concepts, and gain confidence in making a borrowing or investing decision."

You've got a computer on the other end of that phone line. Let your customers use it for something. Make it useful to them.

THIS IS YOUR CUSTOMER'S WEB SITE, NOT YOURS

The one subject everybody likes to talk about most is themselves. Make your Web site a mirror of the individual users. Do not tell them what you want to tell them. Tell them what they want to hear.

Syndicated columnist and MIT research associate Michael Schrage says, "The real value is in the interaction. . . . Real interactivity isn't about giving people more content to choose from, it's about letting people create their own content. The new media challenge, then, is how do you create content that creates content?"

The tools are available to capture information about users and use it on them. The tools are out there for making individual users the center of the universe on your Web site. That's why getting their feedback is so important. In fact, it's worth a whole new chapter.

CHAPTER 8

Feedback

It used to go without saying that a company had to manufacture demand when manufacturing a product. A better mousetrap would languish unless people were made aware of their deep-seated desire for a mousetrap and why a better one was absolutely necessary to their well-being.

Television blossomed into an ideal way to mold public opinion and acquisitiveness. The medium changed the way corporate America communicated with their customers. In *Sponsor* (Oxford University Press, 1979), Erik Barnouw pointed out that the move from the 60-second spot to the 30-second spot on television changed the tenor of messages broadcast into our homes.

> Everyone knows what the job is: instant drama, posing threat and promise. An important corollary is that the promise should be an undeliverable promise. There is scarcely time now for technical persuasions, documentation, "reason-why" advertising. Everyone knows that soap will clean hands, a razor remove hair, and a car transport you from one place to another. To promise such things means little or nothing. But there is no sure formula for being irresistible, for winning and holding those you love, or for rising to the top of the business or social circle. These are the promises worth dangling.

The goal was clearly defined as figuring out new and better ways to make people want the products we were making. Creating demand equaled survival.

In the next dozen or so years, focus shifted slightly. "Create Demand" became "Find a Need and Fill It." It was the task of the marketing professional to scour the country (global marketing belonged only to the few) for a product that people wanted but couldn't find on their store shelves—yet. In addition, the public was no longer a mass audience. They were being segmented through database marketing. Soft-drink companies needed a flavor and a campaign for each market segment. Cars were made to captivate different age groups. Products took on personalities to appeal to more and more diverse audiences.

THE DEMASSIFICATION OF THE MARKET

Then we were hit with mass customization. Henry Ford's, "You can have any color you want as long as it's black," has become "You can have any color you want." The assembly line producing pagers at Motorola was designed to create any of 250 configurations based on customer orders. Mrs. Fields Cookies and Benetton Clothing jumped on the power of a computer in every store to shoot sales information straight to the factory floor. Each day's production was tied directly to the previous day's sales. What flavor are they buying *today?* What color are they buying *today?* Product development and production have become service industries. If you find a product that has universal appeal, you had better exploit it faster than the knock-off shop down the street. Holding a lead in this fast-moving world depends on dexterity.

Sitting in an ivory tower and foreseeing the future is a risky business. Sitting in a corporate laboratory and counting on a scientist to invent the next Post-It Notes is not the model for today's marketer. Today's marketer is out in the street asking people what they want to buy. How do you like our current product? How would you improve it? How can we change our services to better accommodate your needs? What do you want your political candidate to stand for?

This is the type of marketing Don Peppers and Martha Rogers talk about in their book, *The One to One Future.* "The 1:1 future will be characterized by customized production, individually addressable media, and 1:1 marketing, totally changing the rules of business competition and growth."

I always felt that it was not the Vice President of Marketing's job to know what customers want. It's the VP's job to *ask* customers what they want.

THE SURVEY FINDS A NEW FORM

Surveys, focus groups, and market share are the glass-bottom boats we use to guess what the fish are thinking. We are able to ask only a handful or two for their opinion, and we try to scientifically extrapolate the answers out into a sea of consumers. A Web site gives us the ability to ask each of the individuals. A Web site gives us the tool to accurately record every answer.

A hefty envelope arrived at my desk one day from a company I enjoyed doing business with. Perhaps it was a new product update or another special discount for good customers. Maybe it was their annual report on the state of the industry. They usually sent me items worth reading, so it went into my in-basket until I could get to it. When I opened the envelope several weeks later, I found a three-page survey in 8-point type and a five dollar bill. I was surprised and wondered how many five dollar bills had wafted their way through the U.S. Postal Service. I wanted to help this company and was very pleased they thought my opinion was worth buying me lunch. I carefully placed the survey back in my in-basket until I could get to it. I carefully placed the five dollar bill in my pocket. The survey stayed in the basket for weeks; the five dollars lasted until noon.

When I finally dug down into my in-basket far enough to find the survey, I saw that I had missed the deadline. Good intentions or not, five dollars or not, that company did not find out how much I liked their services or what ideas I had for improvement. They would never know that I would buy more from them if only they would change a few simple operations.

Now, we look at the same issue from the electronic perspective. When logging on to America Online in the middle of March 1995, I was stopped short by the question:

Do you own a CD-ROM?

[Yes]   [No]   [I don't know]

In my momentary frustration and my desire to get my work done I answered with the truth. After all, it was the first answer that popped into my head. It took anywhere from two to five seconds to read and answer the question. I immediately forgot about it and went on my way. The next time I logged in, the question was nowhere in sight.

Since then, AOL peppers their customers with advertising. In that short window of time, they learned a critical piece of information about their customers. Since then, AOL has been mailing out CDs.

The survey has gone online. Everybody who dialed into America Online that day had to answer that question. Scientific? No. Controlled? No. Valid enough for clinical trials of FDA-approved drugs? No. Of value to America Online? Infinitely. Instead of asking a few people, we now can ask everybody. Can we ask everybody on the planet? No. Can we ask everybody who buys our product? Only if we're America Online. Can we learn about the needs and wants of those people who visit our Web sites? Absolutely.

ASKING THE RIGHT QUESTIONS

You've put a lot of time and energy into providing an accommodating, interesting Web site for your users. Now, it's time to get something from them in return—demographics and psychographics. Who are they? What are they interested in? What do they like about your products? Your company? Your competition? Your Web site? Probe them, and respond quickly with thanks and praise for their participation and good ideas. This will help create the bond that keeps an individual a customer for life.

Keeping It Simple

When the DealerNet site first went up in 1994 (www.dealernet.com), it wanted to know a few things about the people visiting its Web pages, so DealerNet gave away a car (Figure 8.1).

DealerNet's approach to getting visitors to reveal something about themselves was a wonderful example of simplicity. They asked for the usual information: name, e-mail address, street address, and so on. Then, when they had the user salivating over the prospects of acquiring a new car, they asked a few more questions.

Rather than ask for blood type, shoe size, and eating habits, they went right for the smallest bits with the biggest bang. They wanted to know the year, make, and model of the user's current car. Why didn't they go whole hog? Why not age, income, family size, miles driven per year, plans for next purchase? The philosophy was clear: The fewer the questions, the better the response.

These few answers gave DealerNet the information it needed to carry out its marketing strategy. People were encouraged to answer the questions because they were so short and easy to answer. Then DealerNet asked a key question, "Would you like to subscribe to DealerNet's upcoming monthly e-mail newsletter, *dealerNet Report*—Yes/No."

Figure 8.1   Giveaways like this one at DealerNet are great for collecting information.

You can be sure the person who claimed to drive a 1968 Volkswagen Microbus got a very different *dealerNet Report* than the person who drives a 1995 Mercedes convertible. The latter was filled with trade-in value reports and leasing options; the former described how to get oil stains out of the driveway.

Remember a few sacrosanct rules:

- You shall not send unsolicited e-mail.
- You shall not send junk e-mail.
- You shall not collect, buy, sell, or rent e-mail addresses the way you do in real life.

The DealerNet method, however, is a tacit agreement by the users that they are willing to accept e-mail from you. They *want* to be on your mailing list. Just be sure to deliver value.

How Are We Doing?

The good people at Leon Leonwood Bean (www.llbean.com) want to know what you think, and they get right to it in their survey (Figure 8.2).

L.L. Bean received more than 14 million phone calls in 1996. That represented 80 percent of contacts, the rest coming in the mail and over the Net. If you account for the growth of the Internet over the past few years, it's quite reasonable to say they get 20 percent of their orders online (about 2.8 million orders/e-mails/surveys on their Web site).

If you had that much traffic on your site, you'd want to make it better, too, right?

Is this visit to our website your first experience with L.L. Bean?
  Yes
  No
How has your impression of L.L. Bean changed now that you have visited our website?
  More favorable
  Less favorable
  About the same

I just love it when it's obvious the people in marketing have participated in the design and development of a Web site. The previous question

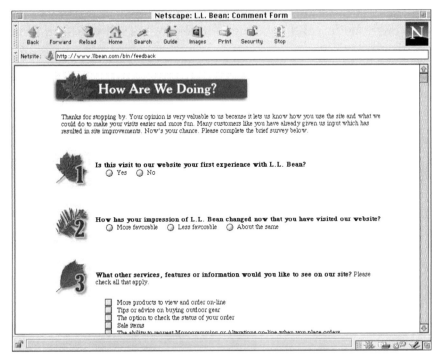

Figure 8.2   L.L. Bean is dead-set on making its Web site the best it can be.

isn't about sales. It's not about merchandising. It's not about advertising. It's about brand. L.L. Bean wants to know if they are helping or hurting their image and their reputation in the real world.

The next question is a direct shot at "How can we make it better?" and "Here are some ideas we like, but we want to know what *you'd* like." Bravo.

> What other services, features or information would you like to see on our site? Please check all that apply.
>   More products to view and order on-line
>   Tips or advice on buying outdoor gear
>   The option to check the status of your order
>   Sale items
>   The ability to request Monogramming or Alterations on-line when you place orders
>   Chat/on-line discussion forums to share thoughts on outdoor adventures: the gear, the destinations, the great experiences

The next questions plumb the depths of buyer misgivings. "This Web stuff might be fun and cool, but is it helping us sell you stuff. If not, why not?"

Have you purchased L.L. Bean gear or clothing on our site?
    Yes
    No
If you haven't, please tell us why not. Please check all that apply.
    I couldn't find the product(s) I wanted.
    It takes too long.
    I'd rather just call.
    It's too difficult to navigate through the ordering process.
    I don't feel comfortable sending my credit card number over the Internet.
    This is my first time visiting the site.
    I'm still browsing.
How would you prefer to place your orders using the L.L. Bean website? Please check all that apply.
    View and order items from the On-Line Product Guide.
    Place L.L. Bean catalog orders on-line using Catalog Quickshop.
    View information and products on-line and place orders by telephone.

Should We Be Doing This?

Communicators Federal Credit Union in Houston, Texas, was organized in April 1937 by 11 Southwestern Bell employees (www.cfculink.com). They're doing a decent job getting their feet wet on the Internet. But they're still not really sure, so they're asking a few questions (Figure 8.3).

First CFCU wants to know how people are connecting to the Internet:

How are you connected to the Internet? (Which dial-up service do you use?)
What browser are you now using?
If you are not using a Netscape Browser, have you considered changing?
What kind of equipment are you using?
What type of operating system do you use?
What speed modem are you now using?
Do you have any of the following? (Soundcard, microphone, camera, etc.)
Do you use any of the following Internet features? (E-mail, newsgroups, chat, etc.)
Do you use any of these money management software programs?

Then, when they've got you in a question-answering spirit, they slip in the only questions that really matter:

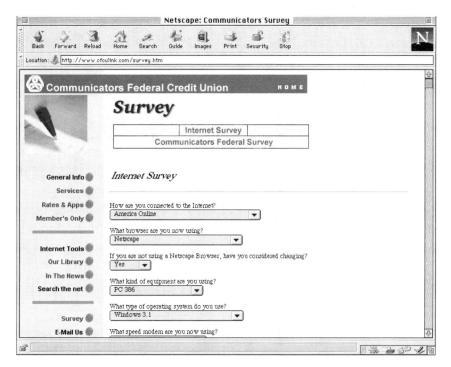

Figure 8.3   Communicators Federal Credit Union wants to know if anybody is out there—and if they're willing to pay.

> How interested are you in accessing your Credit Union Accounts?
> Would you be willing to pay a $2.00–$3.00 fee per month to cover the cost of unlimited access to your account from this WEB site?

Ahh, leave it to the banks. They did it with ATMs already, didn't they? "Here's a way you can do business with us that is so much cheaper for us than having branches full of tellers we can't believe it, and we're going to charge you *extra* for the privilege!" Unclear on the concept.

Going Whole Hog—Black Box

When the Black Box (www.blackbox.com) Catalog went online in 1994, they had the same sort of trepidation, although they never considered financially penalizing their customers for shopping online. Their site was (and still is) full of communications connectivity gear for the serious network afficionado.

Black Box wanted to find out from their customers if this Internet thing was going to catch on. Like L.L. Bean, they started off with a healthy round of Ed Koch questions (Figure 8.4):

How would you rate the value of the Black Box On-Line Catalog?
How do you rate the value of ordering products on-line?
How do you rate the importance of encrypted order processing?
What's the probability you'll purchase products over the Internet?

Would the Internet provide value to their customers? Should they add encryption? Is it a serious sales tool? Rather than make guesses based on their own feelings, extrapolate based on a handful of focus groups, or study the forecasts of industry pundits, Black Box went right to the people who matter.

Black Box takes this line of questioning further by outlining their plans and asking their users to help design the future Black Box Web site:

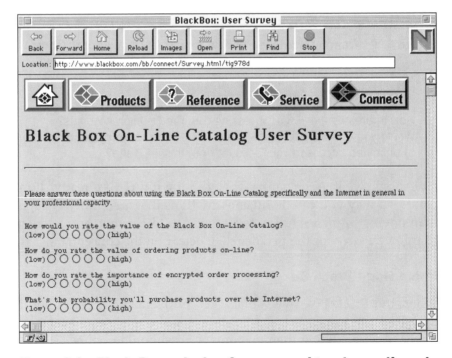

Figure 8.4   Black Box asked a few very poignant questions to start.

We are considering a number of feature extensions to the Black Box On-Line Catalog. These extensions include both additional content and additional functionality. We'd like to get your feedback on which features are more important to you. For the following questions please refer to these definitions of feature extensions to the Black Box On-Line Catalog.

Products

Add more Black Box product information to the Catalog (with information as currently provided in the Products section).

References

Include more general information material describing technologies and product applications (as described in the Reference section).

Ordering

Extend order processing support to include direct on-line ordering by customer number, PO, and credit card.

Support

Enhance On-Line Technical Support, by including FAQs, discussion group support, and e-mail technical contact.

Here's an innovative survey technique that made its Web debut on the Black Box site:

Please indicate how you would rate the value of each of these feature extensions to Black Box On-Line Catalog in your use of it in your professional activities.

For each pair of feature extensions, please indicate which extension you would prefer more than the other one (selecting a radio button closer to the feature implies you more strongly prefer that feature over the other one).

References	○	○	○	○	○	Products
Support	○	○	○	○	○	Ordering
Ordering	○	○	○	○	○	References
Products	○	○	○	○	○	Support
References	○	○	○	○	○	Support
Ordering	○	○	○	○	○	Products

Then, Black Box proved it has true marketing people on its team by asking a series of standard Marketing 101 questions: purchasing authority, industry segment, job title, and so on. Finally, it offered a blank piece of electronic paper for personal comments.

The results were surprising: In 1994 everybody wanted more product information; in 1995 everybody wanted more product information; in 1996 everybody wanted more product information. But the attitude about online ordering changed.

In 1994 nobody was intent on online ordering. Users had a catalog, a toll-free number, and a purchasing agent. But in 1996, 1997, and 1998 that ceased to be the case. People wanted to research the products, determine the right products, and *order* the products while they were there.

It didn't take Black Box long to get the message. The survey came down and the order form went up in its place (Figure 8.5).

A Survey That Hits Close to Home

Mama's Cucina (Van den Bergh Foods, Ragú Sauce) (www.eat.com) (Figure 8.6) is still a fine example of playful brand building and a service to customers. As the first packaged goods site on the Web, it deserves every one

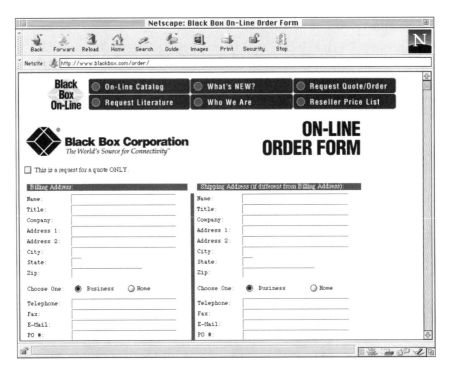

Figure 8.5   No need to ask for opinions anymore. Black Box now asks for the order.

of the almost 20 awards on display in the site's Trophy Room. If you spend half an hour there, you'll learn to not take yourself too seriously.

The questionnaire at Mama's Cucina is nothing if not complete. Its length may have an effect on the quantity of the responses, but the depth is nothing to sneeze at.

Alicia Rockmore was the Associate Brand Manager for Ragú Pasta Sauces when they put up this survey in 1994. She told me they were shocked at the responses they received. Oh, sure, I thought, anybody would have spent 20 minutes outlining their shopping and eating habits in detail in order to get their hands on a "Ragú Surfing Team" t-shirt. I know I did.

But Alicia said that even after Ragú stopped offering the shirts, they got many more responses than expected. Perhaps the tone of this delightful Web site was enough to encourage people to fill out a form that includes so many questions:

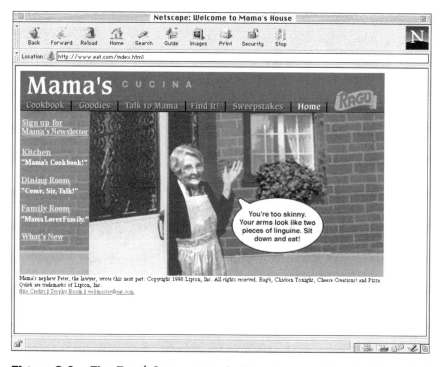

Figure 8.6   The Ragú Sauce people bring you a whimsical touch of Italy.

What is your overall opinion of the site?

How did you find out about Mama's Cucina?

How often do you think you will return to our site?

The phrases listed below may or may not apply to the Mama's Cucina Web Site. On a scale of one to five (1 = Strongly Disagree: 5 = Strongly Agree), indicate how much you agree with each of these phrases: Mama's Cucina . . .

Is enjoyable

Improved your image of Ragú

Is very innovative

Is relevant to you

Told you something important

Is something you would like to visit again

Is informative

Is different from other web sites

Told you something new

For those phrases that you selected "4" or "5," please explain why:

How often do you eat pasta for dinner?

Which of the following products have you used in the past year? (check all that apply)

Are you:

Male - Female

Age:

Married - Non-Married

How many people in your household (yourself included) are (enter numbers below):

Under 3 years old

3–6 years old

6–12 years old

13–17 years old

Over 17 years old

Do you work:

Full Time

Part Time

Homemaker/Do Not Work Outside the Home

What is your level of education?

    High School or Less

    Some College or More

    Graduate Education or More

Mama, write to me when Ragú (check all that apply):

    Offers coupons in the newspaper?

    Features new items on the Web site?

    Introduces a new flavor? Introduces a new product?

When so many of the first Web sites went up because it was possible, the technical crowd carried the most weight. Page design and questions asked were the responsibility of the software and systems people, while the marketing departments stood by in awe. Sites like the Black Box Catalog and Mama's Cucina show that marketing departments caught on pretty quickly and had an important impact on how the company is represented online.

RETHINKING THE SURVEY PROCESS

The World Wide Web gives us the opportunity to think outside the box. We no longer need a number 2 pencil—we have a mouse and all of cyberspace in which to play. A couple of the surveys described earlier are fairly complete, but they're lengthy. As a consumer, you have to *really* want them to know what you think, to spend so much time answering questions. Given the level of interactivity available on the Web, you can create surveys that do not resemble their paper progenitors.

The Conversational Survey

If you want to run a long survey, consider building it out of multiple pages. Each page should contain several questions, which all fit on one screen. When the questions are answered, the user can click on the Continue button and the next set of questions pops up.

This model of feeding users a few questions at a time has a very positive effect on the experience. Instead of receiving one long page that scrolls and scrolls to the end of time, the user is asked to answer only a couple of questions at once. This method makes the user feel as if he or she is participating in the survey instead of just being an input device—being interviewed instead of being shown to a desk monitored by a proctor with a stopwatch and a suspicious disposition. This is the kind of action/interaction that keeps the user involved.

The Intermittent Survey

There is no need to make users sit through a survey session per se. Why not ask on-point questions as they traverse the Web site? A user surfs over and clicks on the minivan selection. At the top of the minivan page is a question box—"Are you looking for a minivan for work or for family use?" A quick click, and the user has given you an important data point.

The Hewlett-Packard printer locator is a fine example. Hewlett-Packard will help you find the right printer for your needs. At the same time, Hewlett-Packard collects a good deal of information about who is visiting its Web sites.

Another method for collecting information about your user's proclivities is tracking the number of people who visit specific pages in your site. This approach is discussed in detail in Chapter 11, "Measuring Your Success."

The Personal Survey

If you take a vacation that you booked through Preview Travel (www.previewtravel.com), they want to know how the vacation went. Did you have a good time? Did the accommodations meet your expectations? Were the flights on time? Would you use this service again? Preview Travel really needs to know in order to keep their customers happy.

Preview Travel uses e-mail to ask these questions. When the calendar tells them you're back home, off goes the questionnaire. Because you've just returned, chances are very good you're willing to tell them you had a wonderful time—all except for that hotel in Montréal that lost your laundry.

BUYING DEMOGRAPHIC INFORMATION

There are a number of reasons to collect an individual's specific identity—the e-mail address. The first is to be sure one individual is answering one question, one time only. An Auto Emporium user could easily indicate a need for a family minivan 5 or 10 times before getting bored. Somebody with a desire to throw your numbers off wouldn't get bored so easily.

Once you have people's e-mail addresses, you can entice them to put themselves on your e-mailing list for future contact. This is such a good formula that you should offer something in return: "Each month our e-Newsletter contains hundreds of dollars in discount coupons you can use online or in our stores" or "Once each month we give away a free widget to one lucky subscriber." A more subtle reason for collecting an e-mail address has to do with the validity of the answers received. After people have identified themselves, they are much more likely to give their answers a little more thought than the individual just surfing through. Asking for an e-mail address is not a simple step; there must be something in it for the user. This is where the buying-and-selling, give-and-take dance begins.

A Web site should be treated just like a trade show booth. You want people to come up and finger the literature. You want them to examine the product. You want them to ask questions. But many exhibit hall habitués are repelled from a booth by an eager salesperson intent on getting name, title, company, address, phone and fax numbers, and shoe size.

Trading Knowledge for Information and Money

Offer information about the company, the products, and the industry. Give users something of value. Prove to them that you have something to offer, and then offer them something better. Begin by dividing up your valuable information into three progressively interesting categories. The first category is of general interest and will attract people to your site. The second category is even more interesting; the third category is absolutely fascinating and almost impossible to find elsewhere. With these three classes in hand, you can begin to barter.

The first class of information belongs on your Web site, prominently displayed and available to all. The second class is a bit more rare, a bit more precious, and worth a little effort to obtain.

"This White Paper is the first of its kind and is yours if you answer the following 12 quick questions."

"We've collected a wide variety of copyright-free images regarding the widget industry. You can download them after helping us improve our Web site."

One rather gruesome example of this was CNET: The Computer Network. This is an all-computers all-the-time television channel for those who don't wish to stray too far from their computer terminals. The CNET Web site (www.cnet.com) (Figure 8.7) wanted you to join their club by giving your e-mail address. This was a tacit agreement that you were willing to receive their newsletter. In return, you got to download a computer animation of how Nicole Brown Simpson and Ron Goldman might have been murdered by a single African-American male (Figure 8.8).

"Digital Dispatch is CNET: the computer network's FREE weekly electronic newsletter for community members. Subscribe now and access CNET's extraordinary re-creation." Rest assured that CNET got a lot of traffic at their site.

Let's hope the pictures, sound bites, and video clips you offer will be in better taste—the sort of information you'd give to the semiqualified individual who spends more than 10 minutes in your trade show booth, the sort of information you'd send to somebody who's still near the beginning of the sales cycle. It's the sort of information you'd rather not give directly to the competition. You save your best for last.

Category three information should literally be worth its weight in gold—so charge for it. If you're in a knowledge business, this is your stock-in-trade. If not, this is the intelligence you've carefully gathered and that is truly unique. A Web site is a fine place for the sale and distribution of your unique monographs, images, sounds, or videos.

At each progressive stage of information sharing, be sure you are on the receiving end of data that is just as valuable. Munificence is a wonderful corporate image builder, but it can be a drain on the budget when carried too far. The people who visit your office can tell you if the waiting-room chairs are comfortable. They can give you their impressions about the physical plant, the way they are treated at the reception desk, and how far they had to walk through the snow to reach the front door. People who call your company can open your eyes to what it's like being on hold, how frustrating your voice-mail system is, and whether your customer service department is worthy of the name.

Therefore, you should look to the people who visit your Web site as the source of information about how your company represents itself online. What impression does your Web site give of the company? Does it look like a Fortune 500 corporation? A nimble start-up? Or a couple of grad students with their own Web server?

Make Them a Coconspirator

When Eastman Kodak (www.kodak.com) had a new home page design that it wanted to test, it asked site visitors for their opinions. It linked its then current home page to the new design and invited people to take a look

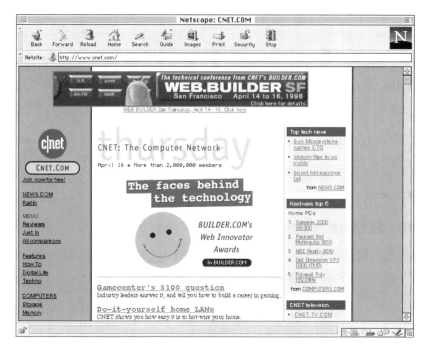

Figure 8.7   The CNET channel offered a newsletter you must agree to accept if you want to download . . .

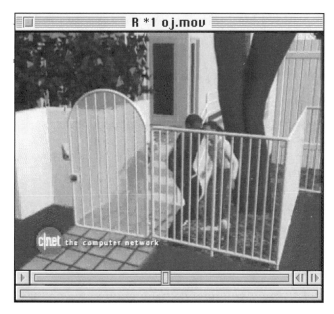

Figure 8.8   . . . a computer animation of the Simpson-Goldman murders.

and vote. The voters had comments about what they saw, which prompted changes. When the voters registered their approval by more than 90 percent, the new page was put online.

If you visit www.yahoo.com you can find its home page (Figure 8.9). If you go to beta.yahoo.com you can find what Yahoo! is thinking about for next time (Figure 8.10).

Notice the predominant "What Do You Think?" and "Please Give Us Feedback" links at the top of the proposed page. These people are serious about catering to their public.

CLOSING THE FEEDBACK LOOP

If you advertise an 800 telephone number on TV, you'd better have operators standing by. If you send a direct mail offer to a list of 500,000, you'd best be prepared for a round of Business Reply cards. If you put up a Web site, you most certainly ought to be prepared to respond to your e-mail.

This is where free-form feedback comes in. Maybe they couldn't find it in the FAQ. Maybe they couldn't find it in the knowledge base. Maybe they didn't even look. Doesn't matter. E-mail is a customer's way of reaching out to you.

It absolutely amazes me that today, as I write this in the middle of 1998, there are still companies like Southwest Airlines (www.southwest.com) (Figure 8.11). For all the flashy colors and online ordering on their site, they simply do not want your e-mail.

At the bottom of their home page is Southwest Airlines' contact information:

Southwest Airlines passenger reservations phone numbers:

1-800-I-FLY-SWA (1-800-435-9792)
En Español 1-800-221-0016
Telecommunications Device (TDD) 1-800-533-1305

Southwest Airlines Home Gate
P.O. Box 36611
Mail Drop 5MD
Dallas, Texas 75235-1611
fax (214) 792-4017

Why we don't accept e-mail

At Southwest Airlines, we want to provide you with the best possible Customer Service by responding to your concerns and questions in a timely man-

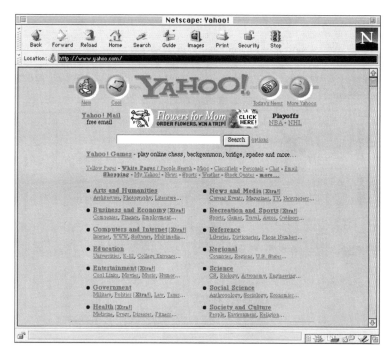

Figure 8.9 Yahoo! wonders how its visitors feel about the current home page design . . .

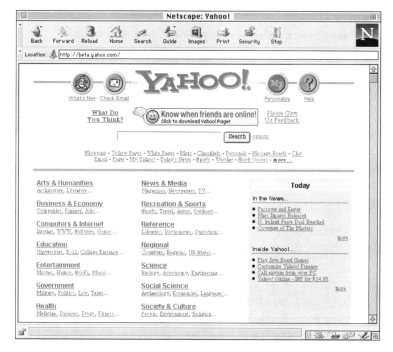

Figure 8.10 . . . and the proposed home page.

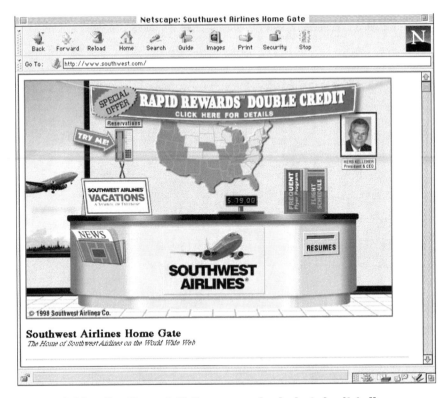

Figure 8.11 Southwest Airlines says look, but don't talk.

ner. At the moment, our ability to support e-mail in a manner consistent with our service expectations is not fully in place. Please feel free to drop us a line at the above address.

Thank you for your interest in Southwest Airlines!

Thank you, Southwest, for your utter indifference.

Respond Quickly

The general expectation on the Internet has always been 24-hour turnaround. This is due in part to crossed time zones, late-night e-mail sessions, and automated Mailbots. It is also due to the informality of the Internet. Responses don't have to be channeled through six layers of management; they just get written and sent. Therefore, have responders at the ready, with ready responses. Build a staff of people to handle the incoming mail from your Web site. Draw on the team that handles the 800 phone lines. They already know most of the questions and have the answers on hand. Bolster this group with a few people who know their way around the Internet, people who know a good idea when it comes in and can acknowledge it appropriately. This is the public relations side of things (where the "public" has become the audience of one).

Respond Personally

The formal reply letter received from a corporation usually confirms that a complaint, suggestion, praise, or threat has been received. It is always boilerplate; it is always more form than substance. This goes against the grain of the online culture and will do more harm than good. Each time somebody registers a problem, makes a suggestion, or asks a question, the response should include enough to let the user know a human looked over his or her words. Just adding a few comments about the message to the paragraphs of outgoing boilerplate on hand will make the difference.

You may put together the fill-in-the-blank, mix-and-match boilerplate that covers the critical 80 percent. Once you thank the user for helping you make your products/services/Web site better, ask him or her to answer a few more questions. The user volunteered an opinion the first time; it's a safe guess that he or she would be flattered to be asked for more.

Go the Extra Mile

It is necessary to give people every means possible to get in touch with you. Accept their e-mail, post your phone number, list your postal addresses, and take phone calls. For the moment, that means training your phone operators in the fine points of your Web site. You want them to be able to say, "Yes, I can help with that!" rather than, "Oh? We have a Web site?"

The folks at GEICO Direct Insurance (www.geico.com) definitely want to talk to you, and they've hooked up their phones to their Web site to do it (Figure 8.12). Click the mouse; your phone rings.

This is a momentary workaround solution to a problem that's going to go away soon. There's no mystery to sending voice packets over the Internet. It's just a matter of time before you'll simply be able to talk through your computer. That time may even have been between my writing and your reading. Then, "Can I help you?" comes with complete knowledge of what page you're on and an idea of how to help you.

Companies like Talx (www.talx.com) have a little button at the bottom of the pages they build for their clients. Talx got started in the interactive

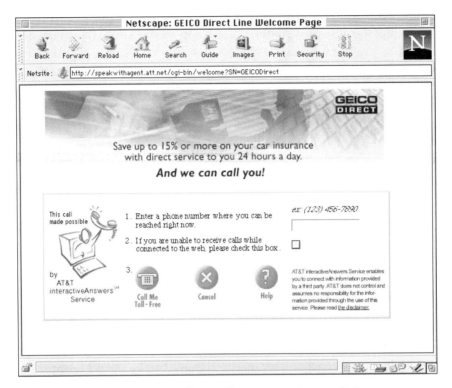

Figure 8.12   GEICO will call you the moment you click.

voice response (IVR) business and realized that the Web could not be ignored, so they combined the two. For years they have been making systems that can solve people's problems by letting them talk to a computer over the phone.

"To change the number of dependents on your W-4 Form, press 1."

The Talx system takes over and completes the transaction by linking the phone to your company's payroll applications. They also make systems that solve people's problems by letting them talk to other people over the computer. If you're doing your own data entry through a browser and you have a question, click the button and the customer service desk or the help desk gets a phone call.

That's good so far, but there's one more step. The screen that you are looking at and questioning is displayed in front of the customer service representative when the call goes through. Instead of, "Who are you? What's the matter? What do you want?" it becomes, "Hi, Fred, sorry you're having a problem with the W-4 Form. How can I help?"

Put that to use on your Web site when you're trying to make a sale, and fewer people would surf off in confusion just when they were about to buy.

GET THEM TO TALK TO EACH OTHER

This topic was brought up in a previous chapter, but it bears repeating here. If you want to know what your customers are thinking, get them talking. I devoted an entire chapter about this subject in *Customer Service on the Internet* and with good reason:

> Beyond posting purified, disinfected data for the masses, and besides answering e-mail from individuals, there is tremendous value in getting your clients to talk to each other. Getting them to talk about you and your products can be a very powerful tool for building loyalty. It can also expose you in unpleasant ways.
>
> Marketers have always used testimonials. Now there is a way to get people to express their ongoing love affair with your products and services in their own words: on line and in real time.
>
> On the other hand, they will also air their dirty laundry. They will be only too happy to espouse your shortcomings. They will be delighted to take their frustrations out on you in public. Kept them waiting on hold longer than they could tolerate? Didn't offer a refund? Didn't even say "I'm sorry"? Now your customers can tell the world in an instant. Is this really such a good idea?
>
> It's a very good idea. Managed properly, these complaints become a wealth of information for product and service improvement. They become the springboard to people helping each other and forming a community of customers. They prove to your customers that you value their contribution. It also shows that your company is embracing this new technology in order to open the doors between you and your clientele instead of using it simply to disseminate the company line.

Getting clients to talk is one thing (and a good thing), but building a community is another thing entirely (and a great thing).

Awareness in marketing leads to branding. Community on the Internet leads to bonding. Bonding occurs when customers are so closely connected to your products they don't just use them and repurchase them; they also recommend them and are happy to make public pronouncements about how your products changed their lives.

One way to move customers toward bondage is to create a place for them to congregate. They'll get to know each other. Then they'll complain. Then they'll gang up on you. Then they'll start helping each other.

If You Build It, They Will Bond

Cisco Systems did more than create automated methods of helping its customers; it created a way for its customers to help themselves. Open Forum was one of Cisco's first customer-only and customer-specific features. A private newsgroup managed by the customer service staff, Open Forum was created for posing less straightforward technical support questions (Figure 8.13).

Here's the process: A customer asks a particularly troublesome question, and the system scours a Cisco knowledgebase for the answer. Poten-

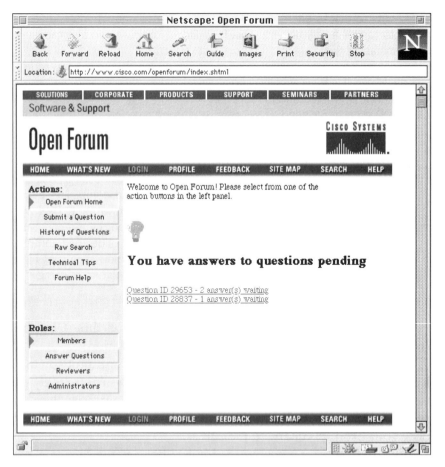

Figure 8.13   Cisco's Open Forum lets customers help each other.

tial answers are shown to the customer; if the answers don't fit or aren't sufficient to solve the problem, the customer can ask again, or the customer can send the question to the engineers. Cisco engineers are tasked with finding the answer. If they do, great. The question and the answer are fed into the knowledgebase for next time. If they don't find the answer, the question goes to the Open Forum, where all customers can take a crack at it.

If the customer sees an answer he or she likes, it and the question are sent to a team of technical writers and senior engineers to check the veracity of the information, as well as grammar and style. Once they clean it up, the question and answer go into the knowledgebase.

As a result of this system, 75 percent of questions are answered before they hit the Open Forum. The bonding happens because of the interesting mix of camaraderie and competition in the Open Forum. Celebrities are created and honored for being willing and able to help their fellow customers.

The reason this customer service application shows up in a marketing book is simple. If you add more value to your products through customer service, your products are more valuable to your prospective customers. And besides, you had better give them a place to talk to each other about your products for one good reason . . .

If You Don't Build It, They Will

Imagine the surprise over at Corel Corporation (www.corel.com) when they heard that people were talking about Corel. Lots of people. In fact, there was a whole Web site set up by Corel customers just to talk about Corel products. In fact, this Web site was so popular and so populated, they were able to sell advertising (Figure 8.14).

When Corel got wind of this site, they rushed right out and bought up the advertising before their competitors could. But that didn't quite make Corel feel comfortable enough.

Their lawyers advised that advertising on a discussion site that could contain questionable information might be construed as endorsement of that information by association. So Corel bought the site—lock, stock, and barrel. This move was far easier in the long run. Now, Corel has the Corel newsgroup page (Figure 8.15).

This area is intended to provide users the opportunity to exchange information, tips, and techniques with other users regarding Corel applications. To

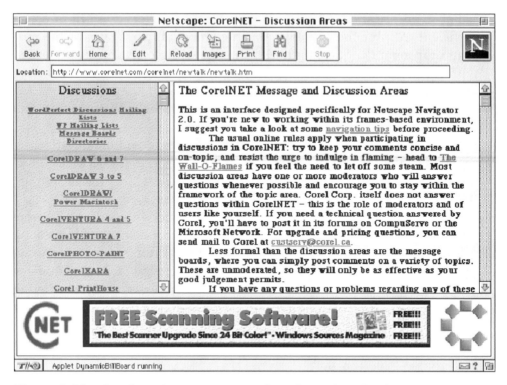

Figure 8.14   Corel customers were such a chatty bunch, they created their own clubhouse.

ensure a smooth flow of information, please note the Expectations of Service and Rules of Conduct for the newsgroups.

Corel understands the power of letting customers talk to each other and understands the power of being the focal point, the starting place, the portal to that discussion. Corel also understands that some rules are valuable and some moderation is necessary.

Expectations of service

Corel's role: Corel does not offer any formal support in the public newsgroups. Instead, Corel technical support staff will monitor and moderate the newsgroups to ensure the smooth flow of information and ensure messaging guidelines are maintained.

Users are free to exchange advice amongst one another, but users must use discretion when receiving technical information from individuals who are not Corel staff.

Figure 8.15   Corel wanted to open the discussion to all while keeping a close eye on it.

Corel assumes no liability for information exchanged amongst users of these message areas.

All responses obtained from Corel representatives will be indicated as such.

Rules of conduct

Appropriate Language: The purpose of the newsgroups is to exchange technical information and expertise on Corel products. Please avoid personal attacks, slurs, and any use of profanity in your messages.

Message Topics: Please keep the topic of messages relevant to the subject of the newsgroup. It's normal for some message topics to drift from the stated subject. However, to ensure maximum impact and benefit for all involved, please keep your messages close to the newsgroup's subject.

Advertising/Solicitation: The newsgroups are for peer-to-peer assistance on Corel products. Participants are asked to refrain from posting advertisements or solicitations not pertaining to the intended use and purpose of the newsgroups.

NOTE: Corel reserves the right to remove, without warning, any messaging that does not fall within the outlined criteria for message postings within these areas.

All of the above is followed by a disclaimer so serious, Corel felt compelled to print it in gray on a white background so it wouldn't be too jarring. Nevertheless, you have to hand it to them for being brave enough to ride herd on some 59 different discussions covering all the different versions of all their products.

Be Brave and Benefit

Philips (www.philips.com) makes a hand-held computer/personal digital assistant/gizmo called a Velo. It runs Microsoft's Windows CE and keeps track of your life for you. In the spring of 1998, Velo owners were a little miffed about some problems they were having, such as a delayed upgrade in operating system and a loose hinge. In fact, they were upset enough to bring it to the attention of Ed Foster.

Ed Foster is a writer for the industry newspaper *Infoworld*. You don't want your customers to get in touch with Ed—his column is called The Gripe Line.

People who wrote to Ed wanted him to know they were not lone voices in the wilderness and pointed him to the discussion of their problems by many others on the Philips Web site. Are you willing to air your dirty linen in public? Philips says, "Yes."

Ginger Moschetta is the marketing manager for Web solutions at Philips, and she's all for it. She knows the value of listening to customers, not just listening to them in focus groups or by reading the amalgamation of their survey responses. She especially listens to them when they complain. An unhappy customer represents two different but very important opportunities: a chance to fix something you may not have known was wrong and a chance to delight an unhappy customer.

People who complain are worth their weight in pain. They are willing to step forward and help you. They are willing to point out the error of your ways so that you can stop disappointing other, quieter customers. They care. And, if you are lucky enough to be able to solve their problem and do it well, they will be dedicated customers for a long time to come.

Letting people gripe and grumble as a group empowers them to be more vociferous. It's the mob-mentality thing: "Yeah! Me, too!" You certainly don't want that to get out of hand, but you do want your customers to feel that you *want* to hear from them and that their opinion is *important*.

Keep an Open Mind and an Open Ear

Your Web site is an opportunity to bond with your customers through enthralling information, entertaining activities, and exceptional service. If you concentrate on getting feedback from them, you will know how to cater to them. If you acknowledge them individually and in public for their participation, they will cling to the relationship.

CHAPTER 9

Value-Added Marketing— It's Personal

The three most important things in the commercial real estate business are location, location, and location. The three most important things in the world of marketing are listen, listen, and listen. We need to keep our attention firmly on the people who keep us in business, the people who buy from us, the people who turn their money into our money.

Do you want to win the game? Then you must take the next step in winning the hearts and minds of consumers in your marketplace—you must offer proof. Not money-back guarantees (although those are good). Not celebrity testimonials (although those can help). Not even free trials (although they are a good start, with a happy track record on the Internet) are enough.

You need to offer proof to your prospects that you understand their needs and desires, understand the industry you're in, and understand your competition. You have to prove that you are a worthy vendor. You must prove you have price, value, status, quality, convenience, and customization sewn up before you make the offer to your prospects.

The most precious commodity on this planet is time. If you expect a prospect to spend any amount of this unrenewable resource, this priceless commodity, thinking about your products and services, you had better offer something of value in return. You are going to have to pay people to consider your products.

It used to be up to us as marketers to figure out which way the parade was going and to get out in front of it. It was up to us to determine what the audience wanted and to give it to them. That was then; times have changed.

Marshall McLuhan became famous for his statement, "The medium is the message," and I stayed up nearly enough nights and smoked nearly enough dope in college to understand what he meant. But, I do understand something else McLuhan said: "The audience is the content."

When Marshall McLuhan said "The audience is the content," he was focusing on what happens inside your head when you watch a play, see a movie, or read a book. The story is different for each of us because we bring a unique lifetime of experience to it.

"The old woman walked into the gray house."

That sentence creates a picture in your mind. But the woman and the house you see are different from what I see. We're different. McLuhan was right about that. Today, the Internet makes his words literally true.

Your marketing materials are no longer the same for all comers. No longer can you measure response based on gross numbers. No longer can you look out at a sea of faces and think of them as a mass market. They are a sea of individuals, and each of them, based on their individual interests and needs, will create his or her own content out of the components you offer on your Web site.

Understanding the significance of "The audience is the content" will make the best of all possible Web sites.

Remember that the Internet culture is acclimatized to a gift culture. All the other players on the Net are giving. Now it's your turn to be a better benefactor than the next guy. You can make your Web pay people for their time in three ways. You can make your Web site fun; you can make it interesting; and you can make it useful. Each of these requires identifying your prospects or customers very well. Something that's fun to a teenager is not fun to her father. Something that's useful to an engineer is not useful to an accountant.

MAKE YOUR SITE FUN

This is tough. Way back when, it used to be easier. A list of knock-knock jokes was fun, and having an interactive game was considered the height of fashion.

Now, you can offer fun and games, but you face two challenges: content match and merit. The first asks whether the "fun" is related to your product. If you're in the software business you might be able to come up with a handful of jokes to entertain your customers. This proves that you are a fun company:

Q. How many software people does it take to screw in a light bulb?

A. None. It's a hardware problem.

Q. How many systems analysts does it take to change a light bulb?

A. The light bulb works fine in *my* office.

Q. How many Microsoft vice presidents does it take to change a light bulb?

A. Five: one to work the bulb and four to make sure Microsoft gets $1 for every light bulb ever changed anywhere in the world.

Cellular One (www.cellularone.com) thought it would provide entertainment for its customers and potential customers. It created the puzzle game and promoted it on the home page (Figure 9.1).

The puzzle pieces are scattered throughout the site; when you find one, you click. A brief message comes up congratulating you on finding another

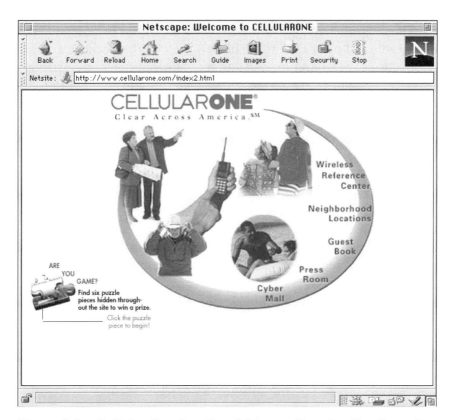

Figure 9.1   Cellular One has the right question: Are You Game?

piece, telling you how many remain to be found, and giving you a link back to the page you were on. My very first question is: What's the prize?

I'm invited to play and it says I can win a prize. But the flow construct just isn't working for me because the game is so boring and the reward is unknown. I'm sorry, Cellular One, but this falls under the category of "Hey kids, let's put on a show!" You can see the marketing people (with little Web experience) huddled with the creative Web people (with little business experience) as they hash it out over lunch.

"We looked over the logs and people are going only to the product description pages. We created all this other great content, and nobody is looking at it. How do we make them?"

"Oh! Oh! I have an idea!" Then he stops to wipe a bit of blood-orange salad from his chin. "How about a game? It's so cool that you can do interactive stuff on the Web, and Web surfers *love* to play interactive games, and we could give away prizes and stuff!"

"Good idea. That's very good. Just make sure it's tasteful."

The second challenge you face when trying for fun on your Web site is the question of merit. What the heck is it for? Why bother?

If you want to accomplish some of the standard advertising goals of awareness building and brand image construction, you could follow some of the big advertisers who are playing serious games.

7-Up knows its audience. A healthy portion of them are young and technically savvy. Rather than trying to lure them to the 7-Up site, they go where the customers are. In this case, to the ShockRave site (www.shockrave.com). ShockRave is a site put up by Macromedia (www.macromedia.com) to promote its interactive, animated tool set and browser plug-in called Shockwave. 7-Up has decided to host a game at the ShockRave site.

We pause for a moment to make this abundantly clear. Macromedia has a software product called Shockwave. To promote it, it set up a Web site called ShockRave where it can show off the software's wonders. 7-Up is sponsoring a game on the ShockRave site to promote its soft drink. See? This Web stuff is simple once you get the hang of it.

The game is about basketball. In fact, you get to play the lead dribbler. Now, this game isn't just sponsored by 7-Up with an ad banner at the top; 7-Up takes center stage (Figure 9.2), or is that center court? Furthermore, you are represented on the court by a 7-Up bottle cap.

That's some serious fun and games. If your market is the consumer, packaged-goods, youth-oriented, fun-seeking, time-to-kill crowd, take note.

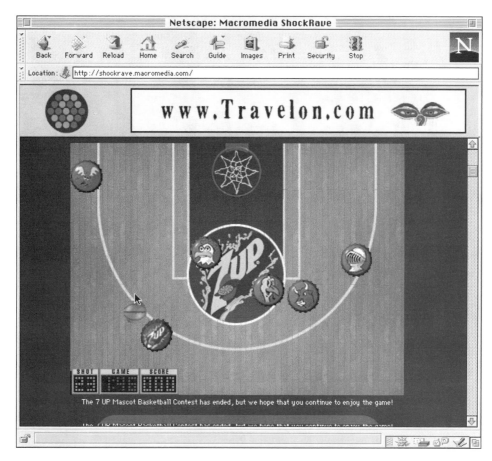

Figure 9.2   7-Up wants its logo branded on your eyeball as you shoot hoops.

If you work for Disney or Warner Brothers, take note. If you work for New Line Cinemas and just produced the *Lost in Space* movie, then the detailed adventure at www.dangerwillrobinson.com (Figure 9.3) is well in keeping with your target audience.

But if you're selling mobile phones, maybe you're better off finding value in other ways.

MAKE YOUR SITE INTERESTING

What do you know? It's a serious question. What do you know more about than most people and that they would find interesting? If you sell umbrel-

Figure 9.3   Lost in Space can be found (and played) on the Web.

las, you might know where to link to weather reports. If you sell wrist watches, you might actually want to describe the factory when asked for the time. If you're Sears, you may want people to know that in "1886—Richard Sears starts selling watches to supplement his income as station agent at North Redwood, Minnesota." And now we're back to the content match and merit challenges again. Is it interesting to your customers or just to you?

AT&T thinks it has lots of different kinds of customers so it has lots of different kinds of interesting things. There are interesting (yet very topical) games at the AT&T Brainspin page (www.att.com/attlabs/brainspin). You can try to find a way to stop the world from running out of phone numbers, learn how Alexander Graham Bell taught his dog to talk, and try to improve bandwidth on the Internet. And there's the AT&T Attic (www.att.com/attlabs/attic) (Figure 9.4), which is filled with such a treasure-trove of stuff, you're sure to waste some time there.

I was caught up for several minutes in the Train of Thought Chronological Tour (www.research.att.com/history/train.html).

1924: The First Fax

1925: High-Fidelity Recording

1926: Sound Motion Pictures

1927: Wave Nature of Matter

1927: First TV Transmission

1929: The Artificial Larynx

1929: Transatlantic Radiotelephone

1933: Radio Astronomy

1933: LP & Stereo Records

1936: Synthetic Speech

1939: The First Computer

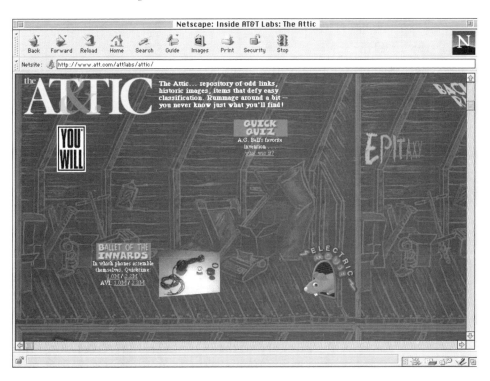

Figure 9.4   AT&T has enough stuff in its Attic to entrance anybody with too much time on their hands.

1939: High-Frequency Radar

1942: The Horn Antenna

1947: The Transistor

1948: Information Theory

1951: Direct-Dial Service

1954: The Solar Battery

1960: The Laser

1960: Communication Satellites

1964: Touch-Tone Phones

1965: The Big Bang Discovered

1970: The Picturephone

1976: Epitaxy Microchips

1977: Optical Fiber Communication

1985: The Smart Card

1989: The Speech-Driven Robot

1989: HDTV

1992: Instant Language Translator

1993: The Computer Videop

I was caught for more than a few minutes in the AT&T Papers and Speeches Archives. I'll probably even quote one of their papers on "Delegating to Software Agents" in Chapter 14, "Looking Toward the Future." You can tell a lot about a person by what he finds to play with in the AT&T Attic.

Now back to our two challenges. Did AT&T find something to distract even me? You betcha. Does this content have value? Depends on your measuring stick. Did AT&T get me to buy anything? No. Was it trying to? No. Did it leave me with a new and better brand image of AT&T than I had before? Yes. Did it have some content that was compelling enough that I told a few thousand of my closest friends? Absolutely. Was it money well spent? I say yes.

If you have the budget and the manpower that AT&T does, you should look into this sort of thing. If you suffer from limited resources, maybe you should skip the find-the-hidden-puzzle-pieces approach.

MAKE YOUR SITE USEFUL

Companies are finding the biggest return on their Web investment by making their sites useful. Some people look at the Internet as entertainment. Lots of people look at the Internet as a form of communication (e-mail, chat, newsgroups). But *everybody* looks at the Internet as a resource. They go there to find information, and they go there to get stuff done.

If your site contains information of value to your audience, they can make use of it as a reference. Every site should, at least, have a list of other Web sites of interest—not of general interest, like Yahoo! or Netscape's Netcenter, but sites that contain information about your industry.

Your site can be useful if it offers the latest news on your market segment. You don't want to be an online news agency? Strike a deal with a company like NewsPage (http://www.newspage.com) that can collect the information for you.

Reveal Your Best Knowledge

Remember AT&T's Papers and Speeches? Think like a publisher for the moment. This is where you go beyond putting papers online because they're interesting. You put information online because it's useful.

InterCorr-CLI International (www.clihouston.com) is an independent research and corrosion testing company. InterCorr-CLI provides test services, corrosion test equipment, and a suite of materials selection software applications. It also publishes an online newsletter, *Corrosioneering.*

> Corrosioneering is InterCorr-CLI's online newsletter. We will periodically post short technical articles that may be of interest to the materials community. This month's topics are:
>
> Metallurgical Developments for Pyrolysis Furnaces for Higher-Temperature Operations and Increased Product Yields
>
> Pathogenic Microorganisms in Water System Biofilm Need Biofilm Sampling
>
> Detecting Corrosion Through Insulation
>
> Specifications for FRP Equipment
>
> Pitting Corrosion Diagrams for Stainless Steels
>
> Understanding How Metals Corrode Can Help Build Better Structures

Industrial metallurgists may find these articles as funny as I find Dilbert. They may be as glued to these documents as I was to the online reports of tornadoes in the Southern states this spring. But chances are, though, that they find these articles useful, so they keep coming back.

Make Their Life Easier

What sort of information would your customers like to have finger-tip access to? What sort of an online database could you create for the benefit of your customers?

Glaxo Wellcome makes prescription drugs. They sell these drugs to doctors, who prescribe them to their patients. How do you get more doctors to know and love your drugs? It's a difficult question because doctors are very busy.

When I went to my doctor for a cocktail of vaccinations before one of my more exotic public speaking tours, I found myself in the waiting room along with others who were there for reasons I'd rather not know. Among them was a man in a suit and tie who, like me, looked too healthy to be waiting in a doctor's office. Then I realized he was a pharmaceutical sales representative. The prospect of him having to sit and wait for the doctor to finish with me made my wait infinitely easier. It also made me glad I was not a pharmaceutical salesman.

Knowing that doctors seldom even have time to log onto the Internet, Glaxo thought about what it could offer that would be easier for doctors to access online than off. The answer: continuing education. Medical professionals are required, just like lawyers and CPAs, to take a certain number of hours of accredited instruction every year. What if they could do it online? That's how Helix was born (Figure 9.5).

Helix instructors are not just the local medicos who were willing to spend some time teaching a class. These are top-notch professionals who can only come to town pre-recorded.

Besides being another of the larger makers of human medications, Pfizer (www.pfizer.com) creates and sells animal medicines for veterinarians. Pfizer asked itself what it could do that would benefit vets and allow it to collect a great deal of information on individual livestock? The answer was the Pfizer Animal Health's Electronic Cattle Drive (Figure 9.6).

Today, buyers of breeding stock want to know more than genetic information alone. They're also keenly interested in health status, how the cattle have been managed, and many other details. Today's buyers are also interested in building long-term relationships with producers of quality breeding stock.

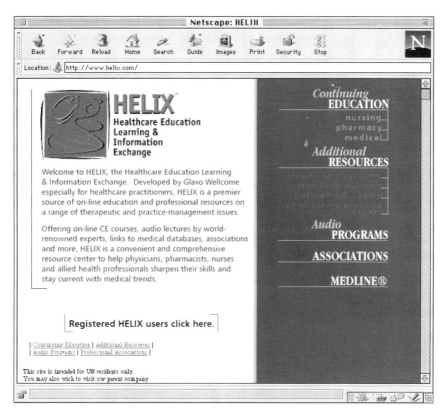

Figure 9.5   Glaxo Wellcome lets medical professionals electronically catch up on their required classroom hours.

When they find the cattle that fit their criteria—and when those cattle stay healthy and perform as anticipated—those buyers will come back to that breeding stock source again and again.

Select source helps differentiate your cattle

The Select Source program from Pfizer Animal Health provides a convenient framework for documenting the health and management history of your breeding stock offerings. It also offers easy-to-follow vaccination and management programs for each of six key breeding stock categories—bull calves, yearling bulls, heifer calves, open (breeding age) heifers, bred heifers, and bred cows. Just choose the program that fits the cattle you are offering, follow the required vaccination and management practices, and your breeding stock will qualify as Select Source cattle.

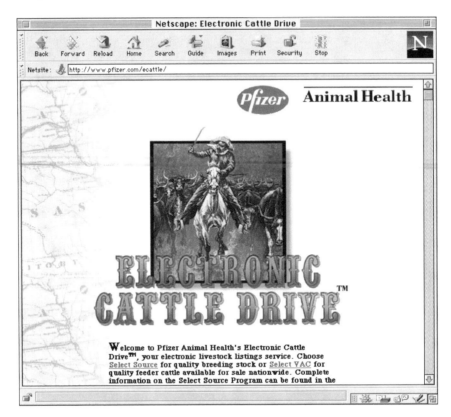

Figure 9.6   Pfizer provides its veterinary customers with an electronic livestock listings service.

Put your cattle in front of potential buyers

As a bonus, your Select Source cattle will be eligible for listing on Pfizer's Electronic Cattle Drive, an excellent advertising service that allows buyers to locate and identify your cattle electronically. For 28 consecutive days, your cattle will be listed on more than 35,000 DTN color screens nationwide. Buyers can also find your cattle listed on their home computers via the Internet. The Electronic Cattle Drive Web site address is http://www.cattledrive.com.

Let Them Access Corporate Data

A corporate database is a valuable thing. It houses the information that is the very lifeblood of your company. It's time to take a deep breath and get used to the idea that you can take advantage of this new computer communication medium by giving your customers access to your live data.

Suggest this to your information systems people, and shivers of fear will run up and down their spines. Fear about network integrity, data security, and computer hackers may make this a tough fight to win. After all, you're only in the marketing department. What can you possibly know about how hard it is to run an enterprise-wide computer network?

The problem is that your competitor is learning how while your firm is standing still. Other companies are finding ways to give their customers limited but crucial access. They are gaining market share because of it.

The reason people get excited about the FedEx Web site is because FedEx thought about it from beginning to end. FedEx knew people wanted the information, wanted it fast, and wanted it complete. They also knew people would have problems with the site and would need instant telephone support. FedEx set the standard. Yes, I know, it sounds like a customer service issue. It sounds like a job for the people in operations. But it is most definitely a marketing problem.

"But I can do that on your *competitor's* Web site." It's a marketing problem.

FINDING YOUR FIRM'S ADDED VALUE

How do you determine what value your firm can provide to your customers and to the Internet? Ask them.

Ask Your Customers. It is not a marketer's job to know what the customer wants. It is the marketer's job to ask the customers what they want. Things change so fast that you must ascertain the needs and desires of the marketplace, *any* marketplace, again and again. Ask customers if they are on the Internet. Ask them if they'd like to be. Ask them what sort of service they would expect from your Web site, and get them involved with the creation and growth of your Web site.

Ask the Internet. Find an appropriate newsgroup and pose the question, "Has anybody seen a Web site that does *this?* If we offered that on our Web site would it be worthwhile? What else should we add?" This is a great way of getting a large number of opinions and doing some prerelease advertising at the same time.

Ask Your Business Partners. Your vendors, your distributors, and your cooperative marketing partners will all have ideas, questions, and resources that will help make your site a better place. Listen to them, give them their own section on your site, and link to their sites. This will make your site a more valuable place for your customers and prospects.

Ask Your Sales and Customer Service Departments. Above all, ask your own people. Your customer service department knows the frequently asked questions. Your sales department knows how people look for information about your products. They also know what else people need in order to consider, justify, purchase, and use your products.

THE WEB IS A PERSONAL PLACE

At first, we all gathered around the fire and listened to the storyteller regale us with bits of our of own history mixed with legend and fantasy. Then we went to the movies. Then television and radio brought the communal experience down to the family level. If you're a baby boomer or older, you remember nights with the rest of the clan, gathered around the glowing black and white box watching "The Ed Sullivan Show" and "Laugh-In" and talking about them in school the next day. It was a close-knit experience, shared by all your peers.

Then came portable TVs, Watchmans, VCR's—and two things happened at once. We stopped watching TV together, and we stopped watching the same things. Now that "Seinfeld" has been relegated to the limbo of syndication, we've lost the last show that almost everybody watched this side of the Olympics.

Computers were never in that category. They were never a group event; they have always been personal.

A Fine and Private Place

How do you feel when you're watching TV and somebody else walks into the room? OK, so maybe you quickly switch back to the PBS special on cholesterol from the Home Shopping Network Sports-A-Bilia special, but you don't mind if they sit and watch you surf. Somebody looking over my shoulder as I type is enough to freeze my fingers. I can work at a pretty good clip until there's another person there who says "Uhh" as soon as I mistype something.

When you sit down at a computer, it's usually *your* computer (at least it's your session). That means you can put the Recycle Bin down in the lower right corner where the Trash belongs and nobody can stop you. You can size the windows the way you want. You can set the margins and change the font size and just make it your own environment.

The worst thing about watching somebody else TV channel surf is that he or she zips right past the good stuff, the serious things of real interest, and then gets bogged down in incomprehensible garbage. Now apply that experience to the Web.

"Don't click there! Click on the Free Stuff button! No, no, not *there.* Hit the Back button. Oh, for crying out loud, you'd think you'd never surfed before—gimme the mouse."

"MoooOOOOooommm! Tell him to quit it!"

A Place of Personal Interest

I have a friend who thought the World Wide Web was, well, OK. Even though I had clearly extolled its virtues on numerous occasions, he just couldn't seem to get interested. Not, that is, until I showed him that he could trade his dearly beloved baseball cards online. Within the week he upgraded his PC, got a modem, downloaded Netscape, and became a cybercowboy.

His wife was overwhelmed by all the choices—they scared her. "How do I know what to look at? How do I know where to go?" I asked her where she went first when she walked into a bookstore. Problem solved.

> "No American is typical anymore. There is no average family, no ordinary worker, and no middle class as we knew it. The State of the Union can no longer be summarized in one sentence because the body politic has become a motley crowd."
>
> Peter Francese, "America at Mid-Decade,"
> *American Demographics*, February 1995

In this day of "You can have any color you want," you must continue to hold out the undeliverable promise to the public. You must still make them understand that your product will make them irresistible, will allow them to win and hold those they love, and will help them rise to the top of their business or social circle. The difference is that you now have a tool to do it for each prospect, one by one.

Don't run away from the responsibility to treat each user as an individual. Change your focus from gaining share of market to gaining share of customer. Measure each customer not as a transaction but as a long-term business partner.

The Web is a personal place full of information of interest to each individual. Unless you are engaged in a battle of joystick skill against another game player, being at a computer is a solitary affair. It's personal. It's work. It's *your* spreadsheet, *your* drawing, *your* document. When you're on the Web, it's *your* surf time.

That's why it's so powerful when the Web site you visit welcomes you back . . . by name.

Web Sites That Greet You by Name

In 1996, when I wrote *Customer Service on the Internet,* Microsoft was beginning to experiment with personal content (Figure 9.7). It was brand new.

Now we've gotten used to configuring My Yahoo! (Figure 9.8) on command. You may choose what you want to see on the Front Page and in what order.

The choices are significant enough to be a little daunting:

Keyword Searches
Lottery Results
Map It
Movies—New Releases
Movies—Upcoming Releases
My Bookmarks
News Clipper
Quotes/Portfolios
Package Tracker
Shopping Top Ten
Ski Report (seasonal)
Sports Scoreboard
Today's Best Fares
Upgrades and Downgrades
Vitamins & Herbs
Weather
Yahoo! Categories
Yahoo! Search
Zacks Earnings Surprises
ZDNet Rumor & Comment

Yahoo! Puts you in the driver's seat. Not just on your own, personal Front Page, but in all of the sections as well. There are choices like the above to be made in every section they have:

Business Section
Chat & Boards Section
Computers & Internet Section
Entertainment Section
Health Section
News Section

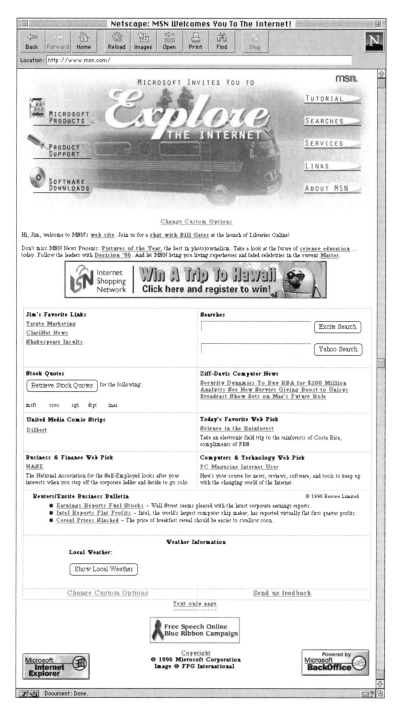

Figure 9.7   Microsoft was one of the first sites to try out personalized content.

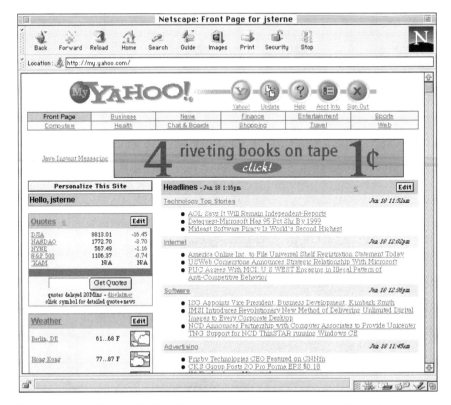

Figure 9.8 Yahoo!'s My Yahoo! is completely configurable.

Personal Finance Section
Sports Section Shopping Section
Travel Section

Yahoo!'s income depends on advertising, which depends on viewers, which depends on your using its Web site more than anybody else's. And for several years in a row, that's been the case.

In April 1998, Media Matrixx calculated that "The top sites remain steady with AOL.com in the lead at home with 48.3 percent reach, followed by Yahoo.com with 42.3 percent reach, Netscape.com with 27.7 percent, Microsoft.com with 24.1 percent, and Geocities.com in fifth place at home with 23.9 percent reach. At work the top sites also remain stable with Yahoo.com in first place with 52.9 percent reach, Netscape.com with 41.1 percent reach, AOL.com with 39.4 percent, Microsoft.com with 32.4, and Excite.com with 27.1 percent reach."

Yahoo! stays on top of that list by offering as much as it can; personalization is one of the big reasons people come back to this site. AOL knows who you are because you have to log in.

How does Yahoo! know it's me when I hit the My Yahoo! button? I didn't log in. I didn't use a password. I'm just another anonymous visitor, but I'm a visitor with a brand on my browser so they know where I've been *this time.* Yahoo! uses cookies, created by Netscape and now used by all browsers.

Briefly put, the Netscape cookie is a file on your hard drive that stores a server-given user identification number along with some useful information of its choice. If the server doesn't recognize any of the cookies in your file, it gives you one. If it does, then it knows something about you. It knows that you are the same person that came to visit three days ago. It can keep track of your every move. It can also look into its database to see what you told it on previous visits. You told it your name? It can greet you personally.

Andy gives great technical advice

For a quick look at cookies in action, try Andy's Netscape Cookie Notes Page (www.illuminatus.com/cookie). The first time you go there, Andy explains all about cookies and how to find out more information and gives you "a big, fat cookie."

When you go back to Andy's page, his server reads your cookie and tells you how many times you've visited Andy's page (Figure 9.9). Yes, you can fool Andy by hitting the Reload button, and adding to his stockpile of virtual nickels, but you can also learn a lot about how cookies work. If your technical staff doesn't fathom cookies, tell them to check in with Andy for an introduction.

Unfortunately, Netscape cookies are not the best way to get the best results. Cookies have a few problems.

Cookie drawbacks

As delicious as the first batch of cookies may be, they have a number of drawbacks. The biggest one is the fact that cookies are plain text files on the client, where they can be easily modified or deleted by the user. Don't like the idea of big-brother corporation writing things on your hard drive for later inspection? Don't like the idea that they're collecting information about you? Dump the file.

Cookies also suffer from being browser-specific. One cookie per browser. Only one cookie per browser, and each cookie belongs to only one browser. Once a cookie is written, it belongs to the browser that was in use at the time. If your customers like to surf with Netscape as well as Microsoft's Internet Explorer, they will have a different cookie with each software package.

If your customer, Bob, lets his office mate, Fred, use Bob's machine for surfing because it has the LAN connection to the T1, then your server will think that Fred is Bob. When Bob goes home and reaches your site via his home computer, he looks like a completely different Bob to your server. He's using a completely different cookie. Did I mention that Bob travels and takes a laptop on the road with him? Different cookie. Different Bob. So now, your server thinks there are three different *Bobs* and one of them is sometimes Fred.

From *Customer Service on the Internet*

It's not just the sites that are in the business of being Web sites that offer customization. Companies that have lots of services to offer, such as Sprint, can use a cookie to help a customer keep the noise level well below the signal (Figure 9.10).

Start off by giving Sprint your name and address and some interesting facts about your company:

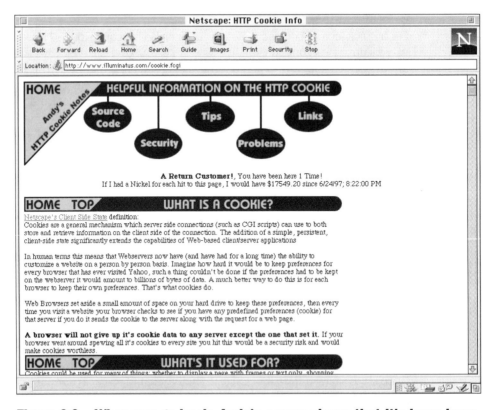

Figure 9.9   When you go back, Andy's server shows that it's been keeping an eye on you.

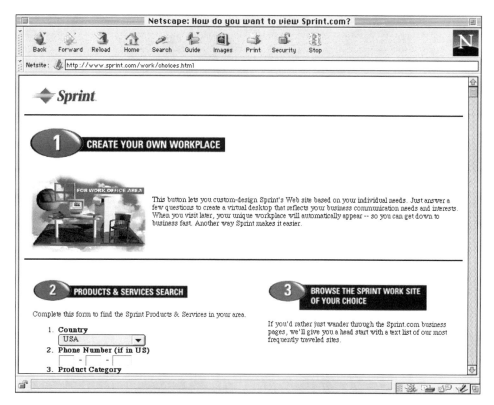

Figure 9.10   Sprint offers a personal Workspace.

Are you currently a Sprint customer?

What is your company's industry?

Does your company do business in the United States, in Canada, internationally?

How many locations does your company have?

How many employees are in your company?

How many employees are telecommuters?

How many employees are in your mobile workforce?

How much does your company spend monthly on telecommunications?

Are you responsible for data? Voice?

Next, choose among a variety of possible product and service areas (Figure 9.11). That way you get a menu bar (on the left in Figure 9.11) that is meaningful to you.

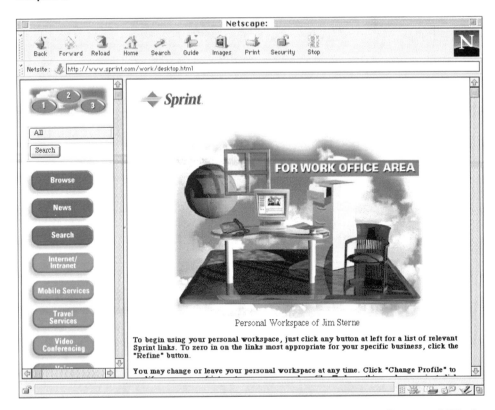

Figure 9.11   Which buttons do you want to see in your Personal Work-space?

General Motors (www.gm.com) takes the same approach, but it does it right from the home page. The third button down on the left side suggests that you "Create Your Own Path. Click to customize this site to your individual needs" (Figure 9.12).

After making some choices about what you like and don't like, GM offers a home page that is more suited to your personal taste (Figure 9.13)

It's not a giant difference. But if I were in the car business, if I wrote about cars, if I loved cars, or if I were in the process of buying a car, this is a nice touch. Anything that keeps me from being overwhelmed with stuff is good.

It may be a subtle distinction, but sometimes personalization is not about getting more of what you want, but about getting less of what you *don't* want. IBM proved it to itself at its Worldwide BESTeam site (www.software .ibm.com/sw-sell/besteam) where it let top-ranking business partners decide how much postal mail they receive.

Figure 9.12   General Motors the way they are.

IBM found that its partners loved to control the amount of junk mail IBM sent them. IBM's not dumb. It knows its all-important, all-significant postal messages build strong partnerships 12 ways. It also knows its partners think most of that mail is junk. The result was more than just happier partners. IBM experienced a significant savings in direct mail costs. A quarter of its partners signed up for mail limitation right away, and it immediately cut 50 percent of outgoing mailings. IBM cut its spending on paper, printing, and postage in half.

The Premier Software Member level is for companies with extensive technical skills for developing and supporting complex business solutions. This level requires three Professional Certifications from IBM. (One of those may be an accepted professional certification from Lotus.)

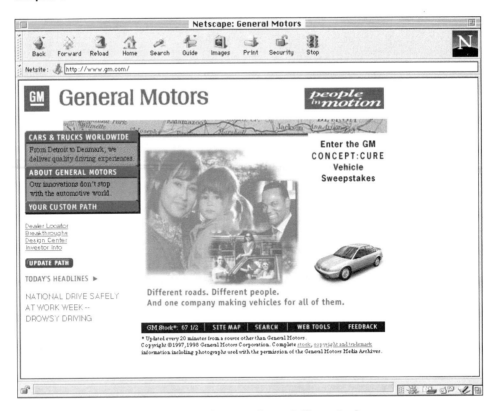

Figure 9.13   General Motors the way I want them to be.

Asking You What You Like

Amazon.com, the online bookstore, started it all (www.amazon.com). They came up with the idea of using e-mail to notify you of new books in which you might be interested. How did they know? At first, they asked. At the bottom of every book page, there's a list of the categories in which they classified that book. Which classification interests you the most? When you specify a category, or an author, or even a title, Amazon.com will send you e-mail when a new book is published that meets your criterion. It's simple. It's neat. As a consumer, I like it; as a marketer, I love it.

As a consumer, it saves me two hours and a hundred dollars every time I wander into a bookstore. As a reader, I try my best to keep track of my favorite authors. Another Jill Ellsworth or Kim Bayne? I want to know. A new Bruce Sterling? How soon can I get it?

But now a new day has dawned. There's a vendor who is willing to scour the shelves, keep track of my favorite authors, and send me e-mail telling me something I really want to know—for free! Amazon sends me an e-mail. I click on the link. I read the review. I buy the book (or not). Amazon.com is simple, fast, elegant, and I always stay up to date on what's being published.

From the seller's perspective, this is akin to the fish jumping into the barrel and handing you a loaded gun. "Sell me!" they plead. "Here's what I want to buy!" they shout. "I want to give you money!" they insist. Is this a seller's market or what?

There's also nothing like being able to accurately predict demand for your goods. When John Grisham puts out another legal-action-thriller Amazon knows how many people want to hear about it, and they know how many purchased his last book when it was released. They know how many copies to buy in advance.

If you are expecting a child, there's a site that wants to get to know you. The Stork Site (www.storksite.com) (Figure 9.14) uses cookies to recognize you and asks some specifics about your anticipated (or newly arrived) bundle of joy.

When you register, you let Stork Site know how far along you are in your pregnancy or when the baby was born. In return, the periodic newsletter and the home page change according to your specific needs. Those needs change depending on trimester, the baby's gender, and the baby's age. If you want the Web to sing your new baby a lullaby, Imagine Radio might not offer enough choices, yet.

Imagine Radio (www.imaginradio.net), is a network of original radio stations "broadcasting" on the Web. It offers a choice of more than 20 original radio stations, featuring 24-hour live news coverage from the Associated Press, 4 stations of talk show programming, and 16 genre-based music stations that range from smooth jazz to alternative rock to classical. All stations are advertiser-supported and free to the listener. Users "tune in" to Imagine Radio with a specially built software "tuner," which can be downloaded for free; the rest is personalization. You pick the station, and you customize your own song rotation—what you want to hear, when you want to hear it.

Divining You What You Like

This is the area where the Web outshines any other form of communication. You can advertise on the Web, you can do marketing on the Web, you can sell stuff on the Web, and you can provide customer service on the Web. Just like everywhere else. But there's one thing the Web does better than any other medium—it remembers.

Figure 9.14   The Stork Site changes to keep pace with your changing life.

When the first edition of this book was published, personalization was still a thing of the imagination. I envisioned some possible scenarios that have come to pass in no time at all:

Collaborative Filtering

After Microsoft and Yahoo! had shown us the power of recognizing visitors and greeting them by name, Firefly (www.firefly.net) surprised us all with the nifty little trick of knowing what we might like. It seemed like magic, but, in fact, it was very easy to understand even though it used a very sophisticated technology. (You know your technology is good when you get bought by Microsoft.)

Firefly had a Web site that asked you for your opinions on various movies. On a scale of 1 to 7, how do you like this one? How about this one? And this? After a while, Firefly had a good idea of what kinds of movies you liked and what kind you tended to give a thumbs down. Now it was ready to make a recommendation.

THE BOOK STORE WEB SITE

Good morning, Mr. Jones. We're glad you're back!

Since your last visit when you picked up *Neal Stephenson's Snow Crash*, he's come out with a *new book*. You may be interested in reading *the first few pages.*

We also have the just-released book on *Marketing Technology* you asked about. Perhaps you'd like to know more about our Thursday *business seminar* series.

One final note: You have 526 Frequent Reader points to your credit. Take a look at the *discounts and specials* you qualify for.

THE LOCAL MECHANIC WEB SITE

Welcome back, Ms. Smith. We haven't seen you here at Bay Motors since *July*.

According to our records and your past driving habits, it's about time for your 60,000 mile tune-up. This is a *thorough* maintenance inspection and service, which should cost approximately $475. If you like, we have several slots open and can set the *appointment* right now.

By the way, based on your excellent maintenance records, John Phillips in sales wanted you to know we can offer you a *hefty trade-in* on your 1996 Honda. Last year's models need to go, and this would be a great time to *trade up.*

If you or I were to create such a site, we'd stuff our database full of stats, such as which movies won Oscars, which grossed the most, which ran the longest, which had the biggest stars. Then, we'd try to match up what you liked against The Best Movies and start making recommendations.

Firefly did it differently. It compared what you liked against what everybody else in the database liked. It found matches between you and the rest of the audience. It could see that you had exactly the same taste as 7 percent of the others, and it knew exactly which movies were at the top of the list of all those people with exactly the same taste in movies as you. Nifty. Do you want to meet people at Firefly? Easy—just click here and we'll give you a list of the screen-names of people who like the same movies and musicians. Take a look at their personal pages on the Firefly site and send them an e-mail. Nothing to it. Easy concept. Tricky technology. They call it collaborative filtering.

Amazon.com thought so and was one of the first to apply this proof-of-concept to a commercial Web site. It's a commercial product called GroupLens from NetPerceptions (www.netperceptions.com). GroupLens does more than filter; it integrates customer preference predictions with business rules and policies. That becomes important when you are personalizing the pricing information on your Web site for consumers versus distributors. Or if your pricing for Asia is different from your prices in Europe. At Amazon.com, it means being certain that an 8-year-old child is not the target of a recommendation for *Lady Chatterly's Lover,* no matter what he *says* his interests may be.

Drastic Times Call for Drastic Tools

A good number of smart people with smart technology are keeping track of what people like and using that information to customize their online experience. Rules-based, case-based, neural-net, and fuzzy logic systems are all getting put to use and are all getting surprising results.

One of the more interesting tools comes from a firm called Aptex (www.aptex.com) (Figure 9.15), which got its start as a credit-card fraud detection company. It makes the software that analyzes your purchases as you make them to see if it's really you. Going on a trip to New York? Going to take in a show and stay at a really nice hotel and do some fine dining? You don't usually do that sort of thing. Your credit-card company knows that. You present your card at the front desk and the nice lady asks you to wait and then hands you the phone. "It's for you." It's your credit card company calling. They detected an attempted purchase outside your normal buying pattern. Is that really you? They'd like your mother's maiden name for verification, please.

Aptex has taken this high-speed, real-time system and given it over to Web sites that want to serve the right content to the right customer at the right time. Collaborative filtering is good, but it's not enough, says Aptex. Business rules are important, but they don't take you all the way. The SelectSystem watches what you do. It's a behaviorally based system.

What you *say* you like is all very nice. But the links you actually click on, the pages you actually read, and the products you actually buy tell the real tale about who you really are and what you really might like to see next.

Your interest in a few hundred different categories is tracked in real time. As you change your focus from work to sports to vacations, the system keeps up, but it still remembers what you were interested in yesterday, last week, and last month. Your profile then is made up of the combination of your implicit interests. Aptex's patented Context Vector mathematical data modeling techniques use proprietary neural network algorithms with 2D and 3D graphical exploration and analysis.

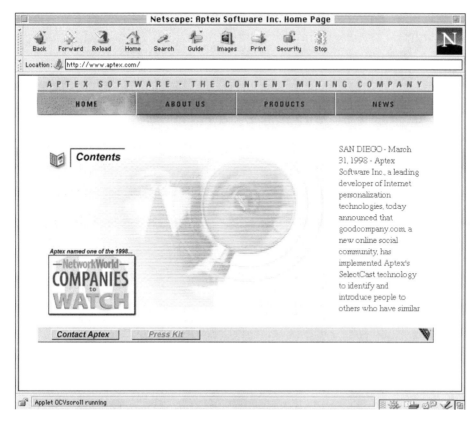

Figure 9.15 **Aptex knows what interests you, making for a very rich Web experience.**

The Aptex technology may be well into the deep end, but its philosophy is simple. If you can capture what people are doing on your Web site and match that to what other people are doing on your Web site, you can start to make some extremely powerful suggestions and recommendations about what they might *want* to be doing or seeing on your Web site.

PERSONALIZING WELL

Don't you hate it when somebody you've never met comes up to you and says, "Oh, hi! You must be Jim! Your wife has told me *so* much about you!" My first reaction is to be grateful that my wife is discreet and not inclined to babble about my song selections when I sing in the shower. My next reaction is that I don't even know if I'm going to like this person and why is he or she acting like a long lost friend. They say familiarity breeds contempt; I say overfamiliarity is far worse.

Familiarity Breeds Contempt

American Express learned this lesson when it started using caller ID. People didn't like it when AmEx seemed to use ESP to recognize them before they even spoke. Answering the phone with "Hello, Mr. Smith, this is Sally at American Express. How can I help you?" was repeatedly met with disdain, distaste, and distrust.

The advent of caller ID did not delight the caller. It was only a matter of time before AmEx allowed callers to identify themselves first. "My name is John Smith, and I have a question about my bill."

"Yes, Mr. Smith, I have your account records in front of me now." That turned out to be quite a coup. Customers got the impression that AmEx's computers were blindingly fast. More importantly, it provided the customer with that all-important feeling of being in control of the conversation. Turns out the correct answer to "Do you know me?" is "Not until you introduce yourself."

We all prefer to shop without being hovered over. Nobody wants to walk into a store where the clerks follow your every move and note each item you glance at. At first, you may just want to be left alone to contemplate the merchandise. Later it's a matter of negotiation dexterity. Frankly, I don't want the car salesperson to know that I've already decided to buy a car and that this afternoon is the only time I have to do so. I want to hold up my end of the illusion of being a savvy, aloof buyer for as long as possible. I don't want the salesperson in the antique store to know that I'm a meerschaum pipe fanatic. That makes bargaining much more difficult when the salesperson knows you're a live one.

A Little Knowledge Is a Dangerous Thing

A wonderful cautionary tale appeared in the *Harvard Business Review* (January-February 1998, page 42). In it, Sandra Fournier, Susan Dobscha, and David Glen Mick suggestion ways for "Preventing the Premature Death of Relationship Marketing."

They warn about asking customers for too much. Just how many times do I have to give the guy at Radio Shack my address? I bought something here last week. You really need my address again so I can buy this telephone cable? They warn that too many companies want to bond with an individual and that the resulting flood of "personalized" postal mail is overwhelming. They warn that savvy customers are feeling put out because they are not Gold Club Members or Platinum Card holders.

I was on a United Airlines flight once, and the captain came back into the cabin to seek me out. When I agreed I was the one he was looking for, (while desperately worried that the only reason he'd leave his seat to look for me was to deliver some very bad news), he handed me his business card and said, "Thanks for flying with us so often." On the back of the card was a handwritten note, signed by the captain. "My crew and I wanted to let you know we really appreciate your 100,000 miles on United. Thanks!"

My first reaction was pleasure at being singled out. But then I noticed the dirty looks from the guys on either side of me. I felt good; they felt crummy. That's two to one. Those *Harvard Business Review* people were on to something.

As interesting as those cautions were, one tale stuck in my mind. It was from an interview they did with a consumer who had ordered some gifts from a catalog. The catalog company sends annual reminders to their customers, assuming the gifts were usually birthday, anniversary, or holiday related. The company is right. I have purchased gifts from the Harry & David catalog for several years in a row; in November they send me a printout of what I bought last year and allow me to check the ones I want to resend. If you buy lots of fruit baskets for lots of office staff, this approach can be quite handy. Good thinking.

But this gentleman had a problem. He had bought gifts for the physicians and nurses who had taken care of his mother during a medical emergency. It was a very unpleasant time and now, every year, he gets a cold, calculated reminder of it.

Use your knowledge wisely.

Pigeon-Holing Too Tightly

Taking the train from London's Waterloo station to the Gare du Nord in Paris is great. You get there faster, and you don't get seasick. But you also don't get to enjoy the wind in your hair, see the sights, or smell the sea air. You are sealed in a metal tube that plunges you beneath the English Channel, and you don't see a thing until you pop out on the west coast of France.

When you profile somebody, you can guess what he or she might be interested in next. But you also put that person on a straight and narrow track with blinders on all sides. Adroit retail practice places the staples at the back of the store to force customers to walk past aisles and aisles of impulse items.

Infoseek President and Chief Executive Officer Robin Johnson feels that search engines should keep queries in context. In *Information Week* (October 14, 1996) Johnson said, "If you do a lot of business searches and type in 'chicken stock,' we're not going to direct you to a bunch of gumbo recipes." But what if gumbo recipes were exactly what you had in mind? How can a computer decide you are either an investor or a chef, but never both?

Sometimes you go to the store as a mother of a sick child, sometimes as a plumber with a leaky faucet. The "milk" you're looking for might be for breakfast, might be baby formula, and might be coconut milk. What if you're trying to find a present for your wife? Will the Sears site not show you the softer side if you spend too much time looking at Craftsman tools?

A Fine Balance

The trick is to be knowledgeable about your guests without being overly familiar. Be attentive without fawning. Be helpful without pigeon-holing people into such small categories that they have to fight your system to find the products or services they want. It's a dance. It's a mutual exchange of data. I don't mind that the woman at the dry cleaner knows my name and phone number. I don't mind that my bank knows my savings balance. I don't mind that Amazon.com knows what kind of books I like to read. But I do mind if that information is used callously.

The trick is to do it well—and that's not easy.

Beyond the fact that it's not cheap and it's not easy, there's another problem with personalization: not everybody cares for it.

THE RIGHT TO PRIVACY

What seems chummy to some is Orwellian to others. What started as your friendly grocer asking about your health and then remembering your answer the next time you come in has turned into a multinational, overly intrusive, oh-my-god-what-happens-if-it-gets-into-the-wrong-hands, mega-database.

You get that sinking feeling that some insidious individual is watching you for some nefarious purpose. Your innermost thoughts might be sold to other merchants who will flood your mailbox with offers you can't refuse.

What kind of mail and phone calls would you get if the Christian Coalition should get their hands on your opinions, attitudes, beliefs, and buying preferences? What if the Pacifists for Animal Rights knew every time you looked at www.nra.org? What if your boss signs up with a service that lets him or her know that you went to Career Mosaic three times last week?

Just where, as a card-carrying member of the data-hungry marketing industry, do you stand on the issue of privacy?

We Like Our Privacy

We even pay an additional fee to have our phone number kept out of the book. That's why it was front page news in California when GTE made a little slip-up.

GTE let the cat out of the bag by releasing unlisted numbers and addresses. If GTE had slipped with only a few telephone numbers, it would have been hush-hush. But GTE managed to blab the numbers and addresses to about 50,000 customers. Were they published in the white pages? No. They were published in a database that GTE leases to telemarketers, along with demographic information. GTE could be on the hook for fines of $30,000 per customer, but that's up to the California Public Utilities Commission. At this point, GTE has sent out a letter offering new numbers, free unlisted listings for a year, and a refund. In the fashion of a true phone company, they declined to let me reprint the letter they sent. They referred me to their lawyers, instead.

That all happened not too long after Lexis-Nexis ran its public relations ship aground by making social security numbers available on its Web site to anybody whose check would clear.

People don't like it when someone spies on them. People don't like it when you know things about them. More important, people don't like the idea that information floating around out there will come back to haunt them.

The first time I tried to get a car loan I was turned down because I was still a student. I waited one month until graduation and tried again. This time I was refused because I didn't have a job. One month later I had a job but was turned down and the bank couldn't tell me why. Finally I opened up an account cosigned by my father, which made me feel about 10 years old again. This time the bank denied the loan because too many people had been checking my credit report in the previous six months.

In his column in *NetworkWorld* (January 12, 1998), Scott Brander lamented the data-gathering side of our society. He pointed out that more information is being gathered about us than we suspect.

The cashier at the airport records your license number as you exit, "for inventory purposes."

Automatic toll-collecting machines keep track of when you pass by so they can provide you with a detailed bill (and someday perhaps a speeding ticket if you take too little time to go from entrance to exit).

Swisscom, the Swiss telephone company, has records detailing every move that a million of its cellular phone users have made over the past six or more months, accurate to within a few hundred meters.

A U.S. luxury car manufacturer advertises that with a call to its 24-hour help desk you can get directions from where you are to where you want to go. The company doesn't happen to mention that the car is using satellites to keep track of where it is and can, upon a request via radio, report its location.

The FCC is requiring all U.S. providers of cellular phone service to be able to accurately report on the location of the origin of any cell phone call to help support 911 emergency call centers.

Fortune Magazine reports that NTT in Japan has a prototype system with which the company can report, on request, the location of any cell phone in NTT's system that is turned on, down to the floor of the building the phone is on.

Many U.S. trucking companies use radio tracking systems to monitor the location of their vehicles.

This all is more Orwellian than Orwell ever was.

But it gets much worse. What if you have genetic tests done in preparation for parenthood and that information is released to your insurance company? The fact that one of your genes shows a propensity toward a heart condition could knock your insurance premiums off the chart. And who would want to hire somebody who was genetically challenged?

Remember the movie *Gattica* (Figure 9.16)?

As a boy, Vincent discovers he is different from his younger brother Anton, a petri dish baby who possesses the perfect genes for success. Where Anton is strong and tall and has perfect eyesight, Vincent is weak and sickly and wears glasses that give away his genetic inferiority. Where Anton earns his parents' constant praise, encouragement, and admiration, Vincent is coddled, pitied, and kept at home.

Jason Catlett runs a company called Junkbusters (www.junkbusters .com) that covers personal privacy and the Web. He e-mailed me the following example of target marketing run amuck:

Dear Mr. Jones:

Our research indicates that you have not bought condoms at SpiffyMart recently. (Your last purchase was eight weeks ago.) Further, you have stopped

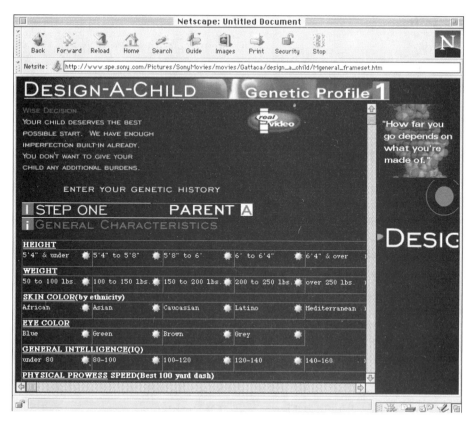

Figure 9.16   The Web site for the movie Gattica lets you genetically design your own prodigy.

buying feminine hygiene products, but you have sharply increased your frozen pizza and dinners usage in the same time frame.

It's clear that Ms. Jody Sanders and you are no longer "an item." (It's probably for the best—she consistently buys inexpensive shampoo, and it was obvious that the two of you were not economically compatible.) The Postal Service database confirms that she filed a change of address form.

We at Hotflicks International offer our condolences.

As the number-one vender of hot XXX-rated videos, we want you to know that our products can help you through this difficult period. When you're feeling lonely, check out our unmatched catalog; we guarantee you'll find something that you'll want to purchase!

Order from this catalog, and we'll throw in an extra tape FREE!

Yours Truly,
Hotflicks Marketing Management

Expectations

We have an expectation of privacy. It's a Constitutional right, right? Well, not really.

A quick search of the text page at www.usconstitution.net/const.html indicates the word "privacy" never appears in the document. We've got the Fourth Amendment: "Right of search and seizure regulated."

> The right of the people to be secure in their persons, houses, papers, and effects, against unreasonable searches and seizures, shall not be violated, and no warrants shall issue, but upon probable cause, supported by Oath or affirmation, and particularly describing the place to be searched, and the persons or things to be seized.

But that doesn't cover the right to know something about somebody he or she does not want you to know. For that, we have to follow the trail of the Tenth Amendment: "Rights of States under Constitution."

> The powers not delegated to the United States by the Constitution, nor prohibited by it to the States, are reserved to the States respectively, or to the people.

That brings us to the Constitution of the State of California, which opens with Article 1, Declaration Of Rights:

> SECTION 1. All people are by nature free and independent and have inalienable rights. Among these are enjoying and defending life and liberty, acquiring, possessing, and protecting property, and pursuing and obtaining safety, happiness, and privacy.

Now, we get to argue until the end of time just what privacy means. That is, we get to argue what it means in California.

According to its own "Case Study of Dun & Bradstreet's Data Protection Practices" (www.dnbcorp.com/press/fed-trade-com.html), Dun & Bradstreet has offices in 37 countries, 26 of which have a level of existing national data protection laws, enacted for the purpose of providing guidelines on the collection, processing, and dissemination of information about individuals.

The European Union Data Protection Directive, which went into effect in October 1998, forces American companies to be a bit more careful than they are used to. One of the rules says that you have to give people access to and the ability to correct their own personal information on data processed in Europe. In addition, you're not allowed to use personal data for anything except the purpose for which it was specifically acquired, unless you have explicit consent. In a nutshell, if you sell somebody a teapot, you're not allowed to turn around and try to sell them tea unless they signed a waiver.

This is an ongoing issue that will involve lawyers and diplomats. To keep your eye on the ball, watch the Web. The U.S. Department of Commerce has a report posted, called "Privacy and Self-Regulation in the Information Age," that's worth a look at www.ntia.doc.gov/reports/privacy /privacy_rpt.htm. The Federal Trade Commission has been warming up to the idea that industry self-regulation might not be enough—the FTC may start regulating soon. You can get help from Peter Swire, Associate Professor of Law at the Ohio State University College of Law. He keeps tabs on the issue at http://osu.edu/units/law/swire.htm.

The legal issues are tricky, but the cultural side of the coin is comparatively straightforward. First, you have to consider that some people feel privacy is pretty much dead anyway.

Just Like Real Life

You think information about you is just between you and the lamppost? Think your financial records, your health records, your shopping habits, your television viewing habits are yours and yours alone? Not quite. Think computers are not already being used to make guesses about how you might act? Think again.

At the Airport

The Computer Assisted Passenger Screening System (CAPS) might hold you up the next time you try to get on an airplane. It's a combination of database and transaction watcher that stops people in their tracks, rather than let them into the friendly skies. If you're in the habit of buying one-way tickets to countries known for terrorism, if you're of Middle Eastern descent, if you like to pay cash for your ticket, you are likely to be questioned, maybe even searched.

The American Civil Liberties Union is concerned about invasion of privacy. Northwest Airlines built and implemented CAPS following a recommendation by the White House after TWA Flight 800 exploded in the summer of 1996. The FAA has handed down the directive that all major air carriers implement such systems by 1999. It's sure to catch some terrorists. After all, the percentage of dumb terrorists in the world equals the percentage of dumb people in the rest of the population.

At the Loan Officer's Desk

Aptex, mentioned earlier for profiling behavior, is an offshoot of HNC Software. HNC has been in the credit card and fraud detection business for decades. Now, it is turning its attention to people who want bank loans, and it bases its profile criteria on some interesting information from some interesting sources.

Your chances of getting a loan are diminished if you have had marriage counseling. Are you buying prescription anti-depressants? Hmmm. Have you been to see a psychiatrist? Tsk, tsk, tsk. Are you going through a divorce. Oooo. Do you frequently buy small amounts of gasoline? Are you using a resumé service? All of the above? You, my friend, are not a good risk for a loan.

In fact, you're more likely to file for bankruptcy than most others, and you're going to have a tough time getting a credit card from Sears. In the last quarter of 1997 Sears racked up $688 million in fraud and bad debts. That kind of pain makes software from HNC seem like a good idea.

On the Web, CyberSource offers a real-time credit check for Web sites that sell. It evaluates how much is being charged, the time of day, the Internet Protocol address the order is coming from, and cross-references that to standard credit reports—all in the blink of an eye, between clicks of the mouse.

At the Insurance Company

If your credit card shows you make frequent purchases at Chicago Extreme Adventures (www.mcs.net/~chgxtrem) and at Barry Beder's EasyQuit Web site (www.smoking-relief.com), and if you neglected to mention these habits on your application form, thanks anyway.

So how do you, as a plugged-in, top-notch, database-driven marketer, get people to agree to give you information about themselves?

Ask them.

Permission Marketing

Yoyodyne Entertainment (www.yoyo.com) is geared toward contests and games. Yoyodyne has a list of 1 million people who said, "Yes! I want you to e-mail me stuff because I want to win!" Here's one no budding Interne-trepreneur could resist:

> Calling All Entrepreneurs! Work for yourself? Determined to be a millionaire? EZVenture is for you! Play EZVenture and you could win a $100,000 investment in your small business. Read new articles every week on topics like Technology, Finance, Leadership, and Sales & Marketing. For every article you visit, you earn an entry toward the Grand Prize. Plus you can win one of the many weekly prizes. Click Here & Register Today!

Sponsored by Inc. Online, Yoyodyne asks for just enough information to target its audience (Figure 9.17). Then, Yoyodyne has the right to send you articles.

Seth Godin, the founder or Yoyodyne, spelled it out well in an article in *Fast Times* (April-May 1998, page 199). Steve Bowbrick of Webmedia (www.webmedia.com) calls it "consensual surveillance"; Seth Godin calls it "permission marketing." "The first rule of permission marketing is that it's based on selfishness. Consumers will grant a company permission to communicate only if they know what's in it for them. . . . You have to turn attention into permission, permission into learning, and learning into trust. Then you can get consumers to change their behavior."

Godin outlined the rules, the tests, and the levels of permission marketing.

The Four Rules of Permission Marketing

1. **Permission must be granted—it can't be presumed.** Buying addresses and sending direct mail are not permission—it's spam, and it's likely to be ignored. Consumers don't want to be bought and sold and then marketed to.

2. **Permission is selfish.** People grant their permission only when they see that there's something in it for them. And you've got about two seconds to communicate that something.

3. **Permission can be revoked as easily as it's granted.** It can also deepen over time. The depth of permission depends on the quality of interaction between you and your customers.

4. **Permission can't be transferred.** It's a lot like dating. You can't give a friend the authority to go out on a date in your place.

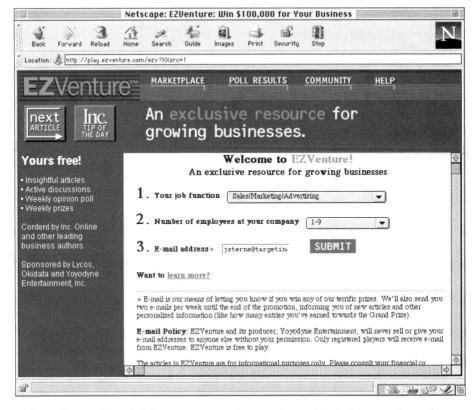

Figure 9.17   How big a company do you have? What line of work are you in? Yoyodyne finds out because people want to win.

The Four Tests of Permission Marketing

1. **Does every single marketing effort you create encourage a learning relationship with your customers?** Does it invite customers to "raise their hands" and start communicating?

2. **Do you have a permissions database?** Do you track the number of people who have given you permission to communicate with them?

3. **If consumers gave you permission to talk to them, would you have anything to say?** Have you developed a marketing curriculum to teach people about your products?

4. **Once someone becomes a customer, do you work to deepen your permission to communicate with that person?**

The Six Levels of Permission Marketing (in Descending Order of Impact)

1. **Intravenous Treatment.** The doctor treating you in the emergency room doesn't have to sell you very hard on administering a drug.

2. **Green Stamps.** Executives suffer through long layovers to gain frequent-flyer miles. Here, the company rewards customers in a currency they care about.

3. **Personal Relationships.** The corner dry cleaner enjoys implicit permission to act in your best interest. A favorite retailer can "upscale" you (recommend something more expensive) without offending you.

4. **Branding.** Given a choice between the known and the unknown, most people choose the known.

5. **Situational Selling.** If you're in a store and you're about to make a purchase, you often welcome unsolicited marketing advice.

6. **Spam.** Where most marketers live most of the time: calling a stranger—at home, during dinner, without permission. You wouldn't do it in personal life; why do it to potential customers?

You want people to reveal themselves? Offer them something in return. I let Amazon track my taste in books because they let me know when there's a new one I'd like. I'm willing to let Intuit know every one of my stock and bond holdings (www.quicken.com) because they tell me what my portfolio is worth as of 15 minutes ago.

1-800-FLOWERS (www.1800flowers.com) pushes firmly on the value of registering (Figure 9.18). They want you to get the most for the least, and a little demographic information is all they ask.

They want to know your birth date. They want to know how you came to hear about them. They want to know five important occasions about which they can send you reminders. They want to know which occasions cause you to send flowers, to whom you usually send them, and whether appearance, prices, freshness, appropriateness, or uniqueness are most important. If you do, you get faster, easier, and more personalized shopping.

At Marketplace1to1 (www.1to1.com), where they know about such things, the Peppers and Rogers Group tells you exactly why you should be a member:

1. You'll receive our free e-mail newsletter weekly.
2. You can participate in the ongoing discussion groups.

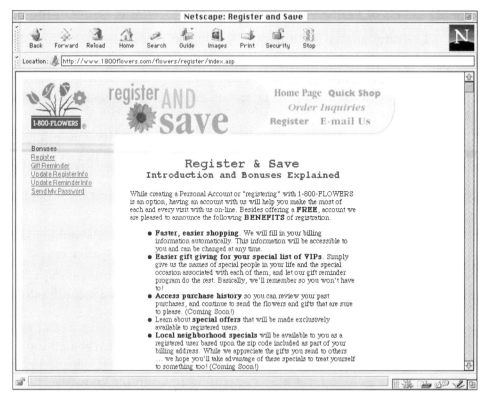

Figure 9.18   1-800-FLOWERS offers all sorts of goodies if you'd only register.

3. You can add companies looking to buy or sell 1:1 products and services to the 1:1 Directory.
4. The site will change to match your interests and preferences.
5. We'll take special interest in your contributions to the community discussions, the 1:1 Directory, and our collection of 1:1 examples, and will consider each (with your permission) for inclusion in our next book of 1:1 "how-to" strategies for the Web.

There is one other thing you can do to encourage people to tell you things—build trust.

Privacy Solutions

First and foremost, your company has to believe in full disclosure. You must candidly explain what information you are gathering and how you are going to use it. You must include a list of third parties with whom you are going to share this information, and you must give visitors the right to update/correct their personal information. You also have to give them the choice and the ability to delete themselves from your database altogether.

A well-publicized Harris Poll in April 1997 found that 79 percent of people asked to fill out a survey on a Web site declined that and 8 percent gave false information. Of those declining and falsifying, 71 percent said they would have given personal information if they had had a relationship with the company, and 63 percent said they would have divulged information had the site offered specific information on how the information was to be used.

Trust Building

L.L. Bean doesn't use fine print to state their privacy policy (Figure 9.19). They want you to feel as comfortable as possible giving them your name, address, clothing sizes, and credit-card number.

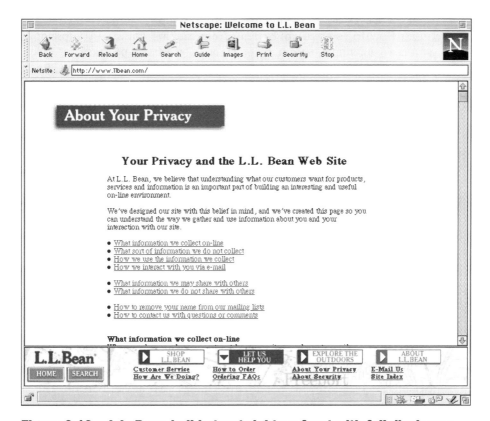

Figure 9.19   L.L. Bean builds trust right up front with full disclosure.

Full disclosure means more than saying "We promise to keep your information safe." It means letting people know if information about them is going to be shared and with whom. L.L. Bean tells it like it is and offers a way out:

> **What information we may share with others** If you provide us with your name or postal address, we may make it available to other companies who want to tell you about their products. (See below if you prefer that we not share this information.) In delivering this information, we may group you with other customers who have bought similar amounts and types of products, but we do not provide any details about you or your household. Return to Top.
>
> **What information we do not share with others** L.L. Bean does not share, sell, or trade e-mail addresses, information collected as part of a survey, or specific details about you or your household. Except to verify credit-card information to complete your order, we do not use or release any credit-card or financial information for any purpose. For privacy purposes, all information relating to our customers is stored on a highly secure server that is not accessible via the Internet. Return to Top.
>
> **How to remove your name from mailing lists** If you prefer not to receive information from other companies whose products we think you might like, please write to the following address. If you have an L.L. Bean catalog, please copy the mailing label exactly as it appears on the back of the catalog and include it with your request.

Branded Trust

Wouldn't you feel better buying from a company that displays a Better Business Bureau symbol of approval on their Yellow Pages ad? It works the same on the Web.

The BBB (www.bbbonline.org) has set up an online program that certifies companies doing business on the Web and offers a BBBOnLine logo for branding your site as a safe place to shop. They also lets the public have access to their database to make sure the branding is legitimate (Figure 9.20).

TRUSTe is a more Web-based approach with more stringent requirements (www.truste.org). They make their point and build their case by pointing to various studies on the subject. Among the surveys' key findings are these:

TRUSTe Internet Privacy Study, conducted by the Boston Consulting Group (March 1997): Growth in electronic commerce will be measurably impacted if Web sites do not address users' privacy concerns. The $6 billion in electronic commerce revenue estimated by the year 2000 could double to $12 billion if users' privacy concerns are addressed.

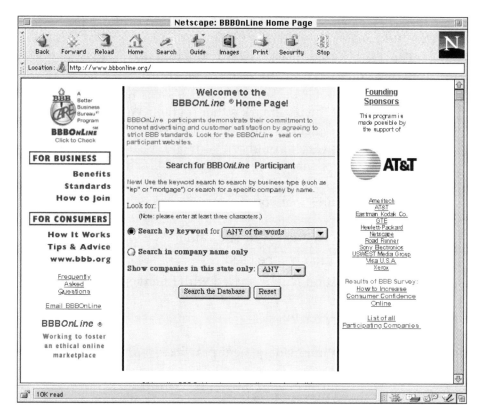

Figure 9.20   The Better Business Bureau lets you use their logo and lets customers see if you earned it.

Commerce, Communication, and Privacy Online, conducted by Louis Harris & Associates and Dr. Alan F. Westin (April 1997): Even if reality proves otherwise, computer users' prevailing perception is that the risk of privacy rights violations is higher for transactions conducted online than for those conducted offline.

7th GVU World Wide Web Survey, conducted by the Graphics, Visualization, and Usability (GVU) Center at Georgia Institute of Technology (April/May 1997): There's a trend toward providing false information online due to privacy concerns.

Surfer Beware: Personal Privacy and the Internet, conducted by the Electronic Privacy Information Center (June 1997): Only 17 percent of the top 100 Web sites post privacy policies.

The TRUSTe Privacy Program helps companies develop privacy statements that describe a site's information gathering and dissemination practices. They provide verification and oversight of the claims a site makes. Then they offer a "trustmark."

The TRUSTe trustmark is an online branded symbol that signifies to users that you disclose your Web site's privacy practices by posting a privacy statement that is backed by TRUSTe's assurance process. All TRUSTe licensees display the trustmark either on their Web sites with a link to the site's privacy statement or directly on the privacy statement. If information privacy practices vary throughout your site, a trustmark linking to the privacy statement for that specific location can be displayed at each specific location.

TRUSTe requires that you disclose:

What type of information your site gathers

How the information will be used

Who the information will be shared with (if anyone)

You have to agree to:

Disclose information management practices in privacy statements

Display the trustmark

Adhere to stated privacy practices

Cooperate with all reviews

TRUSTe has a great "Create Your Own Privacy Statement" routine available at www.truste.org/cgi-bin/wizard.cgi; and there's a copy of the Electronic Frontier Foundation's Overall Privacy Statement in Appendix A.

Mediated Trust

So far we've been looking at the privacy issue from a landlubber's perspective. You collect information on the Web, and you disseminate it (or not) in the usual ways. But what happens if you take a Web perspective? What if all that information can be shared by multiple businesses in real-time?

The reason the privacy issue looms so large on the Web is that the cost of gathering personal information is so astonishingly low. Gather up the phone books for the major metropolitan areas? Yes, it can be done. Cross-reference them with credit reports from the major reporting agencies? Sure. Cross-tabulate that with databases of who subscribes to which magazines? Yes, yes, and more. But that's expensive.

What if the phone company published its phone book online? It does. What if you could get a credit report over the Web? You can. How about direct marketing lists? Who do you think invented merge and purge?

In the January-February 1997 issue of the *Harvard Business Review,* John Hagel III and Jeffrey F. Rayport wrote about a new type of organization—the infomediary. As companies move from fighting over raw materials to distribution to brand awareness, they will end up fighting over information about customers.

Hagel and Rayport postulated that the public will demand payment of some kind for personal information. They got it right so far. Then, they say, because consumers won't be able to negotiate on their own behalf, and because those negotiations would be too costly anyway, new companies will be created to do collective bargaining—infomediaries.

The model states that we as individuals will put our faith, our trust, and our information into the hands of these collectives and let them cut the deals for us. They will protect us from the marketers and advertisers we don't want to hear from and will exchange personal information in return for just the sort of goods and services we want at a honey of a price on our behalf.

Postmaster Direct (www.postmasterdirect.com), Targeted E-mail (www.targetedemail.com), and Bullet Mail (www.bulletmail.com) send you ads based on the profile you create. CyberGold (www.cybergold.com) and ClickRewards (www.clickrewards.com) are just two of the companies that offer promotions and rewards targeted according to your explicit desires. The infomediaries are out there.

Trust Yourself

I tend to disagree with John Hagel III (a principal in McKinsey & Company's Silicon Valley office in California and coauthor of "The Real Value of On-Line Communities" in *Harvard Business Review,* May-June 1996) and Jeffrey F. Rayport (an assistant professor in the Service Management Interest Group at the Harvard Business School in Boston, Massachusetts and coauthor of three previous *Harvard Business Review* articles, including "Exploiting the Virtual Value Chain," November-December 1995).

I think that consumers will be much more comfortable with personal control of information about themselves and that technology will allow that control to be part and parcel of the PC operating system.

I have an innate trust in the power of technology. Complex computer systems are difficult to create. But the further we get, the faster we get there. The more sophisticated things get, the larger the possible gain—and the harder the fall for those who can't believe it can be done.

Lester Wunderman, the coiner of the term "direct marketing" and founder of Wunderman Cato Johnson, thinks one-to-one marketing can't be achieved. At an Internet Marketing conference hosted by Thunder Lizard Productions, in April 1998, Wunderman told the audience that the systems required are so complex and the companies that could afford it are so ill-prepared that so far it's just a bunch of consultants running around spouting the joys of a nirvana never to be. Then he founded a marketing laboratory to find out for himself.

Of the various methods considered, the one with the most attention at the moment is something called P3P.

Under development by the World Wide Web Consortium (W3C), the purveyors of Web standards, the Platform for Privacy Preferences Project (P3P) is intended to let people manage their own information. The user enters personal information into their browser of choice and can then pass on however much of it they choose on to the Web site of choice with a single click. Instead of reentering name, address, and e-mail, just set your browser to give out that and only that. Want to reveal your hobbies and interests? Click over here. According to Joseph Reagle, P3P Project Manager, in a presentation to the Direct Marketing Association in April 1998, it would work something like this:

1. A user sets generic preferences, upon which the agent (browser) automatically acts. The user can now browse the Web seamlessly.

2. A user encounters a site with "exceptional" practices outside his or her generic preferences. Perhaps a sports news site wants to collect his or her favorite teams for a customized news page.

3. The user is prompted if he or she wishes to consider other alternatives, consent to the exceptional practice, or go elsewhere. The user can develop a one-to-one relationship with a trusted site.

You can find the details at http://w3cl.inria.fr/P3P/Overview.html.

In time, there will be enough sophistication in such browser-based systems that they will be able to negotiate on your behalf. But I'm getting ahead of the story. We'll save that for Chapter 14, "Looking toward the Future."

For now, it's crucial to understand why personalization is so important to the continued health of your business.

Payback Time

You put so much time, effort, and *money* into your Web site. Are you going to get only happier customers? No, you are going to give your competitors a heart attack, and you're going to increase profits.

The heart attack is understandable. If your competition has a fabulously interactive, personalized Web site and you don't, you start to feel a bit tight in the chest, don't you? The bottom line, however, is what we live for.

One-to-one marketing isn't *all* about knowing your customers so that you can cater to them. It's also being able to identify your best (read: most profitable) customers so that you can increase the amount of business they do with you.

There is a great tool at the Peppers and Rogers Group Web site that will walk you through the process of identifying those customers (Figure 9.21) (www.1to1.com/ExecPers/default.pl).

The tool asks a series of questions about your industry and your ability to listen. Spend a few minutes, answer a few questions, learn a few things.

Implementation Tips

Chris VandenBerg is the Lead Program Manager on the SiteServer project at Microsoft. He tends to tackle problems from a very pragmatic perspective and keeps end users in mind at all times. At a recent Internet World conference, Chris turned his attention to *his* end users—Web site managers. He offered some advice, which he called "things to avoid."

- Don't roll your own.
- Don't try to sprinkle it on later.
- Don't ignore scalability.
- Don't worry about cookies.
- Don't buy something that doesn't integrate with other Web services.

There are finally enough tools available that do some impressive things for personalization. Use them.

Building a dynamic Web site should be a ground-up affair. No, it's not possible because we have all had our sites up in one form or another for several years. At least prepare for the fact that a personalization engine is going to touch all the corners of your site before you're done. Half-done is worse than not done at all.

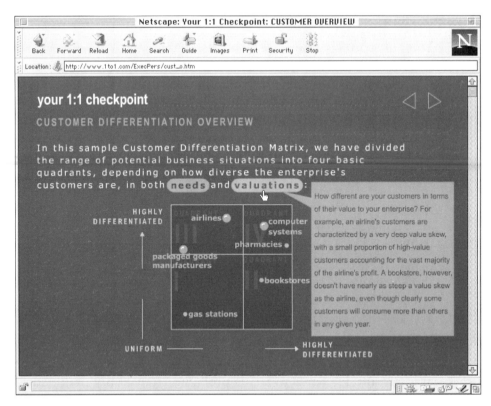

Figure 9.21   Peppers and Rogers outline the difference between high- and low-profit customers.

If you find some technology that works, great. Go for it. But look forward a couple of years and make some optimistic guesses. Will your solution really be able to handle the load?

Cookies are not evil, they are not insidious, and they will not be run out of the village by peasants carrying torches. They are handy tools for identifying people. If some of your customers don't want cookies, ask them to log in.

Customers don't just look at your Web pages. They also send e-mail. They also place orders. They also join in discussion groups. Don't install something that is going to be really friendly until they wander into an unintegrated area that stops them cold and says "Who the heck are you?"

In the spring of 1998, the www.microsoft.com Web site hosted 20,000 new files representing 200MB of new data every day, produced by 500 content creators, and being served by 65 Windows NT servers, which were updated every three hours. One and a half million people a day roam the site in crowds of 100,000 at a time.

When people at Microsoft tell you to choose tools that are scalable and are integrated, they speak from experience.

A Good Resource

Cliff Allen, Deborah Kania, and Beth Yaeckel recently came out with a book called the *Internet World Guide to One-to-One Web Marketing* (John Wiley & Sons, 1998). It's an entire book on the subject of this one chapter. And it's an important subject.

SUMMARY

The success of your Web site depends on how well you can get into your clients' minds and give them what they want, instead of what you want to give them. Make it their place. Cater to their needs, wants, and desires, remembering that what they want and what they need are different things. I may want brighter clothes, but what I need is bleach.

They will all need and want different things. They have emotional needs: the need to belong, the need to own, and the need to win. They have informational needs: the need to be made aware, the need to understand, and the need to get the nitty-gritty details. If you cater to them well, they will reward you with valuable information that will make it easier for you to cater to their needs and wants.

What used to be a simple matter of whipping a few pages together has turned into quite an undertaking. It's not simple anymore. Now that you are well on the way to a superlative Web site that your customers will enjoy, you still need to get the word out that such a wonderful Web site exists.

CHAPTER 10

Attracting Attention

Posted by the author to inet-marketing@einet.net, Tuesday, April 18, 1995, in response to the question: Is simply setting up a Web page enough? How do you let people know about it?

> *Shout it from the roof tops. Write it in the sky.*
> *Promote until your budget pops, until they all surf by.*
> *Announce in proper newsgroups. Mail directly through the post.*
> *Fire up the sales troops. Televise the most.*
> *A 1-800 number won't get you any calls.*
> *Unless you advertise it and paint it on the walls.*
> *Put it on your letterhead. Put it on your cards.*
> *A Web site will be left for dead unless it's known on Mars.*
> *Your Web site can be funny, pretty, useful, crisp, and clean,*
> *But if you don't promote it, its message won't be seen.*

Value Added Marketing is the evidence of your worth as a potential vendor. You can fight for shelf space. You can fight for market share and mind share. You can fight for the hearts and minds of consumers everywhere. But the real fight, the fight that will win you the business, is the fight for the *attention* of consumers—their time.

Each day we are hit with thousands and thousands of commercial messages. The newspaper and the "morning" shows during breakfast, the billboards and the delivery trucks on the road, the signs on the sides of the buses and buildings we pass along the way, all blend together in a blur of commercial broadcasting.

Remember that old saw about half your advertising dollars being wasted, you just don't know which half? It's a saw no more. A study done by Information Resources Inc. (www.infores.com) in March 1998 confirmed it. It analyzed 104 weeks of sales performance for more than 1500 brands in 200+ categories across 50 nationally dispersed markets and determined half of the ads placed were for naught. Every day we see new ways of delivering advertising messages. I was surprised when I first saw ads for the movie *Titanic* on large bags of popcorn at the local movie theater. I didn't expect to see advertising on the little plastic dividers between my purchases and those of the person in front of me at the grocery store. As you drive along California highways, you'll see that they have been "adopted" by local companies (Figure 10.1). It made me wonder where all of it was going to stop (Figure 10.2).

With technology changing so fast, will it surprise anybody when we see this press release?

Figure 10.1   Green freeway advertising is cheaper than a billboard and environmentally correct.

Figure 10.2   We can only hope that it never comes to this.

YOUR NAME IN (NORTHERN) LIGHTS

NEW MARKETING MEDIUM ANNOUNCED

Company Slogans in the Skies Before the Year 2000

SANTA BARBARA, CALIFORNIA 4/1/98—Scientists have announced a new method of using the Northern Lights as a display for advertising. This latest development on the marketing front has large companies scrambling to be the first to sign up with a new service being offered by Target Marketing of Santa Barbara (www.targeting.com). "It's essentially a breakthrough in iono-spheric and magnetospheric physics," says Jim Sterne of Target Marketing. "Years ago, original studies had been focused on the use of low frequency signals to communicate with space probes across vast distances, and now the Internet gives us a large enough platform to control the Northern Lights." Computer models generated back in the early 1980s indicated that a blan-ket of loosely woven copper wire spread over a huge area could generate

(Continued)

YOUR NAME IN (NORTHERN) LIGHTS *(Continued)*

controlled pulses. The intent was communication with spacecraft that had left the solar system. Low-frequency communication has long been used to communicate with submarines far out at sea. It was deemed impractical at the time, however, to construct such a system due to its enormous cost. Today the Internet backbone provides the platform, and the characteristics of modern routers and switches provide the controls.

The clock rates of modern computers and the use of interference pattern techniques can generate signals in the 40 to 50 GHz range. These signals interact with the Ionosphere and can be tuned to cause alterations in Northern Lights contours. Target Marketing plans to display the first commercial messages in Northern Lights one year from the date of this announcement. This announcement has started a bidding war among several corporations.

In individual press releases, Scott McNealy announced a new virtual machine called Javlcicles, Microsoft announced Windows NL, and AT&T and Sprint have petitioned the FCC for new frequency auctions. Bill Gates was overheard wondering how many programmers it would take to make the Northern Lights appear over the lower latitudes.

The people you are trying to attract to your Web site are looking for something of value. Something that is entertaining can be considered valuable. Something that improves their chances at gaining stature is valuable. Something that helps them achieve their goals is definitely valuable. You might offer the most helpful, useful, important, captivating Web site ever written, but if you don't let people know it's there, it will remain a secret. An electronic presence on the World Wide Web is very much like an 800 telephone number: If you don't tell, they won't call.

You can let wired people know you are open for business on the Internet in several ways. However, you must pay close attention to netiquette before you broadcast your sales pitch to the masses. You must also be very certain everything is in its place and works before you let the cat out of the bag.

WAIT UNTIL YOU'RE READY

There are a million details to consider when you launch a new product. Timing the press release, the brochures, the advertising, the direct mail, and the trade shows is nerve-wracking at best. If the brochures show up a week late, the leads pile up, but there's no real harm done. If you announce a new Web site or an additional service on your site and the site's not ready, the harm may be irreversible. People are going to look at your new site within seconds of an announcement—literally. Think about your reaction if the site you want to visit isn't ready.

While you are working away on your computer, a small beep or some other alert indicates a new e-mail message. It's from the SCUBA-L list to which you subscribe to. You've recently posted a question about diving in the Cayman Islands and are hoping for an answer. Instead, it's an announcement about a new Web site dedicated to Caribbean diving. You're interested; maybe there's information there about a hotel you're considering.

If you use an older e-mail system, you highlight the URL in the mail program, copy it, and paste it into your Web browser. If you use a newer version, you simply click on the link and it pops up your browser. Half a minute goes by, and you are greeted with a large "Under Construction" sign. "We'll be up and running soon!" Thinking to check it out later, you add it to your bookmark file and hold a grudge against the fools who announced something that wasn't there.

Two days later, in a normal review of your bookmarks, you come across this dive site address and try it again. Again, you find the site is still not available yet. You delete it from your bookmarks. There are so many resources out there, so many Web sites to see, and so many varied entries in your bookmarks, it's overwhelming. You gave them a shot—two, in fact—and they blew it. Never again.

It takes no time at all for your public to discover if your site is really running. Better make sure it is tested, tested, and tested before you announce.

TRAFFIC EXPECTATIONS

There was a time when the moment an announcement was made, a Web site was overrun by the curious. Remember, there haven't always been 5 million Web sites to choose from. Back then, the mere mention of a new site brought out the hordes. They would come to kick the tires and slam the doors. The majority of them came to compare the new site to their own. Then, they'd tell others what they saw and whether it was a waste of bandwidth or something all of us should emulate.

If the new site was worthwhile, the number of users would swell for about two weeks. After the excitement was over, users would drop to a precious few, the ones who were continually interested in the content. They were customers, prospects, and competitors keeping up with current events. You can't expect the same curve today. Initial visits will be from those with a keen interest in you, your company, your industry, the service your Web site provides, or a new technique it shows off. Then, as word gets out, the number of people with an interest in your product or industry will slowly grow. It's simply a matter of figuring out new attention-getting devices.

PLAN FUTURE ANNOUNCEMENTS

Announcing a new site is one thing, but what do you do for an encore? How do you keep new surfers coming? This is where your people with experience in event marketing come into the picture.

The most fun part of creating a Web site is the tremendous number of creative ideas it engenders. The most aggravating part of creating a Web site is the tremendous number of creative ideas it engenders. You are going to end up with a list of dozens of interesting, useful, and exciting things you could do on your Web site. You won't have the budget or the time, but you will have a need to keep track of the best ideas for rolling out later.

A Web site is always a work in progress. You don't just create it and it's done, like a brochure. Think in terms of a newsletter, a TV show, or a monthly seminar. Each item you create can live forever on your server. When each item grows old and stale, it needs to be replaced.

These replacements can offer an opportunity to make another announcement if the new content or service you are offering is note-worthy; this is Public Relations 101. If you have a compelling story that editors will be interested in, they will be interested because their readers will be interested. If their readers are interested, then they'll tell others. The nifty part about the Internet is that you can go directly to those readers and they can tell others at the speed of light.

ANNOUNCING IN NEWSGROUPS

Used carefully, newsgroups can be a great place to launch a Web site due to the tremendous word of mouth they engender. The key word here is "carefully." Electronic word of mouth is unlike anything you've experienced before. As Ron Richards of ResultsLab (www.resultslab.com) puts it,

> Discussion-group word of mouth is capable of causing product and service appraisals to be distributed with amazing speed and breadth. Sellers must have an interactive Internet presence to compete, and once they have it they are operating in a fish bowl. I've seen products soar, or be destroyed, in just months from it.

If you post to rec.bicycles.racing that your new Web site lists all of your bicycle products, you are sure to incite flames. If you're putting up a Web site that lists bicycle races around the world, you will have no problems whatsoever announcing it in rec.bicycles.racing. However, you are sure to incite flames by posting this announcement to rec.bicycles.tech.

Stay on Topic

People in rec.bicycles.tech may retaliate, and the results can be unpleasant. Consider a real-world allegory. A man runs into a room and shouts at the top of his lungs, "We won the Super Bowl!" If the room is a sports bar, this newsbringer will be greeted with cheers and invited to join other celebrants. If the room is a quilting session of octogenarians, this interloper will be sized for a white jacket that fastens at the back. Be sure to announce where the news will be well received. How can you tell? There are two ways to get a clue: the FAQ file and reconnaissance.

Almost all newsgroups have a frequently asked questions (FAQ) document that is posted regularly. This digest will include the answer to "Is it OK to advertise?" Almost all newsgroups answer this question with a simple "No." Others will provide qualifications. Ignore these rules at your peril. Posting an aberrant message reveals that you have not read the FAQ or, worse, hold it in contempt. The unpleasant response can be damaging to your reputation, your Internet access, and your person.

Reconnaissance will go a long way toward helping you understand the microculture of the newsgroup where you want to place your announcement. Read the newsgroup for a few weeks. See what others are posting, and assess how the group responds.

The Penalty for Misbehavior

The tale of Laurence Canter and Martha Siegel has become legend in cyberspace. Known as the Green Card Lawyers, they were the first to abuse the ability to post to thousands of newsgroups with the push of a button. The wrath they incurred and the price they paid are lessons to all of us. They were warned, they were cautioned, and still they ridiculed Internet customs. In their book, *How to Make a Fortune on the Information Superhighway*, Canter and Siegel describe how they advertised their services for helping noncitizens fill out applications for the Green Card Lottery.

Canter and Siegel started off on the right foot by participating in the alt.visa.us newsgroup. People had specific questions, and they knew the answers. They were willing to share their knowledge, and the result was great. "Within a day or so our electronic mailbox overflowed with individual immigration inquiries. People we had never met wanted to hire us as lawyers."

Then they tried an experiment. They posted an ad for their services in about a hundred alt.culture.(country) groups. In their own words:

> Hundreds of requests for additional information poured in. . . . We also received our first "flames." . . . A few individuals did not like the fact that we had posted our notices to a number of newsgroups. We were informed that when you post to newsgroups, you must post only on the topic of the group. "What," someone wanted to know, "does the Green Card Lottery have to do with alt.culture.japan?" Others advised us to look into "Netiquette," the informal code of behavior certain people believe must be observed when you operate in Cyberspace. Still others were not so polite.

Undeterred by this negative response, Canter and Siegel widened their operations. They posted to 1000 newsgroups and then to 6000. Each time they were met with flames and ill will. Each time they ignored the signals and shrugged it off. You'd almost expect these people to walk gladly through a Japanese home in their hiking boots, raise their voices when their host could not understand them, and insist vehemently that their host bring them a knife and fork for their dinner—even after having been told that these are contrary to local customs and good manners.

It doesn't matter if you think your actions are proper; it matters what your clients think. You must respect the culture of whatever country you're in, even if it's that newly founded realm called cyberspace. The result of their continued breach of netiquette harmed them and others around them.

> Call after call came complaining about what we had done. . . . The amount of (electronic) mail was particularly staggering because a number of protesters decided to do more than just apply bad language to the situation. Instead, they sent mailbombs, huge electronic files of junk designed to clog up our computer by their sheer size.

This clogging shut down the computers at Canter and Siegel's Internet provider. When data overflows a disk drive, the computer objects and goes into a coma. After the system operators rebooted the system, thousands of additional flames were waiting. This actually happened several times. The access provider terminated Canter and Siegel's account. Canter and Siegel went elsewhere and experienced the same situation. The sad part is that many others were using those access providers as well and had their service interrupted for days on end. Thousands of people were said to have requested information just to make Canter and Siegel spend money on brochures and postage. It was rumored that a program was written to dial Mr. Canter's pager every 20 minutes between the hours of 1:00 A.M. and 5:00 A.M.

The stories of revenge enacted by indignant Netizens range from the simple to the unbelievable. Net lore is often spurious, but it is also indicative. In a population this large, there are sure to be those with an equal-but-opposite sense of right and wrong. They may also possess the ability and desire to carry out such acts of revenge.

> In the physical world, the advertiser bears the entire cost of distributing their message to the consumer. Anyone who has mailed any number of marketing brochures can appreciate the very real costs involved in distributing information to consumers.
>
> But this is not the case in the online world where these costs are shared between the advertiser and the consumer. We pay a measurable cost to receive information via the global Internet—from an on-demand shell or SLIP account to a high-speed dedicated leased-line connection. Some pay per hour charges for information, some pay per message. But the reality is that everyone pays in some way for the information they receive.
>
> We all live by certain rules which make it possible for us to live and communicate effectively with our peers. We do not lie, cheat, or steal from those around us. We do not drive on the wrong side of the highway. We do not use rude language in polite conversation. And we do not use our neighbors' property without their permission.
>
> These simple rules are there to allow us to function effectively as a society. Some are important enough to require protection by law while others are part of the social compact we all observe for the benefit and support of human community.
>
> Canter and Siegel have ignored the single fundamental truth of the global Internet. They have ignored the fact that above all else, the global Internet is a community and like any community, participation in it implies certain rules and obligations.
>
> From "Postage-Due Marketing" by Rob Raisch of Internautics
> (and well worth reading).
> (www.internautics.com/raisch/article960910.htm).

The lesson for the unsophisticated marketer is that unconsidered postings can cause direct personal harm. The lesson for the rest of us is that unconsidered postings can destroy any good will you have tried to foster in the Internet community. Do everything in your power to stay off the Black-list of Internet Advertisers (Figure 10.3) (http://math-www.uni-paderborn.de/~axel/BL/).

Newsgroup Participation and Signatures

Canter and Siegel started off on the right foot. They answered specific questions. They were helpful. They received serious leads this way. That was before they learned to spam the newsgroups with their ads.

Let's say you make espresso machines. You read the alt.coffee news-group. When somebody posts a complaint about the difficulties of frothing milk when making latte, you are helpful. You offer a few tips on the fine art of holding the wand just below the surface so that the steam pulls in air as very fine bubbles. Then you mention that your company's Web site has complete frothing instructions in a variety of formats from line drawings (they load quickly) to ShockWave animations (they're more explicit) to

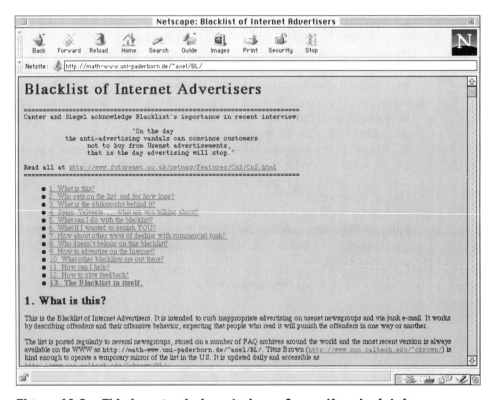

Figure 10.3   This is a good place to learn from others' mistakes.

video clips of Howard Schultz, CEO of Starbucks, personally showing you how it's done. This is offering specific help for a specific problem. You are a participant, not an advertiser.

Wait for a question you can answer. If somebody asks about an upcoming regional bike race, you can write to the group with the answer and add a short "By the way, we have a Web site where you can find all sorts of biking information."

The best approach to newsgroups is to become a frequent poster. Through your participation in newsgroups, people will recognize you as a voice of reason. They will read your postings because they are always well thought out, considerate of others, and helpful to the group. Spend a few months sharing helpful insights and advice, even asking a few interesting questions. In time, people will equate your wisdom with your company and your products. This name recognition is achieved through the use of a signature.

Every e-mail or posting you send can include a prewritten, several-line chunk of information. Your signature is like your letterhead or business card. It may contain your company name, phone number, e-mail address, and personal quote, along with your corporate slogan. It may also contain "Come see the latest at our exciting new Web site at http://www.xzy.com."

It's best to keep your signature as short as possible. Mine is borderline:

```
- - - - - - - - - - - - - - - - - - - - - - - - - - - - - - - - - - - - - - - - -
Jim Sterne                      http://www.targeting.com
jsterne@targeting.com                   Target Marketing
Author: "World Wide Web Marketing"      +1-805-965-3184
"Customer Service on the Internet"            Consultant
and "What Makes People Click - Advertising on the Web"
=========================================================
```

The Announcement Newsgroups

Many newsgroups were designed for announcements. If you have a new Web site or an important new feature to talk about, you should post it to comp.infosys.www.announce. You might also find other newsgroups that pertain to your industry.

There are more than 600 "announce" newsgroups at Liszt, the mailing list directory (www.liszt.com); some are topical:

comp.newprod announcements of new products of interest (moderated)
comp.infosys.announce

comp.infosys.www.announce
comp.security.announce
comp.sys.ibm.pc.games.announce
news.admin.net-abuse.announce
rec.arts.movies.announce
rec.aviation.announce
res.skiing.announce

Some are regional:

ba.announce	(San Francisco Bay Area)
alabama.announce	Of interest to everyone in Alabama (moderated)
brasil.anuncios	General announcements of interest to all (moderated)

Some are event oriented:

akr.jobs	Announcements and discussion of jobs in the Akron, Ohio, area
cam.announce	Local events annouciation for cambridge, uk
news.announce.conferences	

Some are industry-specific:

alt.aapg.announce	The American Association of Petroleum Geologists
alt.building.announcements	Building industry announcements
bionet.announce	Announcements of widespread interest to biologists (moderated)

Some are company-specific:

biz.digital.announce
biz.oreilly.announce
biz.sco.announce
biz.zeos.announce

And some are even product-specific:

rec.games.doom.announce
comp.archives.msdos.announce
comp.os.ms-windows.announce

Above all, remember the public relations aspect of posting to news-groups. Select the individuals who will represent your company in news-groups as carefully as you would select those who would be interviewed on television. Public written announcements, statements, and comments need to be clean and to the point. They need to be proofread to ensure that every http and : and // is correct. Should you have enough of a following, you might consider creating your own newsgroup.

ANNOUNCING ON LISTS

An e-mail list acts just like a newsgroup. The only difference is that your message goes directly to the participants. Instead of their having to go to the newsgroup, your message is delivered directly to those who subscribe to the list. At first this sounds like the direct marketer's dream come true: Self-selecting people with a common interest have all expressed a desire to talk about things that relate specifically to your industry. Posting to lists, how-ever, requires as much restraint as posting to newsgroups, sometimes more.

A list subscriber doesn't look at postings during a free moment as the newsgroup reader does. The subscriber is barraged with messages all day long. People in large organizations who belong to two or three lists will routinely receive more than 100 e-mail messages per day. Your announce-ment comes right to their screen. It had better be on topic.

You may have a Web site that shows the schedules for every dog show on the planet, but you will be flamed if you announce it to all of these at the same time:

Akitas	Bouvier des Flandres
American Bulldogs	Chesapeake Bay Retrievers
Australian Shepherds	Dachshunds/Dalmatians
Basenjis	Doberman Pinschers
Bearded Collies	Flat Coat Retrievers
Belgian Shepherd Dogs	German Shepherd Dogs
Border Collies	Golden Retrievers

Great Danes	Portuguese Water Dogs
Great Pyrenees	Pugs
Greyhounds	Rhodesian Ridgebacks
Kuvaszok	Rottweilers
Labrador Retrievers	Samoyeds
Leonbergers	Shetland Sheepdogs
Mastiffs	Vizslas
Newfoundlands	

Consider hanging out on Canine-L or the Obedience list for a while and then post there.

Yes, Liszt at www.liszt.com *is* the right place to go and find lists (Figure 10.4). Dejanews (www.dejanews.com) seems to be the place for newsgroup searches.

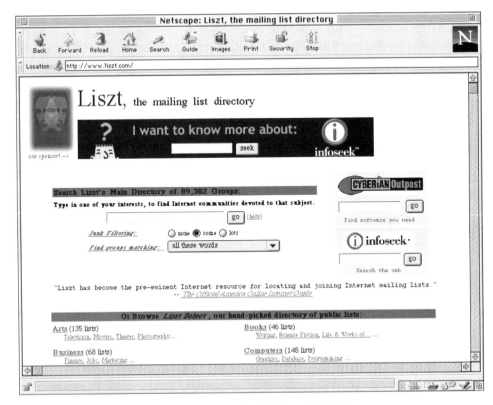

Figure 10.4   Liszt is a great place to find, well, lists.

WHAT'S NEW WEB SITES

What's New pages used to be the way we all found out about new Web sites. Now there are so many new sites every day, they're just not what they used to be. You can get a lot of traffic to your site by getting listed at Netscape's What's New (http://guide.netscape.com/guide/whats_new .html) (Figure 10.5).

You have to wonder about the value of bringing thousands of people to your site who might be just as interested in Buck Owens' Crystal Palace restaurant as they are in nuclear disarmament or JointSolutions' office cat, Kitty. Keep in mind that Yahoo! lists more than 30 What's New pages at www.yahoo.com/Computers_and_Internet/Internet/World_Wide_Web/ Searching_the_Web/Indices_to_Web_Documents/What_s_New/. You have to ask yourself just how useful they can be.

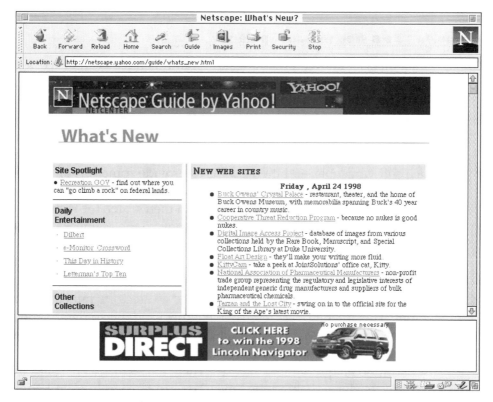

Figure 10.5   Netscape and Yahoo! teamed to create this What's New page.

How are people really going to find you on the Web? Four ways are possible; a fifth is probable. They might type in your domain name (www.your-company.com) because they saw it in one of your regular marketing media. They might hear about it from a friend or on a list. They might click on a link from another Web site that points to your site. They might see a banner ad you have placed on other Web sites. But chances are very good that they will hunt you up in a search engine. Let's start there.

SEARCH ENGINES

It has often been noted that the worst thing about the Internet is that you can't find anything. Seek and ye shall . . . become confused, become lost, become frustrated. It's like having access to the entire Library of Congress with no card catalog. It's like having all the information in all the Yellow Pages at your fingertips but no index. If you're out for a spin, it's fun; If you're looking for something in particular, it's not.

It Wouldn't Be a Web without Spiders

Since this is a known problem, skilled minds have been at work building solutions. That is how the World Wide Web has attracted spiders. According to the Web Robots Pages (http://info.webcrawler.com/mak/projects/robots/robots.html) "Robots, Wanderers, and Spiders are all names for programs that traverse the Web automatically."

What are they doing out there? Collecting information. There are many such software tools, and their goal is to provide some sort of indexing for a chaotic Internet. These automata visit Web sites, study them, and bring the results back to their databases. A user can then search for Web sites of interest using keywords. The value of these tools to the searcher is tremendous. The value of these tools to one who would like to be found is immeasurable.

The major search engines (AltaVista, Excite, HotBot, Infoseek, Lycos, and Webcrawler) are slightly behind Yahoo! as the main way people find stuff on the Web. Your site equals stuff. Yahoo! is a directory, rather than a search engine. The difference is that search engines send out spiders to crawl across the Web and Yahoo! is a hand-built directory. The search engines read every page of your site and store the text in humongous databases. Then inquisitive surfers can query the databases. There are so many Web sites that these engines are always behind the times. You can't expect the latest and greatest information on your site to be indexed for 6 to 10 weeks down the road.

Yahoo! has humans looking at every submission and deciding where to put the listing in its directory. After sending Yahoo! your site information, it can take even longer to show up in Yahoo! than in the search engines. (Tiny bit of trivia: Jerry Yang and David Filo, founders, chose the acronym for Yet Another Hierarchically Organized Oracle.)

Sometimes when you're out there looking for something, it's much easier to traverse the Yahoo! hierarchy than do a text search. That's why the key search engines like Excite now have categorized listings as well as databases (Figure 10.6).

Creating Spider Food

Obviously, you want to attract spiders to your site and have them list you first when somebody goes out to look for that which you sell. Laying out

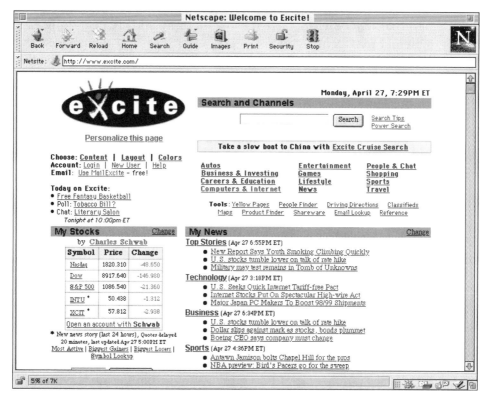

Figure 10.6   Excite is staying competitive with Yahoo! and the others by offering much more of an "Internet front door" than just a search engine.

tasty spider food is much easier than making a sound like a female spider. Begin your spider food production by listing all the keywords people might use to find your company or products. Do you make keyboards? People will look you up by company name, by product name, and by product type. They might also search on:

- Keyboard
- Keyboards
- Peripherals
- Input devices
- Keypad
- Touch screen

Oh, and don't forget key board, keybaord, keybroad, and keeboord.

You might also want them to find you if they search on *computer services* or *installation* or *repair*. Give it some thought, and create as long a list as possible. At that point, you can start hiding them in plain site around your Web site. Different spiders work in different ways, but some basics prevail.

Home Page Title. Your home page is a document. That document has a title. That title is what appears in the very top of your browser window, in the actual browser header bar. The title is not the first words on your home page, but the words that are HTML coded as <title>These Are The Most Important Words To A Search Engine! </title>.

Make sure the title of your home page, and every other page on your site, is the best combination of words you think people will search for.

Meta Tags. The next HTML code you can make use of is the Meta Tag. These words will not be visible to the human surfing your site, but spiders will pay attention. Don't forget to add a <description> on your page. This won't be rendered by the browser either, but it will show up as the description of your site on the search engines.

First Paragraph. Spiders look at the first paragraph on your page as the most significant. They assume that, if you really have something important to say, you'll say it right up front. The tricky part is making this paragraph meaningful to humans while peppering it with spider food.

Proximity. Do you sell tennis shoes? Then a home page that talks about tennis shoe styles and tennis shoe sizes and tennis shoe brands will get listed higher by the search engines than people who sell shoes specifically designed for tennis. The proximity of the words "tennis" and "shoe" makes all the difference. The repetition doesn't hurt either.

Variations. Shoes, foot coverings, sandals, boots, you name it. Search engines are getting smarter by the day.

Given these criteria, Avis Rent A Car is making some serious mistakes (www.avis.com) (Figure 10.7).

Spiders are good little readers, but they can't see pictures. To them, this page looks like this:

Enhanced for Netscape Navigator or Microsoft Internet Explorer.

Download Netscape Now!

Click Here to start.

The Worldwide Fleet
Reservations & Rates
RIDL (That stands for Rental Info Details by Location. Ultra-intuitive.)
Find Us
Talk to Us
Employment Opportunities
Travel Agents
Local Avis Homepages
Negotiated Rate Plans
Special Offers
Special Services Travel Partners
Maps & Directions
Fun
The Avis Store
Site Index

© 1998 WIZARD CO., INC.

That's all the text there is. Spiders *will* see the title and the Meta Tags Avis has put in its HTML. Those tags include these:

<META NAME="description" CONTENT="Welcome to the Avis Galaxy, (www.avis.com). The Avis Rent-A-Car website offers complete car rental information for your leisure and corporate travel plans worldwide. Visitors can review the entire Avis car hire fleet by country, browse driving maps, request rental rates, and even rent a car on-line.">

<META NAME="keywords" CONTENT="Avis, avis, AVIS, Cars, cars, CARS, car, CAR, Car, rental, Rental, RENTAL, rent a car, RENT A CAR,

Figure 10.7   Spiders can't sink their teeth into the Avis page.

Rent A Car, car rental, Car Rental, CAR RENTAL, car hire, Car Hire, CAR HIRE, rent, Rent, RENT, hire, Hire, HIRE, maps, Maps, MAPS, avis rent a car, online car reservation, automobile rate request, AVIS RENT A CAR, ONLINE CAR RESERVATION, AUTOMOBILE RATE REQUEST, Avis Rent A Car, Online Car Reservation, Automobile Rate Request">.

In this case, Avis decided to forgo findability for the sake of design because the search engines are going to give a lot of weight to the words, "Enhanced for Netscape Navigator or Microsoft Internet Explorer. Download Netscape Now!"

Spider Repellent

If you have a large Web site, a visit by a spider may have an impact on your systems. These visits are always unexpected and unannounced. They can consist of a single server asking for every single page you have. If you are IBM, you have more than 25,000 pages. A spider visit can slow your system down. Well-behaved spiders come into a site and look for a robot.text file. This is the file that tells the robot or spider where not to look. If you don't have a robot.text file, it'll look everywhere.

How Do You Rate?

How on earth do you get the search engines to pop your name to the top of the stack when somebody searches for the products you sell? It's tricky, but it's possible.

STACKING THE DECK

From *CIO Magazine*, December 1997

The content is cool, the GIFs are animated, and the back-end applications are tightly bound to the server. And yet, in spite of the time you've invested, you seem to have created a stealth Web site. All that wonderful functionality is going to waste because nobody can find you.

It's not that nobody knows you exist: Your brand name is widely recognized. But when people use Internet search engines to find you, they come up with 126,023 links to other sites that mention your company, your products or services, or your subject matter. The actual link to your site is number 126,021.

(Continued)

STACKING THE DECK *(Continued)*

What's a Web site owner to do?

Stuff the ballot box, of course!

Search engines are highly pragmatic. They don't all work the same way but are, by nature, very programmatic. They look at HTML document titles, meta tags, text, links, referrals—the works—and they pigeonhole what they find. In so doing, the search engines actually evaluate your site for the prospective customer on the other side of the mouse.

It's not hard to finagle the search-engine rankings to get a better slot at or near the top of the page. But that raises an interesting problem, which occurs right where three distinct needs converge.

First comes the need for Web site publishers to make their Web sites visible. After all, you're doing those searchers a service by helping them find you. Right?

Next, there's the need for search engines to provide the most balanced possible view of the Web. Why is that important? Income. Survival. To understand this one, you also have to understand the third piece of the convergence: what searchers want.

Typically, searchers need only one thing. Actually, that's the problem: they need one thing, and they end up with 126,023. So they hope that AltaVista, Excite, Infoseek, Lycos, WebCrawler and other search engines will be beacons in the dark, lighting up that one-in-a-million page with the single bit of information they want. They depend on the engines to rank their findings according to a strict meritocracy.

If searchers cannot find what they want at a particular engine, they will stop going there. If they stop going there, the engines can no longer sell advertising. If search engines can't sell advertising, they greatly diminish their prospects of ever making a major initial public offering.

So let's tally the score: Search engines and searchers need the purest databases possible. But pity the poor Web site that nobody can find. Isn't there a middle ground? Isn't there something you can do to shine more light on the site in which you've invested so much?

To start, you can take some simple, virtually foolproof measures. Title your home page something other than the ubiquitous Home Page. Use meta tags—HTML coding that, among other things, describes a Web page's content—to provide a description of your site that search engines can display. And keyword tags, which let you identify words searchers are most likely to use to find you, can incorporate those important phrases that don't quite fit in the description or on the home page. A men's footwear retailer, for example, might include the following terms in the keyword tag: shoe, shoes, wingtip, brogan, dress shoe.

There are also some things you should not do. Don't overstack the deck. If you use the same phrase too frequently in your keyword tag, the search engines will simply kick your entries to the end of the list. And don't use trademarks registered to others; several lawsuits have already been filed over such infringement.

What's the right formula? Depends on whom you ask. If you've been on the Web more than 10 minutes, you've already gotten spammed with bulk e-mail from people promising to help put your site in the top slot in all the search engines. If you prefer professional help, consider turning to resources like Web-Ignite (www.web-ignite.com).

Anybody can use keywords to steer site traffic. Simply fill the meta tags with sexually related idioms or a few celebrity names and the words "Microsoft bug," and the hits will keep coming. But if you want to attract people who are genuinely interested in your products, then you need to track what happens after they hit the home page. Web-Ignite will concentrate on keyword phrases that attract the people who dig down deep rather than those who just hit and run.

You come up with a technique that puts you at the top of the list today, and you're going to have to check back tomorrow to see whether you're still king of the hill. If not, it's time to create a new technique. You could spend your life doing that. Or you could outsource it to a company like Web-Ignite. But is it the right thing to do?

Unsolicited e-mail is wrong. Yes, it is commercially viable. Yes, a small investment for a bulk electronic mailing can yield a large return. But it's wrong to saddle users with paying access fees and phone charges to download huge packets of junk mail.

When it comes to helping people find your site, I'm not on such solid moral ground. If you can create a better Web site, you'll be more successful. If, like Amazon.com Inc., you can afford humorous radio ads that draw more people to your site, more power to you. If you can build a better banner and place it on the exact spot on the Web to draw searchers to you, well done! If you have bright minds working for you who know how to target direct (postal) mail to drive traffic, then I want to hear from you. So why not offer kudos to those who know the ropes when it comes to keywords?

Because deep down, I want my Web search experience to be pure. I want to find only those pages that really meet my needs, not those that just want to grab my attention.

But the real world now includes ads on public television and interstitial pages in content Web sites. (Those are the ads that pop

(Continued)

> **STACKING THE DECK** *(Continued)*
>
> *up between the time you click and the time the page you wanted finally shows up.) So I guess I'll get used to the idea that the first few pages of my search results will be spattered with the efforts of those who know how to manipulate the system, hoping they're also among those who best meet my needs.*

Getting Noticed at All

The main spiders may find you eventually, but with the mass migration to the Web, there are just too many sites to see. To account for this, they have forms you can fill out to add your site to their list of things to check out. Look at the Yahoo! list to find a current list of registration spots. Going to each one of the search engines and letting them know you exist is certainly possible, but it'll take you forever. That's why Scott Bannister created the original free Submit It (www.submit-it.com) while an undergraduate at the University of Illinois in Champaign.

It is not the only one of its kind, but Submit It automates the process of announcing your Web site to your choice of more than 400 search engines, directories, What's New sites, and award sites. All at the push of a button.

Specific Search Engines

As the Web gets bigger and the search engines get more competitive, one interesting turn is the emergence of topic-specific search engines.

The Internet Sleuth (www.isleuth.com) (Figure 10.8) lists more than 3000 different databases by category and in a searchable index. Need a place to list your hotel? The Internet Sleuth knows over a dozen hotel databases where you should be included. Putting on a convention? How about six different search engines for business events?

And don't forget to check out www.search.com. It knows about 43 places people might look for your hotel.

Don't Forget Your Signature

Be as creative as you can when composing your signature. Add as many keywords as you can while staying within the realm of reason and propriety. Remember, a signature that is too long will do more harm than good.

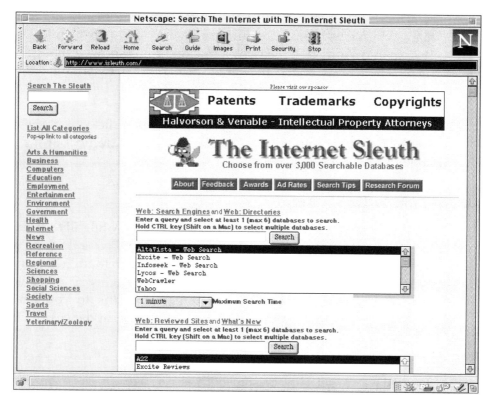

Figure 10.8   **You know the Web is big when it takes a search engine to find a search engine.**

So why put keywords in your signature? Your signature should contain an invitation to visit your Web site.

Your signature will be used when posting to newsgroups and lists, which both can be searched. If you post a recommendation from your bicycle shop on the best axle grease to use for a certain manufacturer's bicycle, you want the person searching newsgroups for the phrase "bicycle racing" to find your posting. That phrase may not appear in your message, so you have to get it into your signature.

Make Them Show You the Money

In May 1997 Viaweb (www.viaweb.com) released a first study comparing the amount of money spent by online shoppers coming from different search engines. Per-capita spending varied surprisingly between search engines, differing by as much as a factor of 3.

The study examined more than a million visitors arriving at 132 sites made with Viaweb software during a 120-day period from mid-December 1996 to mid-April 1997. Viaweb's tracking tools showed that traffic from search engines generated an average of 17 cents per visitor in online sales, with individual search engines ranging from 10 cents to 31 cents (see Table 10.1).

All search engine traffic is not created equal. Clicks from each are not worth a constant amount. It's nice to get lots of traffic, but it's great to know the value of that traffic.

LINKS FROM OTHERS' SITES

Another way to attract people to your Web site is by literally sprinkling the World Wide Web with links to your home page. People looking at travel tips in Hawaii might find a link to your surf shop in Maui. They might find your coffee shop by visiting Quadralay Caffeine Archive (www.austinlinks .com/General/caffeine.html) or come across a link to your shoe store while looking at the Tap Dance Home Page (www.tapdance.org).

Beg a Link

The first way to get a link on somebody else's page is to ask them. Simply ask them. Often, Web builders just want to create a resource for their constituents. If your site offers something of value, it's in their interest to point to it as a service. If another site builder is not willing to create a link to your home page, then perhaps they will create a link to some piece of information

Table 10.1 Search Engine Value

Source	Visitors	Sales	Sales/Visitor
Excite	226,321	$ 26,478	$ .12
Infoseek	217,448	$ 26,170	$ .12
Webcrawler	179,551	$ 17,943	$ .10
Yahoo!	170,522	$ 53,553	$ .31
Alta Vista	164,369	$ 37,067	$ .23
Lycos	24,895	$ 5,302	$ .21
HotBot	16,917	$ 2,513	$ .15
Total	1,000,023	$169,026	$ .17

on your site. A computer repair organization might think it's a grand idea to link to your discourse on how diskettes are manufactured. A natural history museum might want to have a link to your $1.5 million dinosaur egg for sale (www.nis.net/egg) because, well, just because it's such a curiosity.

Borrow a Link

. . . and pay it back in kind.

If you have a Web site of interest to a cooperative marketing partner, you might ask about creating a reciprocal link. A vendor or supplier will quickly see the benefit of this kind of a deal. "Our products are made from some of the best <u>stuff</u> on earth," would link to the company that supplies some of your components. Conversely, your page could boast, "Our parts are used in some of the <u>best products</u> on earth." We all like to talk about our success stories and show examples of our products in use. Host a link to microbreweries in exchange for corresponding links to your beer stein factory. Perhaps the chiropractor will include a link to your vitamin shop.

These links may be even further removed from the day-to-day. Have a contest and give away somebody else's product as a premium. Create a reciprocal link to their site. Discuss a topic that's important to your company but not central to it, perhaps the environment, and point to sites associated with that topic.

Hired Help

New firms are sprouting up all over, offering Internet services of all kinds. One such service falls into a new category called CPR—Cyber Public Relations. These firms will make your announcements for you.

It doesn't take a huge company to pay attention to selected newsgroups, post announcements, register your Web site in directories, and send press releases to the right editors. For example, there's NetPost, run by the energetic Eric R. Ward (NetPost@netpost.com). He describes his services this way:

> My primary activity is conducting personalized, content-specific awareness campaigns for significant Web launches, Web-based events, and Web-based promotions. My method to accomplish this is a combination of carefully researched and selected URL submissions, along with matching your Web launch/event news to *exactly* the right Internet media contacts, editors, writers, reporters, site reviewers, news outlets, news headline services, etc., that are appropriate for your particular news. As a columnist myself for *Ad Age*

magazine, and a 40-hour-a-week Web user, I have an experienced sense of how Web sites and their intended audiences find each other.

You cannot short-cut or automate this process and succeed. The quality comes by looking at the specific content of your site, and then taking the time to research, locate, and submit to outlets that are a perfect match for it, based on its subject, content, and features. This is time-consuming to do, and I thrive on the challenge of it. No two campaigns I have ever done were identical, or could they ever be. The submission campaign I did for Amazon.com Books was far different than the one I did for Rodney Dangerfield's Rodney.com.

My focus is on targeted, content-specific launch submission campaigns to the exact outlets that

a). make sense for your site
b). seek submissions, and
c). represent a legitimate chance for coverage, review, or inclusion

These include:

General search engines

Search engine special guides (Lycos AtoZ, Excite Channels, etc.)

General directories

General announce sites

General announce mailing lists or newsgroups as appropriate

Search engines specific to your site's industry and content

Directories specific to your site's industry and content

Announce sites specific to your site's industry and content

Announce mailing lists or newsgroups specific to your site's industry and content

Human-reviewed Web indexes and guides, both general and in your industry

E-zines

Web-zines

E-digests

Print Internet magazines

Print Internet guides

Internet New's Sites

New syndicates

Web Filtering Services

Web filtering agents

Popularity Trackers

Content Rating's Services

Content Recommendation Agents

Topical Web forum's sites

Internet TV and radio shows (at shows like CNet Radio, TechTalk, NetTalk, and others, my clients are featured regularly)

Print yellow page Web directories

OK, so I'm obsessive about it. I am constantly seeking and evaluating the best of MANY DIFFERENT possible submission sources. And while I do include search engines and directories, these are only a small part of a legitimate awareness-building campaign, and sadly, search engines and directories are all that most folks submit to. This is such a shame, because the majority of the best opportunities for awareness come from sources that *aren't* search engines. I actually do a custom search for outlets for my client's campaigns based on the site content; thus no two campaigns I do are ever the same.

I choose not to get involved in reciprocal linking pursuits, nor paid listings, nor submissions with other strings attached. If you need these, we should talk by phone about my consulting services where I can help you learn how to pursue these more knowledgeably on your own so you don't get taken.

I have clients and references in seven countries.

I take on limited clients, and you don't see my banners slapped all over the Internet in search of business because I have plenty, solely via word-of-mouth and referrals. Rather than attracting everyone to me, I prefer to attract people to my clients and their sites. I will candidly tell you right up front that there are no silver bullets for Web site promotion. Every site has different needs. This is the fundamental failure of any type of auto-submitting services. Your site needs to be evaluated and campaigned for based on its content and merits.

To me, the act of building awareness of a Web site is a process, and an art.

I provide this excerpt not to promote Eric's services, but his ideas. He's been at this since 1994, which, you'll recall, was when the National Science Foundation first dropped out of the picture and removed the Acceptable Use Policy stating there shall be no commercial traffic. In other words, Eric was the first. He's also right on the money. Just look at that list of places he researches for postings.

If you have a serious brand to build or a major site to support, promoting your site this way can make all the difference. It takes dedication and constant vigilance. On the other hand, if you feel you need only to blast 400 search engines and leave it at that, go with Submit It. Says Eric, "I feel that

Scott Bannister's Submit It will cause you the least pain and suffering." High praise, indeed.

Do It Yourself

If budget, time, scope, or just plain orneriness is keeping you from seeking professional help, there's a Web site you should know about. Danny Sullivan has been covering search engines since late 1995. He did some research, posted some of it to the Web, kept adding to it, and Search Engine Watch was born (www.searchenginewatch.com) (Figure 10.9).

BUY A LINK—ADVERTISING COMES TO THE WEB

Advertising on the World Wide Web has become a billion-dollar industry. If you're on the advertising side of the house, skip this section and read my book *What Makes People Click—Advertising on the World Wide Web*. The whole

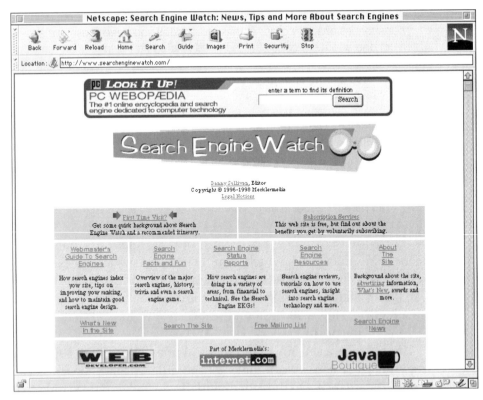

Figure 10.9 **Search Engine Watch tells you how all the major search engines work and how to post to them.**

book covers buying, selling, making, and measuring Web-based advertising. For the rest of you, this section provides the overview, the introduction.

Sponsor a Site

The first efforts on the Internet were to build branded Web sites. They all were supposed to be billboards on the information superhighway, but the traffic on this highway wasn't driving near the Web site created to show off a new product or an old favorite. Traffic was going places where things were happening.

It became clear that you had to make some noise about your site on others' sites. Sponsorship was born. It started out the same way it did on television, and some examples of sponsored sites still exist today.

The Playbill site (www.playbill.com) (Figure 10.10) has everything you want to know about live theater, including a method to buy tickets. Knowing that people looking for a good show to see will wander over to the Playbill site, the producers of *The Scarlet Pimpernel* purchased an ad banner at the top of the page.

Knowing that theater-goers tend to be more upscale, and knowing that the preferred method for buying tickets is credit cards, American Express decided to sponsor the site. You'll notice that "Presented by American Express" is an integrated design element, whereas the *Pimpernel* banner is in the classic, ephemeral ad location at the top of the page.

American Express is fully committed, unlike the advertisers at the bottom of the page (Theatre Central, The Drama Book Shop, the Betty Buckley site, and the Daily Briefing), who are hoping to drive traffic from Playbill with small banners (Figure 10.11).

If you want to go whole-hog with a sponsorship, you can follow Sun Microsystem's lead—IBM did.

Sun (www.sun.com) invented Web event sponsorship quite by accident at the end of 1994. A Webmaster at Oslonett in Lillehammer, Norway, was taking snapshots of the Olympic games by day and scanning them onto his Web site by night. Sun had set up a link from their home page to this unique reporting effort to show off a creative use of technology and the glory of the human spirit. Then they got the phone call.

Oslonett was flooded. Word had gotten out, and the hits came in, but there was simply not enough horsepower in their server to serve the world. Oslonett appreciated the link and the traffic, but they were getting buried. Could Sun do anything to help? Sun seized the opportunity and overnighted a hefty number cruncher to Norway. Within 24 hours, it

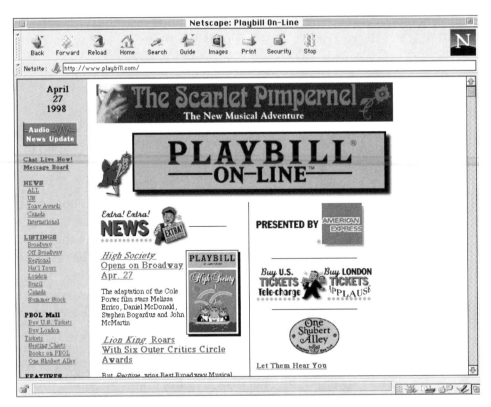

Figure 10.10   Playbill is sponsored by American Express and sells advertising to *The Scarlet Pimpernel*.

became apparent that even more power was needed, but even with more computer power, the phone lines couldn't handle the traffic. The only solution was to mirror the Lillehammer data on another computer at Sun headquarters in Mountain View, California.

Twenty-four hours later, tens of thousands of daily users were getting scores, pictures, and front-line reporting. Forty-eight hours later, lawyers from IBM, the official Olympic games sponsor (with no Web site), were on the phone with Sun Microsystems' lawyers. By the time they finished talking about it, the Olympics were over. A rollicking success for the "information wants to be free" Internet!

While Sun was out finding new events to sponsor, IBM was out sewing up the Web site rights for the 1996 Centennial Olympic Games. IBM became the Official Internet Information Systems Provider for The Atlanta Committee for the Olympic Games. IBM didn't take any chances that they could be overlooked on the 1996 Web site (Figure 10.12).

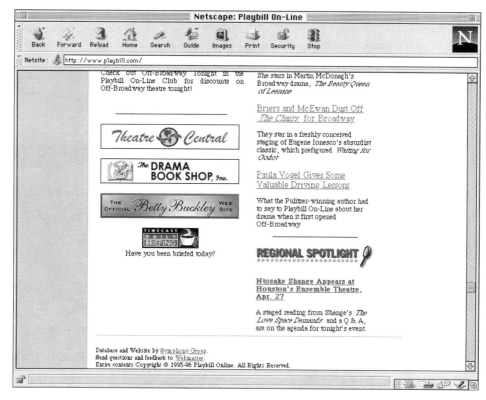

Figure 10.11   Banner ads at the bottom of the Playbill home page are another alternative.

In 1993, IBM signed an agreement with the International Olympic Committee to become a Worldwide Partner to the Games, agreeing to provide and integrate full, end-to-end technology solutions and systems through the year 2000. In Nagano, it cost IBM a cool $100,000,000. That's one hundred million dollars in people and equipment to make the reporting and networking systems run and support the Web site. That's a healthy budget. IBM must feel that they're getting their money's worth because they're ready to do it again in Sydney in the year 2000 (Figure 10.14).

Banner Ads for Quick Clicks

You see banner ads wherever you go. Any site that has sufficient traffic is selling (or trying to sell) banner ad space. The way sites sell that space varies, and some interesting models have emerged. Where you place your ads will have a significant impact on the response you get and there's

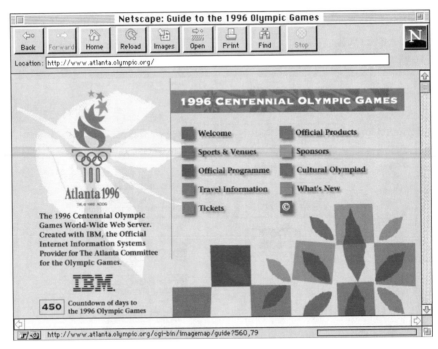

Figure 10.12   IBM made sure they owned the 1996 Olympic Web site.

already some interesting technology out there to help. Finally, there are some tried and true ways to increase your response that have been discovered by going out there and giving it a try. Let's start with the different ways you can pay for an ad banner.

The Four Basic Business Models

There are four basic ways ad space is sold, and they differ significantly. You can buy based on the number of times your ad is shown, the number of times somebody clicks on your ad, the number of qualified leads resulting from those clicks, or a commission on sales. Your choice.

Impressions A freeway billboard is sold based on impressions. Television ads are the same way. You pay on a CPM (cost per thousand) basis.

But the Web is different in one important way. With all the others, the more impressions, the more you pay. On the Web, the better identified the audience, the more expensive the impression. If you want to show your

Figure 10.13 **Not to be left in the lurch again, IBM signed up to be the official provider for 1998 in Nagano as well.**

banner to a thousand people, it can cost anywhere from $5 to $50, maybe even $100. Why? Because the $5 crowd just happens to be there. Imagine there's a billboard on the highway and a thousand people go by. Five dollars, please.

Now let's say that you sell golf carts, and the only people who drive down that highway are the purchasing agents, buyers, managers, and owners of golf courses. As Ron Popiel would ask, "Now how much would you pay?" Don't answer yet! Because we can slice and dice that audience up even finer. Where are they from? What time of day do they drive? The more selections you make from a magazine subscribers' list, the more it costs. Web sites that specialize in a particular type of visitor can charge more to put your banner in their face.

Figure 10.14   IBM gets an early start (870 days to go) on the Olympic Games in Sydney.

For some, that's just not good enough. Procter & Gamble started it when they told Yahoo! they were going to pay only when somebody actually clicked.

Clickthroughs You saw my ad? So what? You clicked on my banner and came to my Web site? Now we're talking!

There are two major flaws and one great benefit with this approach. The first flaw is that it negates branding altogether. When somebody sees your logo, it makes an impression. Whether that person picks up the phone or drives to your store or clicks on your banner at that very moment is beside the point. Branding is about building trust over time. Many studies have shown that Web site ad banners create, build, and secure branding. The clickthrough model disregards the value of branding.

Ali Partovi, Vice President for business development at LinkExchange, has a strong grasp of the value. He says that in tests for The Internet Antique Shop, they put up a banner that said, "Collectibles. Click Here." It scored ever so slightly higher on the clickthrough rate as another banner that said, "Collectibles.net. Click Here." But the obvious choice was to go with the latter because it included a branding message.

People who see the first banner may not be interested in looking at antiques right now. But if they might be interested later, there's no way for them to find that banner again and click on it. Had they seen the second banner, they had a good chance of remembering what Web site to visit. I know I did—three months after the fact.

The second major flaw with clickthroughs is that the seller of the banner space has no control over the creative. You could design and test a banner that got as few clickthroughs as possible. Then the site owner would have to let you run your banner for years until they fulfilled the requisite number of clicks. All the while, your company and/or product name is there for all to see.

The one great benefit, of course, is for the buyer. If you're buying, ask for clickthroughs. Just make certain the numbers reported are audited and correspond to the numbers you get in your server logs. Paying for artificial clicks does not make for good advertising.

Leads So you don't want impressions and you don't want clicks? How about leads? A lead is counted when somebody clicks on a banner, goes to your site, and fills out the form. Name, address, buying habits, time-to-purchase—all the information that tells us this is a qualified buyer. Can it work? Yes. Can it be profitable? Ask Sherri Neasham.

Sherri runs FinanCenter (www.financenter.com) (Figure 7.6). After you spend time configuring the loan that's just right for you, you can apply for that loan online. When you do, FinanCenter sends your application to a mortgage lender, who pays Sherri a nice little bounty for bringing you in.

Actually, it's not so little. Consider the cost of finding somebody who wants to borrow money. You advertise, you do direct mail, you hang cardboard fliers on front door knobs. What does that cost? How many people does it bring in? Divide the former by the latter, and there's your cost-per-lead. The answer turns out to be in the hundreds of dollars. To the mortgage company, Sherri Neasham is one of the least expensive ways to find potential customers around.

The people at CyberGold (www.cybergold.com) are banking on the same concept (Figure 10.15). Let's say it costs you $25 worth of marketing to get the name and address of one person interested enough in your services to read your brochure. Would you be willing to spend $2 instead? Sure you would.

Paying people to read ads sounds completely backward. Aren't ads the things we put up with so we can get our content for free? This thought pattern caused George Gilder to say, "That proves they're not ads. They're minuses!" As an advertiser, you simply pay CyberGold for every person who is willing to read your ad, visit your site, fill out the form, enter the contest, or whatever it is you want them to do.

In their own words, "CyberGold doesn't just hope that customers see your message, it proactively directs visitors to your information and rewards them for responding. CyberGold will reach as many customers as you want, but does it one customer at a time. CyberGold simply refuses to let your cus-

Figure 10.15   CyberGold pays you in cash to read ads.

tomers click and run. It measures effectiveness by verified content read-through and performance follow-through. CyberGold rewards your customers in real time and with real money. You only pay for real results."

Sales You can forget about impressions, clicks, and leads and go for the gusto: sales. It works on the Web just as well as it works in the physical world. One of the best examples is Amazon.com's Associates Program.

The concept is so simple as to be laughable, and the implementation has been brilliant. You want to sell books from your Web site? Become a retail storefront to the Amazon.com back-end delivery system.

Let's say you wrote a book called *Customer Service on the Internet.* Let's say you wanted to sell it from your Web site, but you didn't want to have to take orders, box books, and open an account with UPS. The Amazon Associates Program awaits. Just put up a link to their site from yours (Figure 10.16), and Amazon takes care of the rest.

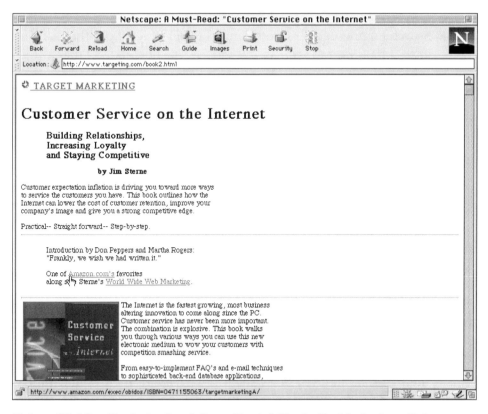

Figure 10.16   Buying a book from Target Marketing is just a click away.

Notice the URL at the bottom of the screen. One click will take the buyer to www.amazon.com/exec/obidos/ISBN=0471155063/targetmarketingA to buy the book. Notice the "targetmarketingA" at the end there. That means if you buy the book, Amazon.com can tell I was the one who sent you and will send me a commission of 10 percent to 15 percent at the end of every quarter.

It takes about 10 minutes to sign up and start earning money as a retail book store on the Internet. It takes a serious out-of-box thinking experience to come up with something so elegant. So what would you like other sites to be selling for you?

The Tariff

Here are some general prices at the moment and to steal a line from Omar Ahmad of Netscape, VWPYMMVPDCCAWH (Void where prohibited, your mileage may vary, professional driver on a closed course, always wear your helmet).

Search Engines, general rotation: $5–30 CPM (cost per thousand)

Search Engines, specific pages: $30–50 CPM (explained below)

Search Engines, keyword buys: $50–70 CPM (explained below)

Small Topic-Specific Sites: $50–80 CPM

Clickthroughs: $.25–1.25 CPC (cost per click)

Cost Per Lead: $1–$200 CPL

Cost Per Sale: 5%–30% of the sale

It will cost you somewhere from $500 to $1000 to have an animated banner created, $1000 to $2000 for a banner that can handle data entry (a form in the banner), and the sky's the limit for Java banners. Of course, you'll have a tough time finding a site that will be willing to serve a Java banner. They're just too big and bulky, and they tend to cause problems for the surfer.

Targeting

Getting your message in front of the right person is as straightforward as placing your ad in the right magazine. If you sell cars, you need to promote them in *Time* and *Newsweek* and *The New Yorker.* If you sell fishing gear, you might consider *Florida Sportsman Magazine* as well as its online version (www.floridasportsman.com).

Put your banner in front of the people most likely to want your products. That's not rocket science. On the search engines, you'll want to buy the Outdoors Fishing page like the people at North of Fifty (Figure 10.17).

On the other hand, if you want to get even more specific, you could buy a keyword. A keyword is what a searcher types into Yahoo! while hunting for that elusive bit of information on the Web. If you sell bamboo fly rods, then your banner will show up every time a fly fisherman does a search on "bamboo fly rods."

But to really get matched up with the people most likely to like what you're selling, consider SelectCast from Aptex (www.aptex.com). This is the same technology described in Chapter 9, "Value-Added Marketing—It's Personal," only this time, it's used to figure out what banner you are most likely to click.

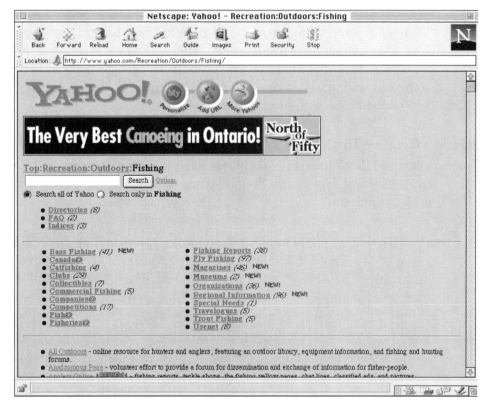

Figure 10.17   Every time somebody goes to Top:Recreation:Outdoors: Fishing at Yahoo!, North of Fifty will be there to catch their eye.

First, SelectCast tracks what you do—your behavior. If this software is used across an ad banner network like DoubleClick, it can get to know you pretty well. DoubleClick serves ad banners to lots of different sites as a service. You give them your ad and tell them you want your ad to be shown to people with certain interests or in certain geographies or at certain times of day, and they take care of the rest. When a surfer shows up at one of those sites, SelectCast starts paying attention to what that surfer clicks. Did you spend more time on this page than that? Did you click on this banner and not that one? Eventually, the software has enough data points to create a profile of you that it can update on the fly.

As soon as you click, your profile changes. As soon as your profile changes, SelectCast compares it to those of other people with a similar profile, sees what banner ads *they* clicked on, and serves the banner they clicked on the most to you. Response (clickthrough) rates tend to go up dramatically with this sort of system in place. That *is* rocket science.

If you're trying to figure out where to advertise on the Web, the real world has caught up. The Standard Rate and Data Service, known better to the industry and librarians everywhere as SRDS (www.srds.com), has come out with its *Interactive Advertising Source Book.* As it was for print, it will be the bible of buying ad space online.

Random Creative Tips

Because I don't have the space here to go into the level of detail I included in *What Makes People Click,* I'll give you some broad hints about what works with banner ads.

Click Here This is the Internet version of a call to action. Don't leave your home page without it. Yes, it sounds trite and even a little obvious, but banners with "Click Here" or "Click Now" do much better in the click race than those without.

Time Is on Your Side There are a couple of ways your ad can stay up longer than usual. When it does, its chances of getting clicked go up. Maybe the site you advertise on offers a framed space for ads. That would mean your ad shows up in one portion of the screen and stays there as the surfer navigates around in the other window inside the browser. You might also consider having the banner follow a surfer from page to page on a Web site, making it a persistent image on the screen.

Banner Burn Out Studies indicate that if users haven't clicked on a banner the first three times they see it, they simply aren't going to. Don't let your banner get overexposed to the same surfer.

The Seven-Word Limit The standard banner size is 468 pixels wide × 60 pixels high. That's not very big. Getting your point across in a small space that is likely to be scrolled off the screen in the blink of an eye is a challenge. Given the small amount of time and the small amount of space (think font size), seven words is a good limit.

Keep It Small LinkExchange only allows banners with a file size up to 7K. Others go to 12K, and some even more. Some sites will let you serve Java banners with streaming video. No matter what they allow, consider the poor surfer. Waiting for ads to download is worse than waiting for the dentist. At least at the dentist's office you can find the hidden pictures in the seven-year-old copies of *HighLite Magazine.* You want your banner to load ASAP, giving it more exposure time.

Bright Colors Attract the Eye Cliff Kurtzman from Tenagra (www .tenagra.com) had just done a major beautification upgrade of their Tennis Server site (www.tennisserver.com) when he noticed a huge drop in the number of clickthroughs his clients' banner ads were getting. His conclusion and advice to others? Put your banner on ugly sites so they're the most interesting thing on the page.

Use bright colors to attract attention. Be aware of the color schemes of the sites where you want your banners so you can be sure to contrast without clashing.

Animation Is Unavoidable The eye is drawn to things that move—it's part of being an animal. So make your banner move. Annoying? You bet. Effective? Yes, indeed. Does it hurt branding? It can. If your banner jumps and bounces and flashes and gives people headaches, you're not doing your brand any favors. But if it quietly draws attention to itself, no harm done and more clicks per impression.

Interact Banners can include data entry boxes, voting buttons, and more. Give people something to do on your banner. Some banners can even take the order for whatever you're selling without taking the surfer away from the page they're on.

One of the better implementations of this approach was a banner for the Web Marketing 98 conference put on by Thunder Lizard Productions and created by e/y/e/s/c/r/e/a/m interactive (hey, that's how they spell it.) It was a combination banner that invited you to enter your e-mail address to get an e-mail sent to you immediately with all the conference details and a button that invited you to Click Here. You could either get the info sent and continue surfing or go to the site and find out more.

Always Use Your <Alt> While waiting for pictures to download, the surfer is faced with the textual place-holders for those banners. Most of them say "<alt>", which indicates no text was placed in the HTML identifying the graphic.

The majority of the rest say, "Click Here" or, even worse, "Support Our Sponsors." For heaven's sake, put in a few words for branding and attention grabbing. It doesn't cost any more.

Test, Test, Test In direct mail, the A-B split is what you do to find out which envelope got opened most, which list had the best prospects, and which offer got the most responses. On the Web, you can make splits from A to Z without licking a stamp. So test everything, but do it in a controlled fashion.

Start with the offer. Do more people click for Buy One, Get One Free or for Buy Now and Get 20% Off? Test it and see. When the offer is nailed, try out different language—Click Here versus Click Now, versus Click! Now!!! Try a few things and see which gets people to do as commanded. You've got the right offer and the right words; what about color and layout? Test multiple designs and see which work best.

When you have the best banner you can make, try it out in different places. Different Web sites draw different types of people, who may click on different sorts of banners.

Just keep trying. Make sure the deal you sign with the content sites where you will place your ads allows you to publish multiple banners over time. It would be a shame to be stuck with one banner and not be able to try out alternatives.

Beyond the Banner

Banners aren't the only way to get people to your site. There are many other types of ads online. Once you get visitors beyond the clickthrough, you'd better give them a bridge to cross from the site your ad was on to the site you own. First, a few banner alternatives.

Interstitials You're playing a game like You Don't Know Jack (www.bezerk .com), and suddenly your entire screen is overtaken by an ad for 7-Up (Figure 10.18).

Some interstitials show up between the page you're on and the page you wanted to go to. Some show up as whole new browser windows. This type usually times out after a little while. The thought is that you'll see it, read it, and click on it. If you ignore it, it'll go away.

I always wonder about the creative types who think this is a good idea. It's intrusive. (So what? So are the ads on television.) It keeps me from seeing what I really want to see. (But the ad might have something in it you want to see even more.) The extra window might crash my machine if I already have windows open. (You need more memory.) Most of the time, they time out before the message even downloads. Dumb. (You gotta get a faster modem!)

Right.

Push There are still lots of people who use programs like PointCast that continuously send you information. How is that even tolerable? You sign

Figure 10.18   An interstitial is an ad that is in your face, like it or not.

up for the sort of information you want them to send you: news about technology, weather in San Francisco, sports scores for your favorite teams.

PointCast is a screensaver that pops up when your keyboard is idle. It is completely advertising supported. Translation: Your ad shows up on the screens of computers all over the world whenever nobody is in the room.

E-Mail Sponsorship Remember all that talk about e-mail lists and newsletters you can write and mail out to those who subscribe? Turns out there's money to be made selling ad space on them.

Besides running the Tennis Server, Tenagra Corporation runs an e-mail list from that site. Sign up for the Tennis Server INTERACTIVE, and you are welcomed with the following:

> Thank you for subscribing to the Tennis Server INTERACTIVE; your first copy of the newsletter is on its way.
>
> A key part of our service, Tennis Server INTERACTIVE provides notification of updates to the Tennis Server, news about tennis information on the Net, as well as other tennis information of general interest. And it is FREE! Periodically, tennis-related polls and surveys may also be e-mailed to people on the list. Some of our mailings also contain commercial tennis-related information and opportunities from Tennis Server sponsors.

Tenagra has figured out how to earn a living sending e-mail. They also run a list for their Year 2000 Web site (www.year2000.com) and the very popular Online Advertising Discussion List (www.o-a.com), both of which not only keep the Tenagra name in front of the people they care about, they also turn a profit.

THE OLD-FASHIONED WAY

I remember the day my father came home and showed us that his new business cards included the telephone area code. Direct dial was in; operators were out. Several years later, his card included a telex number. Then it acquired a Zip code for his postal address. Later, his fax number replaced the telex, and the additional four digits of the Zip code appeared. Now the race is on to see if his e-mail and Web address will be printed on his card before he retires.

Don't forget your traditional promotional methods. Put your Web address in your print ads, in your direct mail pieces, in your television spots, on your letterhead, and on the marketing specialties you hand out at trade shows. Not only will this attract people to your Web site, it will show the world that you are a forward-thinking company.

There's also good old public relations, which is worth an entire book by itself. You might pick up *Publicity on the Internet: Creating Successful Publicity Campaigns on the Internet and the Commercial Online Services* by Steve O'Keefe (John Wiley & Sons, 1996). Don't let the date fool you; it's packed with evergreen advice. Spend a couple of minutes reviewing what Eric Ward can do for you via his Urlwire service (www.urlwire.com).

When the press *does* come calling, make sure the welcome mat is out and easy to find. One look at the Intuit Just For Editors page (Figure 10.19) will show you how to do the job right, all the way down to screen shots ready for downloading and printing.

Figure 10.19   Intuit knows how to cater to the press at its site.

BE PREPARED

If you're good at your job and attract lots of attention, you may suffer from overpopularity. There are limits to the number of users a particular machine can handle. There are limits to the speed with which users can get your home page to show up on their computer. If you exceed those limits, you have a navigational problem that can keep people away. If you're taking a couple of kids to school, a car is fine. If you're driving the neighbor's kids too, you'd do better in a minivan. If the transportation for the whole school rests on your shoulders, you should own your own bus company.

The best way to avoid your users getting the cold shoulder is to use more equipment than you need. Unfortunately, this approach is incompatible with most budgets on earth. Plan, discuss, test, and then keep a constant (automated) eye on the type of throughput your server is experiencing.

One of the most dramatic conflicts on the World Wide Web has been between Microsoft and Netscape: the browser wars. Both companies, however, agree on one thing: More capacity means happier visitors.

Within two weeks I had talked to the people at Microsoft and Netscape responsible for making their respective servers run smoothly. I had a private meeting with Michael Moore, who is responsible for www.microsoft.com, and I introduced Omar Ahmad, Webmaster and Director of Infrastructure at Netscape, at a public conference. In the meeting in Redmond and in the presentation at the conference, they said exactly the same thing: More capacity means more page views. And neither company sells hardware.

Somebody is going to visit your site for a certain, set period of time, let's say six minutes. Either they see 6 pages in 6 minutes, or they see 12 pages in 6 minutes. The more visitors see, the more likely they find something they like, the better they feel about your company. Both gentlemen said that the instant they added more capacity, the number of viewed pages went up. A lot.

Above all, ask your users. Did it take too long? Did they have trouble logging in? You might be surprised to find that your big, expensive machine seems too slow to most of your users.

Don't create a Web site that's a hidden gem. It should be tied into the rest of the company's marketing plans, programs, and messages. Whatever nifty, new, exciting experience your Web site offers, you will need to set aside some time, budget, and people for the task of promoting it.

Otherwise, you might end up shipwrecked (Figure 10.20).

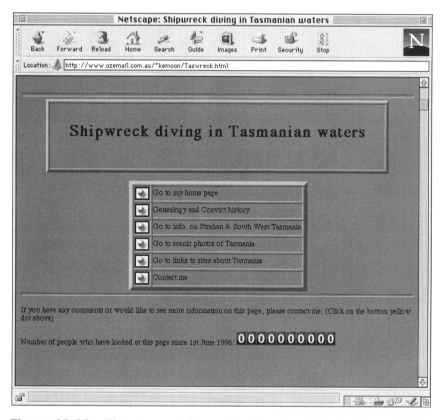

Figure 10.20 **Things must be pretty lonely at the bottom of the sea in Tasmania.**

A BIRD'S EYE VIEW OF ADVERTISING ON THE INTERNET

Clickthroughs may be artificial.
Branding can be beneficial.
Pushing ads is superficial.
Pop up ads are interstitial.

E-mail spam is sacrificial.
E-mail spam's a blasted bore.

Direct response can bring in cash.
Animation adds some flash.

(Continued)

A BIRD'S EYE VIEW OF ADVERTISING ON THE INTERNET *(Continued)*

Privacy and cookies clash.
Java makes my browser crash.

E-mail spam brings naught but trash.
E-mail spam just makes me sore.

Banners spawn in mass profusion.
Making money's an illusion.
IPOs spell cash infusion.
Legislation brings confusion.

E-mail spam is an intrusion.
E-mail spam just makes me roar.

Banner selling's one tough story
Due to so much inventory.
Tightly targeting your quarry
Is the road to clickthrough glory.

E-mail spam revenge is gory.
E-mail spam means legal war.

This industry is young and learning,
Each investor daily yearning.
Many trying, many hurting
While we with fame and flame are flirting.

E-mail spam just leaves me burning.
E-mail spam strikes to the core.

So, that's the take from my perception.
If you think you take exception,
Feeling that I need correction,
Bring it to the List's attention.

But PLEASE don't spam me anymore.
To e-mail spam say, "Nevermore."

CHAPTER 11

Measuring Your Success

You have carefully determined your goals, planned your strategy, and assembled the right people. You have acquired the needed equipment, convinced upper management to give you the resources, and created a process to get good content online, in time. The text is crisp, the graphics are stunning (without being too big), the links have been tested, and the navigational tools are in place to help people get from page to page.

You've announced your site far and wide, received attention in the trade journals for your unique use of the technology, and have had photos of your site appear in *Advertising Age.* Product managers are clamoring to take you out to lunch to convince you that their new contest should get top billing in your What's New section. Only one question remains: How do you know it was worth it?

WHAT DO YOU COUNT?

Everybody with a Web site will proudly tell you how many "hits" they got in the first day, week, and month. Perhaps the only one who can really brag about this number is an organization that got 800,000 hits in the first day. They didn't advertise. They didn't post. They didn't announce. They didn't even read the previous chapter. They simply turned on their server. At first a few hundred people found this site by guessing at the standard, www.company.com. They bragged about their find to their friends. The word got out on the newsgroups, and the hits just kept on coming. The site still holds the record for the most hits in the first day: *Penthouse* magazine.

When somebody brags to you about the number of hits they got, remember that this number has various ways of being counted and is of dubious value. Keep this near the top of your mind when somebody wants to sell you a link on a site and starts waxing rhapsodically about "readership."

MEASURING HITS

How many times do people reach across the Internet to access the electronic equivalent of the cover of your brochure, your home page? This will tell how well you've spread the word. If your Web site promotion is strong (or if your company is known for photographs of unclothed women), you could be visited by a lot of people (or young guys). The number of hits to your home page will tell you how many people heard that you had a home page to hit. It will help you gauge the effectiveness of your PR efforts over time. But there are several technical facts to consider before announcing that hundreds of thousands of *people* have visited your site.

Hits Can Be Deceiving

Let's say your home page has a main graphic image, your logo, a list of five items with different graphic bullets next to each one, a "new" emblem next to one of them, and a menu bar at the bottom. One person visiting your home page racks up 10 hits. How does that work?

The first moment a visitor clicks on a link to your Web site, he or she fetches a page of HTML. That page issues a separate file transfer request for each image to be displayed. One home page plus 9 image files equals 10 hits. So you have to take whatever raw number your log tells you and divide by 10. If only it were that easy.

Then, of course, there's the question of the value of such a measurement.

How Valuable Is a Hit Anyway?

Now that you know how many times your home page was requested, you have to consider the significance of that activity. It may be the number of times visitors picked up your brochure at the trade show. It doesn't tell you if they read the whole thing or used it to wrap their used chewing gum. You only know that they might have looked at the cover. They might also have hit the Stop and Back buttons before your page even arrived.

Magazines can tell you how many issues were mailed and how many were sold to the newsstands. But, like Web site hits, they can't tell you how many people actually read your ad. You need a better appraisal. Of those who check out your home page, how many delve deeper into the content? How many actually got down to the product information? How long did they stay? These figures would indicate how well you crafted your Web site.

Measuring Specific Page Hits

Knowing how many times people requested specific pages within your site can be much more informative. You can get a feel for what information is most important to people. You can see which products are more popular and which are being ignored. You'll get a feel for which areas can be ignored or deleted and which need to be beefed up. You'll be able to tweak your navigational systems to help people get around. But the numbers aren't as intelligible as they seem.

Personal Cache Confusion

Page caching is one problem that will cause your traffic to be *under*counted. Two kinds of caching problems haunt us: personal and institutional. Each individual's browser caches pages, and whole corporate sites can cache pages.

When an HTML page is downloaded, it is copied into a cache file on the local client computer. This allows the user to revisit that page without reaching across the Internet again. This design helps keep extraneous traffic off the Net and makes it much faster to look at a previously viewed page.

When measuring visits to your Web site, there is simply no way to know how many times one individual looked at a specific page. He or she may have looked at the cached version over and over, without grabbing a fresh copy or recording a footprint in your log. Printing your pages can have the same effect. Do you use some sort of percentage calculation for pass-around or photocopy readership when you analyze your collateral? You may want to do the same for caching and printing. What should those figures be? Good question. Ask your site users.

Institutional Cache Confusion

Let's say your organization sells IBM equipment. Lots of your employees use the IBM Web site from their desks. You have a firewall. All of this traffic goes through your one portal in the firewall.

As a good Net citizen, you have the ability (and some would say the duty) to store a copy of the IBM home page on your local (proxy) server. That way, whenever employees want to look at something at IBM, they make a "local call" to your server. When they click on something on that cached page, they make the "long distance" call to IBM. Every page that's viewed gets cached until the disk space runs out, then your proxy server starts deleting the oldest pages. How can IBM record the number of times their home page was read from a foreign server? They can't. Factor that into your measurements as well.

How Interested Were They?

The logs show the time each file fetch was made. They looked at this page for only a few seconds, but they spent three minutes on that page. This gives you terrific insight into their level of interest, right? Wrong. If they stop to answer the phone, talk to their office mate, feed their goldfish, or work on a spreadsheet while perusing your site, the logs won't tell you. You only know when they asked for the files that weren't cached.

Tracing the Path

As users select links to traverse, the log dutifully records their actions. The home page has five or six choices. Which do they pick the most? Each of those second-tier pages has five or six choices. Where do they go from there? Print ad professionals and retail shelf-space marketers pay close attention to where the eye travels on a magazine page and in a grocery store. You'll want to be just as diligent on your Web site. But, wait. Some important information is missing from this detailed log—we can't tell who the individuals are.

HTTP (HyperText Transfer Protocol) records exactly which files were requested, when they were requested, and which computer requested them—not which person. The logs show only the name of the computer (computer.company.com) without giving you the vital knowledge of which user did the surfing. Indeed, the log may show only the IP address (e.g., 204.69.234.7), leaving you without a clue as to the identity of the organization from which your site was surfed.

Another fly in the ointment comes from the fact that you might be visited by somebody from gate1.shellus.com or gate2.shellus.com. These computers act as firewalls for Shell Oil Company. If two people from Shell visit your site, they may both be recorded as gate1.shellus.com. You can also expect lots of hits from computers named proxy.aol.com (America Online) or onramp.net or netcom.com.

When trying to trace a path, be sure to read the logs for the "referred by" footprint. This will tell you from what server the user linked. People may have found you on a cooperative marketing partner's site. They may have found you through a search at Lycos or Yahoo!. They may have pulled you out of their bookmark file.

MEASURING SESSIONS

Mark Gibbs (www.gibbs.com) asks his clients to consider the following scenario for an online sales catalog: A Web site user begins at the home page, looks at the index, finds a particular product page, and then looks at the guarantee. In 9 cases out of 10, people who have looked at the guarantee do not buy the product. What's wrong with the guarantee? You need to address the basic question of the quality of your marketing materials. Despite the technical wizardry at hand, your presentation must still be compelling. If you can measure the paths taken by the majority of visitors, you can test different language, different layouts, and different offers.

You need to know which of your pages is looked at the most. It helps to understand what time of day your servers are getting their most traffic. It can't hurt you to track which of your white papers is being downloaded the most often. But to *really* know what's going on your site, you need to track individuals.

MEASURING INDIVIDUALS

Anonymous hits on your server can tell you only so much. It's sort of like counting the number of times the front door to your store opens. You don't know if it's one person coming back four times or two people coming in together. You don't know if people came in the side door. But if you stop and interview them, if you scan their membership cards on the way in, if you have them identify themselves, you have the opportunity to collect a wealth of information. If you have them log into your site, you can track their path, measure their stay, and ask them questions along the way.

The World Wide Web and the HyperText Transfer Protocol are stateless. They won't tell you anything about individuals. They deliver files upon request but know nothing about the requester beyond what computer he or she last came from.

There are four ways to get around this statelessness problem: embedding URLs into your links, using cookies, asking people to log in, and outside help with all of the above.

Embedded URLs

You don't have to serve static pages. In fact, chances are excellent that within a couple of years all pages will be created at the point-of-click out of dynamic databases. Lots of tools exist today for just that purpose. When you create a page on the fly, you can insert a user ID number into the links on the pages you send out to distinguish one visitor from another.

Somebody looks at your home page. On the way out of the server, the server appends the ID 27 to each of the URL links embedded in that page. When the surfer requests another page, the browser sends the request for the page with the number 27 at the end. Now you know that this is the same person who looked at your home page. The next page gets the same treatment, and now we can follow this individual as he or she clicks from page to page.

Unless the surfer bookmarks a page. Then we can't tell if he or she is today's number 27 or a number 27 from three weeks ago. Or unless the surfer e-mails the URL to a friend. Then we can't tell which is which. Or unless the surfer hits the Reload button on the home page. Then he or she becomes number 28, and all bets are off. There has to be a better way.

Using Cookies

Cookies work much better and can even store information about the surfer on their own machine. Cookies were described in Chapter 9, "Value-Added Marketing—It's Personal," along with their drawbacks. Better, but not infallible.

Will Our Mystery Guest Log In, Please?

Getting people to log in to your Web site is the only way to be certain it's really them. Once they log into your Web site, you can use embedded URLs or cookies to follow them around and see where they go. They've already logged in, so you have a positive ID. Then you can keep track of the fact that customer Jones likes the search tool and customer Smith likes the index. You can see that customer Brown has been spending some time reading up on a newer model than she owns at present. Time for a sales call?

You'll have to work pretty hard to convince them to log in. It's a bother. If they're customers and logging in allows them access to purchasing transactions and records, that's fine. But the casual surfer needs a lot of incentive to create, remember, and use a username and password.

Getting Help

If you're selling advertising on your Web site, you *must* have a third party verify your numbers. After all, people are giving you money based on what you say you've served, and independent verification is prerequisite. If you're interested in the numbers for your own internal use only, you don't need an auditor, but some outside assistance might be nice. If nothing else, consider some of the tools that can help make sense out of your server logs.

The first thing you want to know is which of your pages gets the most attention. All Web log analysis tools will show you. They'll also give you some sort of visual output like WebTrends (www.webtrends.com) (Figure 11.1).

The Organization Breakdown from WebTrends' product line shows a breakdown by types of organizations (.com, .net, .edu, .org, .mil, and .gov.) (Figure 11.2).

Accrue Insight (www.accrue.com) adds an interesting report to the mix. This one (Figure 11.3) looks at the path people have taken to and from your home page. This helps you get an idea of how people are navigating your site.

Figure 11.1   One of WebTrends' reports gives you a comparative look at the popularity of your pages.

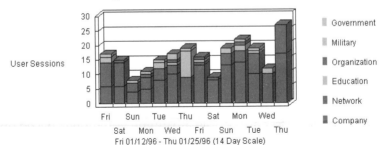

Figure 11.2   One of WebTrends' reports shows the distribution of types of organizations visiting your site.

As Accrue describes it, "This interactive display shows the paths taken through a site. It can be live or historical. A user specifies a focus page within a site, and the pages which referred to that site are displayed on the left, the pages subsequently requested from the focus page are displayed on the right. The referring and requested pages are sorted by the frequency of requests."

Lots of tools do this sort of thing. Readers' Polls, Editor's Choice Awards, and Web Tool of the Week declarations of which is the best change on a minute-by-minute basis. Telling them apart is the hard part.

A Good Book

For a good read, the real nitty-gritty, a CD with some of the tools, and a cross-reference guide to different log analysis products, take a look at *Web Site Stats* by Rick Stout (Osborne McGraw-Hill, 1997). Visit Rick's Web site at www.websitestats.com.

MEASURING EDITORIAL EXPOSURE

Did you create an industry stir at the introduction of your Web site? Did the trade press lavish praise on your bold, forward thinking? Did you garner more ink than you would have had you spent the resources elsewhere? Don't forget this important gauge of marketing success. Alicia Rockmore at Van den Bergh Foods was very pleased with the attention Ragu garnered for being the first packaged goods product on the Web. Its story was picked up by the computer press as well as the food industry journals.

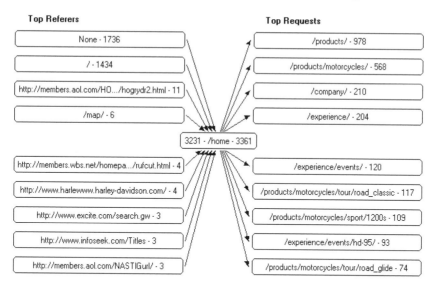

Figure 11.3   Accrue Insight keeps tabs and reports on how people click around your Web site.

It's too late to be the first in your field to get on the Web and enjoy the spotlight. But you can be the first in your industry to offer interactive, personalized services that the competition hasn't even thought up yet. Go out and get yourself some ink.

MEASURING THE LEADS

How many people raised their hands and said, "I'm interested in your products"? How much does it cost? How long did it take? How did that compare to all the other methods you're using to get leads?

If you spend a dollar on a magazine ad, a dollar on a direct mail piece, and a dollar on a Web promotion, which one nets you the most leads? Which one netted you the most qualified leads? Which one netted you the most closed leads?

MEASURING THE SALES CYCLE

A salesperson can spend a lot of time explaining a product to a prospect. The theory, the history, the references, the warranty, and more may need to be imparted before the prospect turns into a customer. If you have a product or service that falls into the long-lead-time category, you should look to your sales force as a measure of your success. Do your salespeople notice that their prospects are better educated? Asking more sophisticated questions? Making purchase decisions faster? Do they find more and more people are asking questions based on what they saw on your Web site? If sales management at your company sees that sales are being closed faster and identifies the company's Web site as one of the reasons, you can claim your efforts have been worthwhile.

MEASURING REVENUES

Finally (and the most difficult question for any company doing business on the World Wide Web today), are you making significant sales you wouldn't have made otherwise?

Consumer Sales

When I send in my two proof-of-purchase labels for my Ragu Net Surfing Team T-shirt, the folks at Van den Bergh Foods can be pretty sure I bought two jars of Ragu Sauce because of its Web site efforts. Colorado Boomerangs (www.pd.net/colorado) might be able to tell if it has increased its sales of the Kilimanjaro Hook by counting its Web transactions. But it'll have to factor in how many sales were lost from other channels. Everybody who used to buy the Kilimanjaro Hook from in-flight magazine ads might be buying them on the Web now.

Are sales made on a Web site actually new sales? Don't discount the novelty element. Good customers might want to shop your Web site just for fun. This is where a good survey can help you collect the qualitative information you need to complement the sales statistics you'll compile as a matter of course.

Business-to-Business Sales

If your product has a long lead time, the question of increased sales is much more difficult to answer. How well are others doing? The World Wide Web as a testing ground and an experiment is over. The jury is in.

It used to be that those doing Web sales and marketing poorly didn't want to mention it. Those doing well feared giving away their competitive edge by crowing too loudly. That's over. Dell Computer is selling $5 million worth of equipment from its Web site every day. It works. Companies not doing Web sales well are going out of business.

The Toughest Part Is Tracking

The mechanisms are not in place yet to track a lead properly from the Web to the cash register. But the Web is perhaps the best tool ever to help us do just that. The World Wide Web puts the front end of our lead tracking and contact management systems in the hands of the public. People who are interested in our products and services can enter their own information (a great way to ensure proper spelling).

A good deal of programming is required to tie a Web site to an automated fulfillment system or a contact management system. The value of automatically tracking a prospect from lead to sale is well worth the effort for many companies.

In the 1995 version of this book, I wrote:

> There is a need for tools to make this bridge between Web server and field sales and back-office systems. Given this need, and the velocity with which entrepreneurs are attacking this marketplace, it won't be long before products appear that fill this need.

It wasn't.

Rubric (www.rubricsoft.com) has coined the term "Enterprise Marketing Applications (EMA)" as a way of describing software systems that really tie the company together. According to Rubric, EMA automates a closed-loop process that tracks marketing dollars spent to revenue dollars generated. If Rubric can do it, it's a major breakthrough. Companies have always stumbled trying to figure out which part of their marketing investment is providing a return. All signs look like Rubric can indeed do it.

First, Rubric's software walks you through a process of Integrated Campaign Management. It's a workflow application that lets you identify and track inbound and outbound leads in all sources and formats: Web, e-mail, seminars, trade shows, telemarketing, and so on. Then there's Marketing Process Automation. This automates the Continuous Relationship Marketing (CRM) processes that use profiling to generate personalized e-mail, dynamically generated Web content, postal mail, faxes, and phone calls. This moves prospects across the *trust continuum* to increase their likelihood of making a buy. Rubric is automating Peppers' and Rogers' one-to-one concept.

The reports that Rubric's system generates are the envy of any marketing executive. From the gory details of the individual purchase (Figure 11.4) to the 30,000-foot-level graphical summary of marketing ROI (Figure

11.5), every marketing manager is going to want this software, Web site or no Web site.

Make It as Simple as Possible

If you are selling a product on your Web site, make the buying process as simple as possible. Once we have made a purchasing decision, we want to get out of the store as fast as possible. Once we've reached the end of a fine meal, waiting for the check can spoil the glow. Make it easy to find the Buy button and easy to make the transaction. If you are promoting products for sale through distributors and retail outlets, make it easy for people to buy. Present a list of stores, dealers, and retail outlets by state or telephone area code. Let people know you want their business.

After Amazon.com had been up and running for a year, I sent them a nasty-gram. Why, I wanted to know, did they make it so hard? Yes, I under-

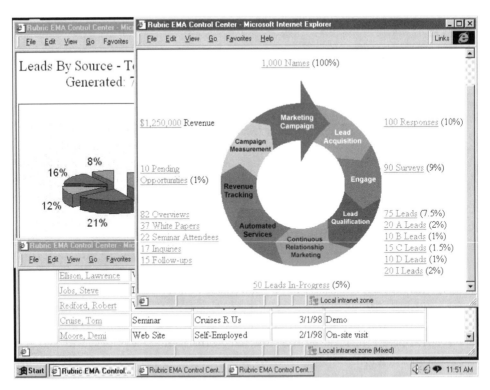

Figure 11.4   Rubric reports show the results of each marketing effort you make and the cost-per-closed-lead. Quite a tool.

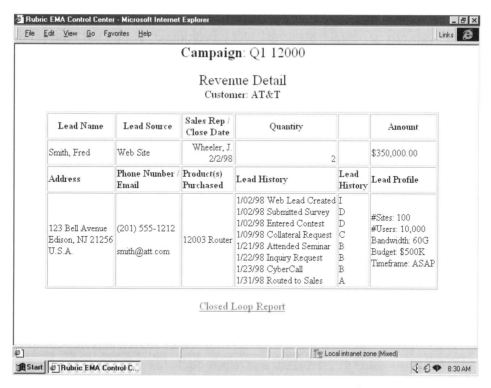

Figure 11.5 Knowing which marketing events resulted in each sale is a real eye-opener. Marketing ROI in person.

stood that first-time buyers were squeamish. Yes, I could see the reason they made people plow through seven screens, reassuring them at every click that they could change their minds and that their credit cards would be safe and that they they still had a chance to review their order before clicking Submit.

But I was a long-time buyer. They already had my credit-card number. I wanted it shipped to the same old address as always, and no, it was *not* a gift for which I had to pick out wrapping paper. Why can't I simply *buy* the book? I don't pretend to have any influence over what Amazon.com does, but it was very gratifying, a month or so later, to see the 1-Click feature (Figure 11.6) that invited me to buy with just one click.

It's so simple and works so well that Amazon got e-mail from people questioning the automation. So they changed the next screen that comes up to say "Thank You. (Yes, it really was that easy.)"

Forrester Research thinks online shopping is going to follow the same growth curve the rest of the Net has enjoyed. They predicted online retailers would ring in $4.8 billion in revenues in 1998 and $17 billion in 2001. They also had some advice for Web sites that sell. According to senior analyst Maria LaTour Kadison, "Retailers must ease site navigation, lower purchase risk, speed checkout, and increase loyalty. Retailers should also forgo current profits for share. During the next three years, heavy spending will be required for promotion, technology, partnerships, and staffing."

FEEDBACK RECEIVED

The final measure of success will be the vote of confidence you get from your clients. When you do ask people questions about your products, your

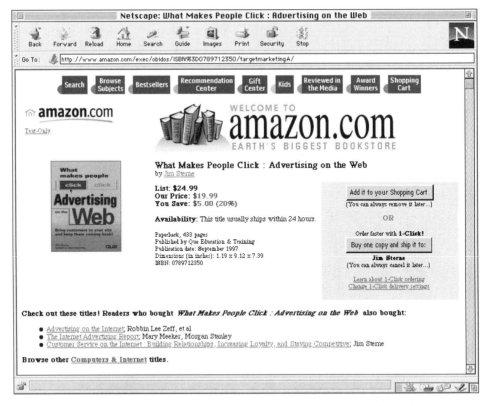

Figure 11.6   The Amazon 1-Click button is the easiest shopping experience on the whole World Wide Web.

company, and your site, what is the ratio of casual users to active responders? What is the quality of the information you gather from your visitors? Do they take the time to give you some insight into their likes and dislikes about your products? Do they offer suggestions for new product features and propose new ways to conduct business? Do they express delight at your new, superior customer service?

The folks at Ragú discussed the length of their survey extensively. Finally deciding on the long version, they were very surprised at the number of people willing to take the time to answer as many as 40 questions. They were overwhelmed by the amount of comments they received. "This is the real fun part," according to Alicia Rockmore, Associate Brand Manager. "Being able to communicate with real consumers one-on-one in a cost-effective way is a real pleasure. People tell us they are now more inclined to try our products because they like our Web site. Others tell us they've been using the products for 25 years and why they love one flavor over another. It's tremendously rewarding, and the rest of the company gets to enjoy them too because they're so easy to circulate."

You'll know you've done a good job when this information comes in consistently enough and at a high enough signal-to-noise ratio to become an integral part of your product development cycle.

A Few Thorny Issues

In the first edition of this book, Chapter 12 discussed trying to convince the boss that you needed more funding. It was a compendium of concerns that the people upstairs would hit you with to keep you from getting approval to test the waters. The need for more funding will never go away, but the issues you need to worry about have changed a lot.

First, let's debunk some of yesterday's problems and get them out of the way. Next we'll revisit some that haven't changed. In Chapter 14, "Looking Toward the Future," we'll open up some concerns you haven't even dreamed of yet.

MEASURING THE MARKET

Everywhere we look we see that the Internet is booming. But who's out there? What is the demographic picture? As little as a year ago the spurious answer was simple: People with higher than average intelligence (they could figure out how to get their computer online), higher than average income (they could afford a computer), and lower than average social skills (they'd rather communicate through a screen and a keyboard than in person).

I have a newspaper article I clipped from the daily paper in Sydney in August 1996. The headline reads, "Web Surfers Almost Normal." I got a kick out of it at the time, but we've been getting more and more normal every day.

The question is answered. The fight is over. People are getting online. Your mother has Internet access. Yes, the prerequisite computer means the numbers skew a little in the higher income bracket, but the price of a PC that can surf the Web is less than $1000 for all the bells and whistles and less than $100 for something used that can do everything but the heavy lifting.

The Internet market is almost normal. Your customers are online. Forrester Research says half of us will have e-mail within five years, and that's more than half your customers. By the time half your customers had fax machines, you had one, right? Case closed.

SECURITY

In the first edition, I devoted more than eight pages to explaining Internet security and credit-card payments and what it would take to make the Net safe for consumption. It's now a dead issue. Done deal. The Web is a safer place to buy than elsewhere. It's easier to filch your credit-card number from the dumpster behind that posh restaurant you go to on your anniversary. On the other hand, the merchant's Web site with the attached database of credit-card numbers starts to look pretty good to the would-be card hacker. That's why firewalls are so important and security software companies are doing so well.

This issue belongs to your IS department or to the company that hosts your Web site. This is not something to be sneezed at, but it is something that should be part of your corporate infrastructure, not the marketing budget. Everybody uses the Web, the same way that everybody uses the telephone and the fax.

CHANNEL CONFLICT

If you're used to selling through a distribution chain, you have to give some serious thought to competing with your own partners. You'll have to find a way to work with them that lets you sell directly without cutting them out of the action altogether.

Territory

If you now sell by territory, you have some serious planning ahead. Territory is meaningless to the Internet. One solution some manufacturers are using as a stopgap measure is to list their distributors on the Web site. They convince users to buy and then show them where the goods can be acquired. The drawback here is *procurus interruptus.* The users want to buy. The users are looking at the product they want. Just when they are being told how your products are superior, just when they are learning about your excellent service, just when they decide to acquire your stuff, they can't. If you make people take another step to order your products (call an 800 number, go to a local store, print out and send in a coupon) you stand a good chance of losing the sale.

Steven Klebe from CyberSource has seen it over and over again. "In all the stores we're put online, the numbers come back proving it. For every additional click you force a user to make, you lose sales."

You might consider closing the sale by taking the order on your Web site and passing it along to the dealer or distributor nearest to the customer. You might even set up a hierarchy of dealers who enjoy various levels of partnership based on sales volumes, co-op advertising expenditures, in-store displays, and so on. Top-flight distributors might even earn a page on your Web site promoting the other products they carry.

INTERNATIONAL PRICING

The Internet is nothing if not global. A Web page in Bangor is seen in Bangkok. That means prices for your products in Salt Lake City will be seen in Sri Lanka. Fortunes have been made by matching the proper pricing to specific territories. Now, specific territories hold no meaning.

Do you show a special Web site price? "Buy on the Web for a discount!" If you do, get ready to get nasty calls from your normal distribution chain. You might quote prices after users have filled out a request. What size? What color? What quantity? By the way, where do you live? The price displayed will be based on the answer to the last question.

Pricing isn't the only problem; there's also language. The solution at Case is to offer regional pages, starting right from the home page (Figure 12.1).

Simply choosing Europe as your location isn't enough information to determine what language you wish to read, so Case gives you the choice of English, German, French, and American English (Figure 12.2).

I got involved in a debate at a recognizable, but please-don't-tell multinational company asking me for advice on whether their home page should be English or American.

Figure 12.1 Case sells tractors all over the world and lets you know that right up front.

From: <xxx@xxx.com>
To: Jim Sterne <jsterne@targeting.com>
Subject: King's English vs. American English
Date: Tue, 17 Feb 1998 17:42:03 -0600

Hi, Jim: I met you when you were speaking at a conference in San Fran last year (and I even bought and read your *World Wide Web Marketing* book!). I am the Webmaster for xxx—a new TRADEMARK for all the existing xxx companies around the world which are part of the xxx group of companies. The Web site I work with represents all of our companies around the world, although most (90 percent) of our business dealings are conducted in English either in the UK or the United States.

Questions 1) What is your opinion about consistency of language VERSION use (King's English vs. American English) within a single Web site? 2) If English is our chosen language of business, would you recommend we use King's English, American English, or some combination on our site? 3) Could I HIRE

Figure 12.2   From Europe? What language would you like to speak today?

you (immediately!) to write a short summary of your opinion (King's English vs. American English) backed by some convincing facts and logical examples?

I'm trying not to reveal my hand in terms of where I stand on this issue, but it might be all too clear. Please let me hear your thoughts, Jim.

Thanks very much.

I was quite intrigued (and flattered) and responded thusly:

To: <xxx@xxx.com>
From: Jim Sterne <jsterne@targeting.com>
Subject: Re: King's English vs. American English

>Questions 1) What is your opinion about consistency of language VERSION use >(King's English vs. American English) within a single Web site? 2) If >English is our chosen language of business, would you recommend we use >King's English, American English, or some combination on our site?

Sorry for the delay in getting back to you.

OK, English is the stated language of record. But which one? The first question is, who is the company? Is it an American company or a UK company? Or is the HQ elsewhere?

Next, but perhaps the most important question of all: Who are your customers? The answer is, all of the above.

I recommend to all my international clients that they localize their Web sites. Here's why. A Web site is not a corporate brochure. It's a single individual's experience. It's not your publication, it's an electronic relationship.

Now, if I call the good people at Rolls-Royce Motor Cars Limited and spoke with somebody with an American accent, I would be appalled! My whole sense of that firm is exceedingly British and not a whiff of Yank. All of the years they've put into creating a strong brand would be dashed to bits in a jiffy.

But xxx is truly an international company. That means I expect to be serviced by a local branch. I want to talk to somebody I can relate to. If I get a representative who is about my age, went to the same school, remembers the same popular music—well, that makes the learning easier and the relationship smoother and I just feel all around better about it. Provincial? You bet!

If I'm a Frenchman and I go to your site and it's all in English, you are not making points.

If I'm a Brazilian and there is a portion of your site written in Portuguese, I'm delighted. Until I realize that it was translated by somebody in Lisbon. The language is right, but the idioms are all wrong.

You run into the same problem if you hire somebody who graduated from the University of Mexico to translate pages for Web site visitors from Spain.

I always recommend catering to the people you are selling to. Make the effort to really *localize*!

So, we now turn to the issue of the King's English or the 'Mercan version. I vote for both. Your products are not the same in both places. Your pricing is different. Your services vary.

I say you have the King's behind the Union Jack and the U.S. version behind the Stars and Stripes and maybe even a tip of the hat to our friends to the North behind the Maple Leaf.

The home page? Tell me—where is HQ?

Surfing the Web is a very personal experience. Anything you can do to make it easier and more comfortable for your visitors, the more valuable your site will be to them and the more return you'll reap.

>3) Could I
>HIRE you (immediately!) to write a short summary of your opinion (King's
>English vs. American English) backed by some convincing facts and logical
>examples?

Jump back, Jack. No way, Jose. Later, Dude. (Now translate those into the King's English!)

After another message from XXX, I replied once again and settled the issue:

To: <xxx@xxx.com>
From: Jim Sterne <jsterne@targeting.com>
Subject: RE: RE: King's English vs. American English

At 11:37 AM -0600 2/23/98, xxx at xxx wrote:
>To clarify, we have no HQ. We are trying to portray that we are truly
>international. However, if we DID have a HQ and it was London, I'd say we
>should use King's English (honest). But since we are trying to portray that
>we are everywhere, SHOULDN'T THE DEFAULT BE AMERICANIZED ENGLISH?
    Yes, sirree, Bob.
>Let's put it this way: I'm guessing that the use of King's English would
>strongly imply that we have a London HQ. However, the use of American
>English would not necessarily imply a U.S. HQ because more people would
>assume we are defaulting to a more commonly accepted form of the
>language.
>IS THIS LOGIC OFF?
    Nope. Since the goal is to be international and of-the-Net, then you need
to use the language of record, which is the colonial version.
>Perhaps I'm being too arrogant about my homeland by assuming that
>American English is not just the language of choice, but the language
>VERSION of choice.
    You're right on.
>In your opinion, am I blissfully ignorant and arrogant?
    I hate to get in the middle of an argument between husband and wife.
You two will have to work this one out on your own.
>For the
>sake of communications consistency (and because I was a journalism
major),
>I STRONGLY resist any attempt to mix English language versions.
    Hear, here!
>What would you do?
    Punt. (Ooops! Isn't that something you do on the Thames?)
    I say American English. (And that's a certified, expert opinion.)
    Cheerio!

Languages can be tricky, but your problems aren't over yet. The next issue is availability. Case Corporation makes tractors and construction equipment and sells them everywhere. The problem comes when somebody in Asia or Africa wants a tractor that's available only in the United States, or a farmer in London, Ontario wants one that's available only in

London, England. Even worse, they put in a stop order on the equipment they thought they wanted because they'd rather wait until the X-325 you're shipping to France is available in Germany as well. That's the predicament with internationally available information, and it's a pain in the cash flow.

Give people a choice of countries from which to view your site, and then put the proper information behind those doors. If you get a lot of overseas traffic, those doors can also lead to servers located on the correct continent for faster access.

INTERNATIONAL TRADE LAW

The Internet is nothing if not global.

> The fact that the Internet is a truly international network complicates government's role in its development as a commercial environment. In trying to set the rules of the game, governments are realizing that on the Internet, all laws are local—that is, they are enforceable only within a country's physical borders. Even the First Amendment is merely a local ordinance. As such, "local" laws that try to restrict the flow of bits across the network, such as export controls and intellectual property rights protection, are unenforceable.
>
> The Internet as an international network is thus not only a difficult environment for governments to regulate, but it is an environment that is causing governments to effectively lose control over their borders and frontiers. In an environment where intangible goods and services can flow unrestricted to any destination in the world, French media content laws and Singapore's press restrictions become both irrelevant and absurd.
>
> "The Internet is Revolutionizing Business, But Who is Setting the Rules of the Game?," Jeffrey J. Bussgang, Harvard Business School

For the most part, we have relied on international letters of credit, trade agreements, and the credit-card companies to alleviate the rigors of buying and selling across borders. When the transaction is discrete, from one country to another, the import/export laws are tenable. But the question of who owns cyberspace is one that will be determined in the courts. It will take a long time. If you have a son, daughter, niece, or nephew in law school, advise him or her to consider a career in international trade law.

INTERNATIONAL CULTURE

As a general rule of thumb, a crack marketing team on its toes can wrangle the tangled laws holding sway over the sale of goods between one country and another. Just don't go overboard dressing up your products until they resemble snake oil. International culture, on the other hand, is a different kettle of fish. The cultures of different countries must be taken into account when marketing on the Web.

As an example, the previous paragraph is almost incomprehensible to somebody who learned English in school instead of in practice. It should read:

> Generally, a competent marketing team can cope with the laws governing the sale of goods between one country and another. Just don't make unsubstantiated claims about your products. However, international culture is a different situation.

Not as personal. Not as colorful. But not as easy to misunderstand.

Chevrolet's marketing faux pas has become famous. Chevy introduced their new Nova back in the 1960s. They marketed it in Mexico and South America. Nobody seemed to realize that "no va" is Spanish for "won't go."

A hospital was built in Santa Barbara in 1923 at the top of Salsipuedes Street. The founders were pleased with the name of the street and wanted to use it for the hospital. That was until somebody pointed out that the lower end of the street ran through a low part of town. It got its name because of the regular flooding. It was explained that "salsipuedes" is a Spanish term meaning "get out if you can." St. Francis Hospital is still in operation.

An e-mail making the rounds included these other gems:

Coors put its slogan, "Turn it loose," into Spanish, where it was read as "Suffer from diarrhea."

When Gerber started selling baby food in Africa, they used the same packaging as in the United States, with the picture of a beautiful baby on the label. Later they learned that in Africa, companies routinely put pictures on the label of what's inside because most people can't read English.

The name Coca-Cola in China was first rendered as Ke-kou-ke-la. Unfortunately, the Coke company did not discover until after thousands of signs had been printed that the phrase means "bite the wax tadpole" or "female horse stuffed with wax" depending on the dialect. Coke then researched 40,000 Chinese characters and found a close phonetic equivalent, "ko-kou-ko-le," which can be loosely translated as "Happiness in the mouth."

In Taiwan, the translation of the Pepsi slogan "Come alive with the Pepsi Generation" came out as "Pepsi will bring your ancestors back from the dead."

Ford had a similar problem as Chevy in Brazil when the Pinto flopped. The company found out that Pinto was Brazilian slang for "tiny male genitals." Ford pried all the nameplates off and substituted Corcel, which means "horse."

Japan's second-largest tourist agency was mystified when it entered English-speaking markets and began receiving requests for unusual sex tours. Upon finding out why, the owners of Kinki Nippon Tourist Company changed its name.

If you're selling globally, you want to be aware of how your words and images are perceived. A wise old owl in the Western Hemisphere is seen as a dull-witted bird in Southeast Asia.

Do's and Taboos Around the World by Roger Axtell (John Wiley & Sons, 1993) has an entire chapter on gestures. It includes some enlightening information about a gesture very common to Westerners:

> Fingers Circle: Widely accepted as the American "okay" sign, except in Brazil and Germany where it's considered vulgar or obscene. The gesture is also considered impolite in Greece and Russia, while in Japan, it signifies "money," and in southern France, "zero" or "worthless."

Using color to imply meaning can also backfire. In America a blue ribbon is rewarded for first place. In England, first place gets a red ribbon. In America, black is the color of mourning. In the Orient, white is the color of mourning. Unless you are promoting a regional business to regional customers only, be prepared to think a bit more globally.

INTELLECTUAL PROPERTY

When the copy machine became a staple of businesses far and wide, copyright and trademark worries ran rampant. It had become so easy to duplicate somebody's art work or treatise. On the World Wide Web, duplication is an inherent part of the system. When you link to a company's home page, you have made a copy of it on your computer. That copy is interpreted by your browser so that you can view it. Replicating words from the browser into a new document is as easy as highlight, copy, paste. Graphics on your screen can be captured or downloaded individually. You can send 20,000 copies to your many friends and relations. Once again, copyright and trademark worries are running rampant.

Whether you are concerned about people stealing your words and graphics from your Web site or duplicating hard information that you have sold from your Web site, there is one truth to remember: The means of making copies have changed, the law hasn't.

You still have all the remedies available to protect yourself from harm, and you still have to prove harm to use those remedies. It may be easier today for somebody to rob you at gunpoint due to the number of guns on the street, but it's still illegal. It may be easier for somebody to copy your entire Web site, but it's still illegal. Eventually, new laws or penalties may emerge regarding the online world. Until then, we deal with the problems we face with the laws we have.

For those interested in keeping abreast of the changes in legal issues surrounding advertising and marketing, take a look at the Advertising Law Internet Site (www.webcom.com/~lewrose/home.html) (Figure 12.3). It is maintained by Lewis Rose, an advertising and marketing law partner with the Washington, D.C., law firm of Arent, Fox, Kintner, Plotkin, and Kahn.

And, as always, seek the advice of counsel.

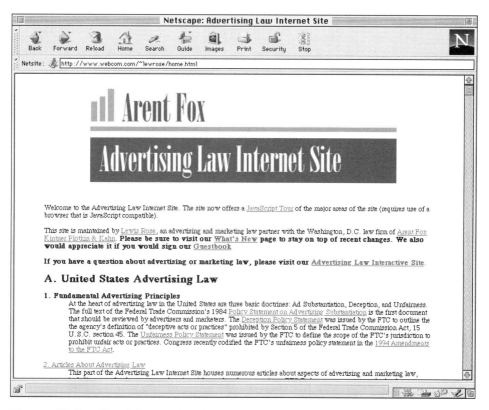

Figure 12.3 **The Advertising Law Internet Site might just keep you and your company out of trouble.**

SUMMARY

Some of the issues discussed here should be cause for concern, some cause for expense, and some cause for real fear. None should be cause enough to make you think you can wait until things improve. While the statistics are being gathered, the security is being hammered out, and the international law is being tested, your competitors are learning. What does it take to create an interactive marketing organization? What resources are needed? What skills are needed? What new procedures need to be put into place? Now is the time to learn the answers to these questions. Learning comes only through doing.

So where do you start? Chapter 13.

CHAPTER 13

Where Do You Start?

The longest journey starts with but a single footstep, right? Well, congratulations. If you've read this far, you can easily be said to have taken more than one step. Now you have your work cut out for you. Your first task is to continue your education and don't let up. This information changes so fast, it's your responsibility to keep up to date.

UNDERSTAND THE INTERNET

Go to a seminar. Take a class. Read some books. Join a discussion list. Get some tools. Surf the Web. Find out what's going on in cyberspace. Become familiar with the landscape before you start building.

- Use HTML to design pages with graphics, sound, and hypertext documents for use on the World Wide Web.
- Design Web pages that are easy for customers to use.
- Incorporate an online multimedia strategy into your marketing plan.
- Avoid committing serious breaches of Internet etiquette that could damage your business reputation.
- Play with some page design software.
- Look into outsourcing.
- Get your Information Systems department involved.

For a more technical look at creating Web pages, read anything by Dave Taylor (www.intuitive.com/books/books.html).

The best source for information about the Internet is the Internet itself. If you want to learn to grow crops, go to the library and rummage through several hundred years of literature on the subject. If you want to learn about changes in the computer industry, go to the magazine rack once a month to try to keep up. On the Internet, things change so quickly that you have to be on the Internet on a weekly (sometimes daily) basis just to keep pace.

There are two appendixes at the end of this book. Appendix A is the Electronic Frontier Foundation's Overall Privacy Statement. It's worth a look. The other is Appendix B, intended to help you find a tremendous amount of information on the Net itself: "URLs You Owe It to Yourself to Check Out." Once you get started, be sure to use an alarm clock. Otherwise, you might end up going with the flow.

CONSIDER THE COMPETITION

Surfing is very hazardous due to human nature and the nature of the Web. When you "spin the dial" on your television set, you know that the choices are fleeting. You can either watch the documentary on cleaner wrasse in the Caribbean, a rerun of the "X-Files" you missed last time, or another syndicated rerun of "Seinfeld." But you can't watch all three, so you get selective.

On the Web, it's easy to succumb to the supposition that what you want will be there when you get back. You're looking for international export regulations, and you happen to come across a link to inexpensive flights to the Pacific Rim. You know the export rules and regulations will be there, so off you go. You follow a link from the flights to the hotels and eventually turn away from the computer after an hour with your itinerary intact and a vague feeling that you left something unfinished. It's not until the next meeting when you arrive without the regulations that you remember.

While you're out snooping around on the World Wide Web, take a look at your competitors' sites. Be careful the first time through to keep your customer hat on. What would it be like visiting that site if you didn't already know everything there was to know about your industry?

Consider the layout of the site, the amount of information, the ease of access, and mentions of future plans. The second time through, you can compare product specifications, look over the Our People Make the Difference section for likely recruits, and see if there are any changes in their list of distributors. Bear in mind that you are looking at the end result of months of effort. Your competitor is on the other side of those pages think-ing up new and different ways to improve their Web site. If you mentally establish this version as the site to beat, you may hit your target (but the target will have moved). Be sure you're thinking ahead to anticipate where they're going.

ESTABLISH YOUR GOALS

A quick look back at Chapter 4, "Using the World Wide Web for Market-ing," offers a reminder of the possibilities:

- Improve corporate image
- Improve customer service
- Find new prospects
- Increase visibility
- Perform transactions
- Expand your market
- Meet your customer expectations
- Reduce costs

Be sure you have the right buy-in from the right parties who share the same goals. Conversely, be sure to spout the appropriate goal when in the presence of the appropriate backer.

Put your goals in writing. Pin them up on the wall so that those who come later can make decisions and take action according to the mission. Make it clear what the company wants out of this investment. Don't get greedy. Don't try to establish every potential benefit as a goal just because it can be identified. That's the recipe for overcommitment and underper-formance. The result will be disappointed senior executives, low staff morale, unhappy customers, and nonbuying prospects. Instead, spread your goals over time. Let everybody in the company see what is expected. It will also help you plan better.

SECURE A CONNECTION

If your company has a connection to the Internet, find out about getting it to your desk. If your company doesn't have a connection, this may be one of the lengthiest processes you'll face. Determine your needs, scout the vendors, and work with your Information Systems people. Many a good

Web site design has come up short by delays in getting connected. Remember that a good deal of network integration is going to have to take place, so give yourself plenty of time. Don't be surprised by the lead times quoted by your internal technicians. Plan on taking whatever the phone company quotes for hookup lead time and doubling it.

Take care not to underconnect for your needs. Let's say you're going with an outside vendor to develop and run your server. The server needs a dedicated, full-time, high-speed link to the Internet. You may not. On the other hand, if your team is composed of more than three people, you want to give them the ability to call up Web sites right and left. Don't saddle them with a slow connection that will inhibit their enthusiasm and their productivity. Rest assured, your need for bandwidth will grow, not diminish, with time.

ROUND UP THE PLAYERS

Who is required to properly create and maintain a Web site? You'll need strong participants to provide knowledge on a wide variety of topics.

Technical expertise needed:

- Operating system management
- Web server management
- Internet connection support
- Internal network support
- E-mail system support
- HTML programming
- Order processing
- Back-end programming

Marketing expertise needed:

- Marketing programs management
- Product management
- Public relations
- Market research
- Graphic design
- Copy writing
- Lead tracking

Other help required:

- Customer service
- Sales management
- Product application support
- Legal support

Look for the players with the sparks in their eyes. The individuals on this team aren't going to be reassigned to this task; they are going to have it added to their continuously lengthening list of chores. It won't even show up in their job description at first. So make sure they are the ones who want to get involved because it's fun, the ones who love the technology and will stay late and come in early. Look for the people who check their e-mail before going to bed.

Later, as it becomes obvious that you need to pay more than part-time attention to this project, balance the team with the proper mix of technical, marketing, and operations people.

DESIGN THE SITE

Whatever you decide to do here, be sure you do it with full knowledge that you are creating a sand castle, not a bronze statue. The result will be more like a play than a novel. It will not stand the test of time but will be recreated frequently. In other words, don't become too attached to anything too early, and be ready to change.

Think about all of the principles of Web design as you go, but don't agonize too long. The things you will learn along the way will be more important than all of the principles in this book.

If you get stressed about anything, get stressed about the sequence of items on your major menus. The home page menu, each of the secondary page menus, and each of the tertiary menus are critical. It's not so important that they be in exactly the proper order but that they are in an order that *is* good enough to stand the test of time. Once people have become accustomed to those menus, they will depend on them to remain stable.

Hewlett-Packard started with pastel colors and the very popular network-around-the-globe motif (Figure 13.1).

Their menus took a radical turn in the next rendition, and customers were confused. It took a moment to reorient and figure out what to click (Figure 13.2).

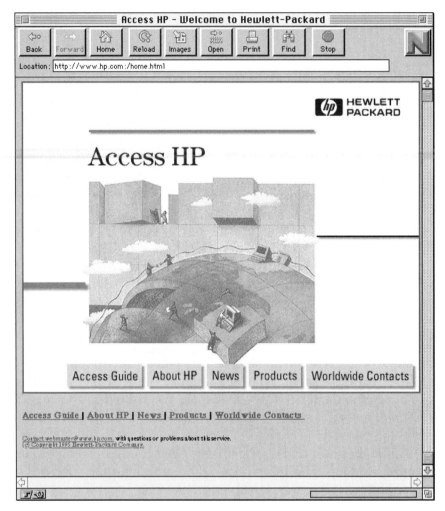

Figure 13.1   HP's first home page had a lot of graphics and a few buttons.

The Eskimo changed with the changing seasons, and HP decided the menu might be more important than the art direction after all. They moved the menu up to the top of the screen, but most importantly, the choices and their locations stayed the same (Figure 13.3).

ESTABLISH WEB OWNERSHIP

Who gets to decide what the home page looks like? Who indeed.

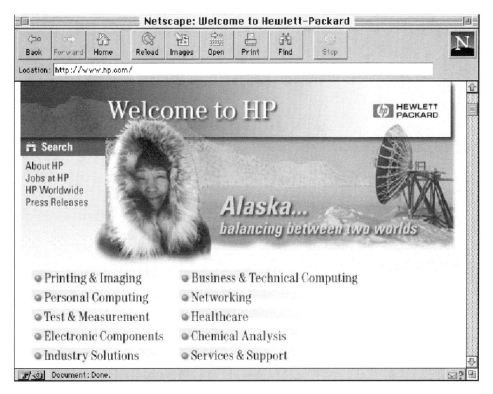

Figure 13.2   HP's customers got thrown when the menus changed.

An organization larger than one division will quickly run into the Grass Roots problem. The Grass Roots problem sprouts from the ease with which Web pages are created. It takes root in the desire to present an independent departmental image to the world. It flourishes where there is no control from the top—no landscape architect. It quickly spreads throughout a corporate Web site until it is overgrown with a myriad of conflicting styles, navigational aids, and cross-purposes.

The Grass Roots problem becomes more apparent when disparate divisions have links to each other scattered throughout their pages. Four major issues need to be resolved when multiple corporate factions create Web sites:

Who owns the format?

Who owns the content?

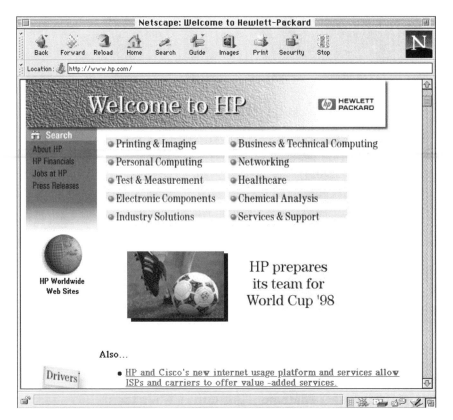

Figure 13.3 **Once HP had trained their customers on the sequence of menu items, they left well enough alone.**

Who owns the technology?

What is the process?

Format Ownership

Corporate culture will have the greatest effect on the control of format. Some organizations have a deathlike grip on every word and image that leaves the confines of their offices. Some organizations push autonomy to extremes.

Apple Computer has always been noted for encouraging the individual and promoting intrapreneurship. As a result, they had to come to terms with their technical support staff in Austin, Texas, in 1994. The staff had created www.info.apple.com and presented a lot of valuable information in an appealing manner. The look and feel, however, were sufficiently different from the www.apple.com Web site created by Apple's marketing arm in Cupertino, California, that it caused confusion and discord when a viewer bounced back and forth between the sites. Apple found out that a certain level of control was necessary to make the user experience as smooth as possible. After several meetings, Apple was able to take advantage of the best of both and create a more homogeneous effect.

The need for a stylistically integrated Web site may be fairly easy to understand, but some will balk at the imposition of specific graphics or a set layout. After all, it can be argued, this medium asserts freedom of information, disregard for authority, and self-expression. Individuals with a need to express themselves should be encouraged to acquire personal home pages from a local presence provider.

A style guide will be your best tool to control a desire to be different. Introduce solid formatting advice to those who will create content. Include the corporate restrictions on page length, file size, navigational methods, and general look and feel. Make it a workbook rather than a rule book. You want people using it as a resource, not a dart board.

Establish the formats for content delivery to help you manage the wide variety of technologies required to create content. If you accept only straight ASCII text, HTML, and .gif files, it will make your life easier. But you must make allowances for the last-minute change that comes to you in a Quark XPress or PhotoShop file. Be prepared for new tools to come along that will make writing HTML a quaint historical ritual. Base your restrictions on your capabilities to preserve impartiality and inspire quality.

Content Ownership

The small firm will bestow format and content ownership on those who can, will, and want to be on the World Wide Web. It's not always fun, and not everybody likes to be responsible for being on a worldwide stage. The large firm must understand the limited value of a limited Web site for image purposes only and assign content ownership across divisions, departments, and products.

Content belongs in the hands of the team managing a given product or responsible for a specific field. Human resources should be responsible for posting job opportunities; marketing communications should deal with the trade show schedule announcements, and investor relations should post the financial reports.

Product managers work closely with engineering and manufacturing to create products. They also work closely with marketing communications and public relations to describe the products. They have the mix of product knowledge and market knowledge needed to represent their products in public. Product managers are close enough to the product to comprehend their audience. Will the audience respond better to a celebrity endorsement, a photo gallery, or a contest? Will the company make more sales in the long run by lowering the price or publishing the specifications?

It will be the product managers' team's responsibility to create the content. They will need to keep in touch with customers and salespeople to constantly refresh their published information. They will also need to determine the right promotional programs to offer on the Web.

Technology Ownership

Internet access, servers, cables, backups, and e-mail do not belong anywhere near the marketing department. The technology belongs to the technologists. The marketing department doesn't run its own printing presses; it shouldn't run its own Web server. Connecting to the Internet and running a working intranet are part of a company's infrastructure. The marketing department uses the phones all the time, but it isn't responsible for the PBX system.

Testing links, making sure files are getting out, and checking that contest entry forms are properly collecting data all belong to the people in information systems. If your company doesn't have an IS department, or if it's too busy with the millennium bug, outsource. Don't hire a bunch of network administrators to live in the marketing department. They won't be happy, and neither will you.

Process Ownership

The term Webmaster has fallen into disfavor. It was the right moniker when the job was primarily technical. The marketing department wasn't involved at first, so it let the technical gurus do whatever it was they were doing. After all, it wasn't really marketing back then.

Now, the lead person managing a Web site has any of a dozen titles. Web Manager, Web Project Leader, Chief Web Editor, Director of Electronic Customer Communications, you name it. This position belongs to a leader. It requires a people-person who can be counted on to make decisions and keep the morale high. It needs somebody with enough high-level, big-picture vision to see the horizon and enough stick-to-it-iveness to see where the weak links are and get in there to fix them when need be.

Ownership Ownership

While the Web Team Leader is directing traffic and putting out fires, you need to have a handful of people involved who can see over the horizon. The only way you can really take advantage of the World Wide Web is when the upper-most levels of management are on board. They have to understand that the Web really does change everything and your company is not going to be left behind. How to convince them? By any means available.

Get the Backing

By now you should have enough information on the cost and effort required to make the case for resources. Here's where your skills at corporate persuasion come into play. When John Patrick, head of IBM's Web efforts, needed to get corporate buy-in, he managed to hook the big cheeses with a little showmanship.

Just before an all-IBM-manager meeting, Patrick and several of his team members showed a demonstration of the World Wide Web to Chairman Lou Gerstner. They had mocked up the start of an IBM home site as well, with Gerstner's photo prominently displayed (Figure 13.4). Under the photo were these words:

> Hello, I'm Lou Gerstner, chairman of IBM. On behalf of all of us at IBM, I'd like to welcome you to our World Wide Web server.
>
> Through our server, we'll try to make it easy for you to learn about our technology and some of the things we're doing at IBM—and also make it easier for you to share your ideas with us. We'll update our information on a regular basis and do our best to keep it interesting and informative. We're committed to the Internet, and we're excited about providing information to the Internet community. I hope you'll check back here often.

Gerstner was as impressed as we all were the first time we saw the Web in action. He was surprised that it could handle audio as well, and he agreed to record the introductory message. The demo was shown again to several hundred IBM managers at the meeting, complete with IBM's commitment to the Internet in the chairman's own voice. After that, it wasn't very hard to get the different divisions to cooperate.

Figure 13.4   The shot seen and the audio heard around IBM.

Whatever tactic you use to get people hooked, this is the time to bring out your enthusiasm. Even if the CEO doesn't get it, doesn't want it, or just plain doesn't like it, your unadulterated vivacity can win the day.

The best way to convince others of the value of the Web is to find a Web site that would interest them. Keep it in your bookmark file for the demo. If they like computers and technology, the idea of the Web alone is enough to excite them. When you're talking to your technically inclined friends or coworkers you can feel the energy rise as you come up with new ideas. But when you get home and talk to your family or neighbors, it only takes 17.5 seconds for their eyes to glaze over.

You can avoid this unbelievable lack of interest by relating it to their specific interests. If the CEO likes to play golf, take him to the GolfWeb Players Club (www.golfweb.com):

Game Improvement
Instruction Targeted to Your Game

Performance Tracking
Just Like the Pros! Track putts, greens hit, fairways hit, and more

Rankings vs. Peers and Pros Alike
How Do You Stack Up? Compare your scores and stats

Compete with Other Golfers

Create Your Own Custom Leaderboards

Nicklaus Flick Instruction 20% Discount on Faults & Cures Programs

Member-only tips and drills

Plus:
Discounts on Golf Travel
Discounts on Golf Merchandise
Your Online Golf Handicap
Your Golfer Profile Web Page
Weekly Players Club Newsletter
Tournaments and Events

If the CFO is a scuba diver, show him or her the Dive Travel Planner (www.divetravel.net/planner/index.html) (Figure 13.5).

The idea is to capture their imaginations and get them to apply what they see to your industry. If they can get excited about it, then they can come up with interesting applications.

What do golf and scuba diving have to do with home remodeling? Get them to think about interactive applications and they, too, can come up

Figure 13.5   Your CFO will understand the power of the Net after one look at the Dive Travel Planner.

with something like the Dream Remodeling Program at www.dreamre-modeling.com (Figure 13.6).

Now that you have their attention and they're willing to reach for their wallets, you'd better have a plan in mind. What are you going to accomplish, and what's it going to cost?

PLAN THE IMPLEMENTATION

With a design in mind and the contributors identified, it's time to propose a plan of attack. Here's where you determine how much you can accomplish in a few months. Try to list the minimum Web site features and services necessary to:

- Attract the attention of the press
- Attract the attention of your customers
- Show your competitors a thing or two

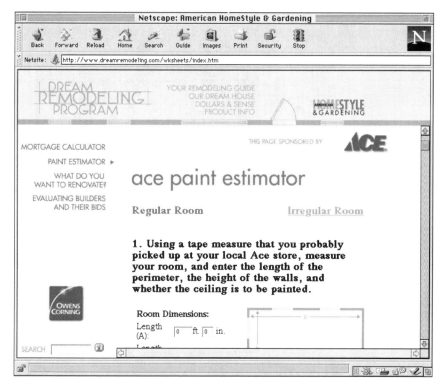

Figure 13.6   Interactivity and imagination can combine to help upper-level managers "get it."

The ultimate question here is this: What do your customers want? If you remember only one thing from this book, remember this:

What do your customers want?

Then it becomes a simple question of how much are you going to have to pay to give it to them. If only the answer were simple.

PRICE OUT THE PROJECT

How long is a piece of string? How much does a software program cost? How many bells and whistles do you need to satisfy that critical question: what do your customers want? NetMarketing (www.netb2b.com) (Figure 13.7) has done a fairly good job at keeping up to date on how much you can spend on Web site construction and maintenance.

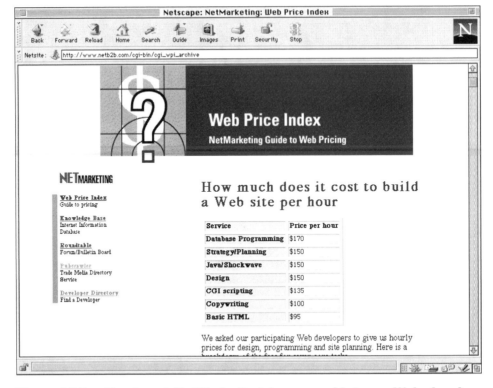

Figure 13.7 **Check out NetMarketing for some hints on Web development costs.**

Once the minimum features are listed and priced out, their creation becomes a matter of project management and resource allocation. Who's on first? What's on second? How soon will the software be ready?

BEGIN THE CONTENT COLLECTION

With a green light from management, you can turn the content providers loose. Before you invest in bigger equipment, upgrade your server, or

NetMarketing's Web Price Index is a monthly look at how much marketers expect to pay for Web services.

The study looks at three hypothetical companies and their ongoing Web needs. The first chart looks at pricing for the entire corporate site. Subsequent charts break those services down and give a piece-by-piece look at Web pricing.

write any more HTML, get the content collection process in smooth running order.

The information itself may already be in brochures, catalogs, notebooks, and databases. You have a good deal of work to do to decide what should go on the Web site, collect it, and get it into a transferable (and acceptable) format. In addition, the content providers will need some time to think about presentation order, response desired, and programs to run (such as giveaways). So hold frequent meetings with or send out frequent e-mail to all the content contributors. You don't want them to get too far off the beaten track. At the same time, you want them to be inspired by their colleagues. One good idea can spark hundreds.

GET THE TOOLS

Assemble a handful of Web page development tools and create a few classes in their use. It'll take some elbow grease to find the best tools and more than that to become comfortable and proficient in their use. Allow time throughout the life of your Web site to review and try out new tools every month. This marketplace is very hungry for products, and more than enough vendors are willing to make a buck off the feeding frenzy. Become the purveyor of the technology, and you might be able to assert control over which tools should and should not be used. It may come down to an issue of compatibility; if content providers use some other nifty tool, the pages they create may be incompatible with your server.

Kim Bayne (www.wolfbayne.com) tells the story of creating a perfectly decent page in standard HTML in a text editor and sending it to an assistant who edited it in Microsoft Word. Word adds a few extra characters when you Save As . . . HTML, which the third-party graphic artist did not know, so he deleted them. By the time the page was ready for Kim to review, it looked nothing like she had intended.

Don't forget to assign somebody the task of creating training materials for all your content providers: classes, handbooks, tutorials, and best of all, the internal Web page that shows everything they need to know about "How to Build a Web Page at XYZ.com." Include access to the latest versions of the tools and discussion areas.

PROTOTYPE AND TEST

As this is a software development endeavor, it's best to think of this project in terms of a new software package. Once upon a time, a prototype was a final version that nobody had seen yet. An alpha was a final version that you showed only to your most trusted friends, asking for their personal opinions. A beta test version was a final version that you were willing to try out on some willing customers so they could help you find any last-minute bugs. The first release was a tested, documented, out-the-door version everybody could be proud of.

It's not like that anymore.

Personal computer software seems to hit the street in beta, dressed up as final release. What's being called final release these days is shot full of bugs, missing features, and simply not ready for prime-time (much less mission-critical) applications. The World Wide Web has turned things a bit topsy-turvy. Everybody using Netscape is using a beta version. New versions are available for downloading almost monthly. The code is actually pretty good. Yet, in calling it "beta" code, Netscape Communications gets off the support hook. Many companies are following suit. Now that people use World Wide Web browsers for mission-critical purposes, they're more inclined to use the older, tried-and-true versions.

Because your Web site is a public document, it and all of the underlying software that makes it tick had better be bulletproof and bug free. You do not send out draft versions of brochures or direct mail letters. You do not print thousands of product labels with concept sketches on them instead of finished artwork. By the same token, you had best be sure that your Web site is properly tested before you invite people to take a look.

Three levels of testing are required: technology, navigation, and overall ability to understand.

Test the Technology

Of the three, the technology testing is the easiest to quantify but the hardest to consummate. Either it works or it doesn't—it's software. Unfortunately, many variables are at play. It may work because it's being tested on a 19-inch monitor at millions of colors attached to a Pentium II PC running Windows 98 and Netscape 5 running on a gigabit local area network— well, you get the picture. Change a variable, and you change the game. Put as much effort as you can stand into testing the technology, then be forever alert for user complaints.

Test the Navigation

Navigational testing is not so easy to quantify, but after a while you figure you've got it right. This is the phase where you find out if your user interface makes any sense to anybody but you and the guy at the next desk. The most important thing about navigational testing is to use fresh blood.

After as little as five minutes of viewing a new Web site, a visitor develops an expectation of what's to come. After an hour of using a Web site, and providing feedback along the way, a user has become too well acquainted with it to be of any further value as a tester. Bring in new eyes to look over your creation. Ask testers to browse. Ask them to play. Ask them to look for a specific piece of information. Can they browse fluidly? Does the site hold their attention? Can they find what they're looking for? Can they compare two different offerings?

Ask your favorite customers to take a look and be brutal in their evaluation. Coming at the project with a fresh eye and from an entirely different perspective, they can give you insights and ideas for the future. More important, they can tell you where your links are vague and your prose boring. They will point out if the pictures are too big or too few. They will also be delighted that you asked.

Test for Comprehension

We face the overall ability to understand questions everyday in marketing. Does the brochure get the point across? Is there too much detail? Not enough? This is the test that goes on forever. It relies on information you get back from users after you're up and running. When you think you've heard the same criticism repeatedly, ask this of every user: "We're thinking of changing things around here, and we'd like your advice." If you keep in mind that it can never be good enough and that you will never be finished, you'll do just fine.

And ask your customers what they want.

ESTABLISH A TEST SUITE

Creators of content may not understand the need to test their creation on a daily basis. Computer systems people do. They know that a networked application is subject to new and unusual changes on a frequent basis. Encourage them to automate testing where they can to ensure your server is online, the links are still legitimate, and data collection is working as expected. It's a straightforward task to set up a client machine that intermittently issues HTTP requests. It can measure the results and report any misgivings.

Links between pages quickly become too complex for human testing. If one page points to three others in three other departments, it's hard to keep track of who's making changes. One change made to a page in New York will make your page in Dallas look broken. Customers don't care who is to blame; they will just think your products are no better than your Web site. Again, automation can play a role here. If commercial tools aren't robust enough, have your systems engineers create a few simple routines or invest in some tools to exercise every link, every day.

Your Web site will be calculating answers, looking into databases, and completing transactions. It will be responding to people who have never used your software before. It will be collecting data on who uses your site, what they've asked for, and what they've revealed about themselves. This is another area requiring diligence. Test the systems yourself, carefully read through user complaints and suggestions, have a standard set of reports produced at routine intervals, and review the reports for anomalies.

PREPARE THE PR PLAN

You will need some lead time to put together and pull off a good PR campaign. Take extreme care not to release information ahead of the game. The danger of people coming to your unready site is real and is harmful. Sufficient time is needed to line up the monthly publications with exclusives and inside reporting opportunities. The weeklies tend to be hungrier, and the local dailies shouldn't be overlooked. They often come up with some very interesting and very usable quotes.

Planning the electronic campaign will take a fair amount of effort. Place specific attention on which announcement Web pages furnish instant response and which take a few days to a couple of weeks. The people responsible for the PR side also need a head start to monitor appropriate newsgroups. When to post announcements must dovetail with the training of staff members to continue to monitor the newsgroups. Once a message has been posted, you must stay on top of responses—both good and bad.

CREATE THE PROCEDURES

Content will need to be analyzed for format, technical accuracy, spelling, and feasibility. Create a review process that's clear and simple. You want to be fair, but you also want the content providers to live up to a certain level of quality. If you are able to keep the level of excitement high among all your participants, the result should be a bidding war:

"My team's modifications should go in with this week's round of changes because we've added this really neat interactive game."

"Ours should go in because it's timed for the announcement of our newest product." "We're running a contest, so it's very time-sensitive."

You'll face these pleas, and more. Without a set procedure and close adherence to the style guide, you can be inundated with requests for inclusion in the periodic site update. Prepare yourself. Implement a couple of tiers of review: department, division, Webmaster committee. Make sure the reviews happen in a timely manner. Only yesterday's newspaper is older than old marketing programs—get them online as soon as resources and reason allow.

Conduct periodic workshops for those who repeatedly fall short of the criteria. Show them where and how their content can be improved in order to be accepted. The wider the range of products represented on your Web site, the better for all.

Make use of the carrot and the stick.

The Carrot and the Stick

The carrot motivates; the stick punishes. Both are necessary but neither is easy to handle.

You were the first person to create a Web site for your company. It was fun. You were the first to promote the Web within your company. It was important. Now you are the first to be responsible for the other people in your company who have created their own Web pages. It is daunting.

Remember how you felt when the Web was new, exciting, and mercurial? Your job required that you be equal parts technical savant, graphic artist, and psychic visionary. The objective went from maintaining the status quo to intentionally stretching the envelope—first into a tube, then into a wormhole. You were leading the way by being the outlaw.

Now that you're at the top of the heap, you're responsible for managing the work of distributed Web developers. They are intent on blowing away tradition and customs to create the new, the unorthodox, the next insanely great thing—just like you were. Now it's your job to keep them in line.

When product managers from the far-flung edges of the company create brochures, direct mail pieces, or magazine ads, it's unlikely the results will look alike. And there's no reason they should. The people who might buy a Kenmore washing machine don't expect the ads to look the same as those for Craftsman tools. Besides, those ads show up in different publications or are mailed to different people. Why should they be similar?

On the other hand, when people come to a Web site, they see all of your products under the same roof. And while those products may be positioned very differently, your pages should include elements to help the consumer recognize that their parentage is the same. A ThinkPad is not the same as an AS/400 is not the same as an S/390, but there should be no question that they all come from IBM.

Your job is to create the high-level, common look of the site. The size and placement of the logo, the color scheme, and the general layout of the pages will tell visitors they are still spending time with your company and haven't drifted off to the home of a dealer, distributor, or cooperative marketing partner.

Celebrate similarity

Once Web visitors have finally figured out what to expect at the bottom of every page, don't pull the rug out from under them by allowing different divisions to create their own toolbars. Establish a standard set of buttons or a standard implementation of a frame for the index and apply it across the board.

We are discovering that the power and glory of the Web is its ability to deal with a marketplace of one. Toward that end, you should address people in Japan differently from the way you address them in Norway. But there need to be corporate standards and filters to ensure that brand equity is not frittered away and that loose translations don't embarrass the company or confuse the customer. If the division that makes modems insists on a button bar that is distinctly different from that of the group developing mobile phones, where and how do you draw the line? How do you impose and enforce your corporate perspective?

The World Wide Web Consortium, which is forever trying to adopt standards to keep up with a changing marketplace, has incorporated style sheets into HTML. But even if your authoring tools don't incorporate style sheets as a technical feature, you should adopt the philosophy behind them. Your company's style sheet should include those elements that are dictated by the corporate communications department. How should the logo be used? What is the standard, checked, sanitized, and approved description of the company? What is the corporate color scheme? Add to that consistent navigational devices, and you're off to a good start.

Follow up the imposed corporate standards with corporate guidelines. Suggest helpful techniques or procedures that worked for you when you were inventing the wheel. Recommend common look-and-feel widgets. And then bring out the carrot and the stick.

Use sticks and carrots

Of course, the size, shape, and power of the stick is up to you. Each company deals with threats, demotions, and terminations in its own way. Nevertheless, you must have something you can wield over the recalcitrant. In some cases, it's tight control of the server. No approval? No hosting. In more distributed organizations, your leverage might be the ability to reach into a server from afar and remove offending pages. It might be the ability to leave a mark in somebody's Permanent Record. Or it might be as simple as, "Remove that link from your home page to our home page or you're fired."

Whatever the penalty, it must have behind it the force of someone sufficiently high up to have power over remote miscreants.

But the stick will get you only so far. If you want people to do what you say and bend to your rules, you've also got to plant some really good carrots.

To start with, appeal to common sense. The corporation needs to look like one entity to the outside world; users will be able to navigate better; and so on. Then make them some offers they can't refuse, beginning with all the wonderful things that will happen if they use common tools for page development. The most obvious benefits, of course, are training and support. A central team can get to know the products well enough to teach and run a help desk. Developers in individual business can get up and running faster and won't have to face hours on hold trying to reach manufacturers. The central team can critique dozens of products rather than each business unit doing the Comdex Crawl.

Furthermore, the approved toolset will create pages and graphics in approved formats. As a result, Web work can go live faster. And approved tools and file formats will become doubly valuable when combined with approved procedures. Rather than threaten that the wrong tools and processes will spell certain death, demonstrate how the proper tools and procedures will promote pages into prompt production.

The fastest carrot on the Web

Your average content provider is under the gun: New material must be posted fast and frequently. When marketing department creatives hold a brainstorming session, they want to show off their brilliance immediately. Your job is to show them how—if they use the standard look and feel as well as the recommended tools and procedures—their content will hit the Web at the speed of light. Then add the clincher: Web-based workflow.

No marketing department—or any other department for that matter—is going to turn down an automated Web content hosting process. Write your copy, tweak your graphics, drag your files over to this browser, and drop them in the approval bucket. If it's easier and faster to use the tools and follow the rules, they'd be fools not to do so.

A horse in the wild runs free but is of no value to the farmer or rancher. The horse tethered to a stake cannot run at all and will soon lose its spirit, then its health. But the horse in a corral has enough room to run without running away. Divisional, departmental, and business-line page authors and content creators must be treated the same way. Give them enough freedom to express themselves and represent their products without tying them to a stake. But don't leave them entirely to their own devices.

"Customer Interface: The Velvet Glove,"
Webmaster Magazine, June 1997

Automate the Process

According to Suzanne Neufang, director of interactive media at GTE, automation means major dollar savings. Tens of thousands of dollars and cutting the time to get content on the Web from weeks to days mean happier content providers. An article in *Net Marketing* magazine (March 1998, page 29) discussed content automation with a number of large-company Web managers.

> "The real key for us was getting content as close to its owners as possible," says Suzanne Neufang, director of interactive media for Stamford, Conn.-based telecommunications company GTE, which updates its site twice a day.
> Using homegrown authoring and administration tools, nontechies at the company now cut and paste content into a CGI form themselves rather than submitting it to a Webmaster, who would first convert the material to HTML.
>
> *Management strategy*
> The content is automatically indexed and linked to other parts of (the) site, then electronically routed, edited, and approved on a staging server before going live.

Ask the Right Questions

You may remember what Mae West replied when asked to use the word "horticulture" in a sentence. If not, ask your father. Either way, her point is well taken. Sometimes it's harder than tolerable just to get people to think. Following are a few questions you might want your content creators to answer before launching onto another round of careless creation.

PROPOSAL FOR PUBLISHING ON THE WORLD WIDE WEB

The proposal will be used to evaluate the project to be included in the company World Wide Web site. Please furnish as much information as possible to speed the approval process.

The Project

Project Name
   What does the proposing group call this project?

Project Identification
   Assigned by review committee for future reference

Project Description
   What will this addition to the Web site do?
   How will it look?
   Provide a diagram of the page calling tree.
   What are the expected results?
   How will those results be measured?
   What is the life expectancy of this project?

The Audience
   Who is this project for?
   How large is this segment?
   How is this project directed toward them?

Response Mechanism
   How will response to this project be managed?

Competitive Analysis
   Who is doing anything similar?
   How successful are their efforts?
   Why is this project better?

Promotion
   How will this addition be publicized?

The Players

Business Unit
   Identifies the chain of command

Project Manager
   Primary stakeholder

Response Manager
   Responds to incoming data

(Continued)

PROPOSAL FOR PUBLISHING ON THE WORLD WIDE WEB *(Continued)*

Design Manager
    Lays out the interface
Content Developer(s)
    Writes, draws, paints
Processing Manager
    Designs the back-end processing

The Tools

What graphics and HTML tools will be used for authoring?

What tools will be required on the server?

What new software will be required?

What tools will be used to manage response?

What training will be required to use these tools?

The Technical Dimensions

How many pages, graphics, and MB will be added to the server?

How much data will be collected?

How many visitors are expected over time?

How many pages will they view per session?

How much data will they download per session?

How often will pages be updated?

How much material will be changed per update?

How will the project be tested prior to going live?

Guideline Deviations

How will this project vary from the Guidelines?

What is the expected benefit of these deviations?

Is this a request for a waiver or a Guideline alteration?

The Cost

Define the funds required for:
    Training
    Design

   Copywriting

   Graphics creation

   Back-end development

   Integration

   Testing

   Fixes

   Documentation

   Promotion

   Updates

Where will the funds come from?

The Timeline

Define the time required for:

   Training

   Design

   Copywriting

   Graphics creation

   Back-end development

   Integration

   Testing

   Fixes

   Documentation

   Promotion

   Updates

   Success determination

Potential Risks

Define the risks associated with this project.

How can these risks be minimized?

How will potential problems be dealt with?

The Alternatives

How else might this project's objectives be met?

Why is this approach the best alternative?

(Continued)

PROPOSAL FOR PUBLISHING ON THE WORLD WIDE WEB *(Continued)*

The Lost Opportunity Cost

What is the risk of not producing this project?

Measuring Success

How will we know this project was worthwhile?
What constitutes success?
When will we know?
How and when will a no-go decision be made?

LAUNCH

Make sure all the players are tuned up and ready for the big day. Then make a splash. Have a party. Raise some excitement. Get people talking. Heck, go all out and take the weekend off! Just check your e-mail before you go to bed.

ACT ON THE FEEDBACK

Individual product managers will need more than content formatting workshops. They will need to understand the response side of the equation as well.

Respond Quickly

Frequently, marketing programs are put together and launched with only cursory regard for the follow-up procedures. A couple of days' delay in getting out a brochure in response to an inquiry may be tolerated. People have a certain expectation that the U.S. Postal Service will not deliver instantaneously. People have a different expectation on the Internet.

Help each content provider carefully plan and prepare support for an online marketing program. Get him or her to understand the need for 24-hour response and weekend auto-responders. When a question comes in, your company will be measured by the hour. Make sure your product experts are electronically available to the front-line representatives, and make sure all involved have adequate access to the tools they need and the knowledge to use them.

Put Stock in the Suggestion Box

Pay very close attention to the people who are willing to send you their comments. People who read brochures very seldom have anything to say about the medium. Web site visitors can be induced to give you feedback. If they take the time to give you input, they deserve a serious thank-you—not a form e-mail saying you appreciate their interest and observations, but something personal. Encourage them to continue to be a part of this growing, changing entity.

This is how you find out what the customer wants.

CHAPTER 14

Looking toward the Future

When will there be 100 million people on the Internet?
What time is it?

Tomorrow will bring new methods of communication, new competitive challenges, and new demands from your customers. Keep a very open mind.

In my opinion, the prospect of near-universal connectivity, most visibly illustrated today by the Internet, redefines at least three of the four P's of Marketing immediately, and probably the fourth shortly thereafterward.

If the majority of customers exhibit any predictable behavior regarding their networks, the "Place" of the business transaction becomes a logical one, no longer just a real one.

"Promotion" must acknowledge this behavior and at least add a new dimension, which will turn advertising on its head since the best 'Net presence is a content-rich and user-selected one. "Product" will evolve in ways that emphasize the network-based features, whether this be distribution of software to enable remote-control access over distant processes, or service/product extensions into Netspace.

In short order, as these developments attract more people to Netspace, "Price" will be set based on an entirely new set of variables. So, at the root, the discipline will be grounded in the same four basic aspects as ever; those aspects, however, will be totally redefined over time.

Robert Hamilton, Federal Express

THE TECHNOLOGY

There are more scientists and engineers alive today than have ever died. More technology allows us to make more technology faster. The more things change, the more things change. The enormous potential for capitalistic gain, coupled with the ability to produce technology at blinding speeds, means that keeping track of the changes around us is more important than ever.

I had to laugh when I reread this chapter from the 1995 edition. The anticipated technologies all seemed so remote then and so routine today.

We were going to get animated pictures that could actually move. You'd be able to enjoy a text-chat with a friend and even see his or her photo every time he or she added to the conversation. Then you could click on a link and take your friend to the next Web site with you. Virtual Modeling Language would let you "fly" through 3D landscapes instead of just clicking on flat pages.

Sun Microsystems was playing with something called Java that would revolutionize distributed programming. Sun was so excited that they posted a list of astonishing applet examples, including:

- An Animated "Under Construction" Sign (with audio)
- Scrolling Images
- Speaking Clock
- Wave Form
- Tumbling Duke
- A Simple 3D Model Viewer
- Some Animated Titles
- A Simple Spreadsheet
- Dynamically Generated Color Bullets
- Live Feedback ImageMap
- Fractal Figures
- A Simple Bar Chart Applet
- A Multilingual Word Match Game

Believe it or not, that was breakthrough stuff in 1995.

Audio has become mundane. We can listen to a local broadcast of a local sporting event from the other side of the world. Streaming video allows us to see the CEO's presentation to the stockholders without having to fly to the meeting. Internet telephony has become a major industry segment all by itself.

In the first edition, I included an April Fool's joke about the ScentMaster, a PC add-in board that uses chemicals to generate scents, from Idaho Computing. "The first olfactory or 'olaf' board," said the press release, "the $199 ScentMaster consists of a 16-bit board, three external chemical vials, and a small spray-emitter module. The chemicals last up to six months and refills are $5.99 each."

"The scent board functions much like a sound card, interpreting files with an OLF extension. Instead of playing sounds, however, the ScentMaster mixes three chemicals (primary scents) to produce the desired effect."

Several years later, I found myself checking the date on an issue of "Time Digital" that told the same story. This time it was April 27, 1998, and the story was no joke:

> Watching video or listening to music on the Net is becoming old hat. But a few scientists are busy working on a real shock to the senses: the prospect of electronically transmitting smells by computer. Companies like Cyrano Sciences are developing electronic noses, which use chemical sensors and artificial neural networks. The noses can be trained to recognize odors for telemedicine, mine-hazard detection, and quality control in food, beverage, and perfume industries. After converting a real-world scent to a digital pattern of ones and zeros, the nose could, in theory, forward the scent to another PC, where a system with a preset array of odors could generate that very smell. It may sound farfetched, but the U.S. government is funneling money into firms like Artificial Reality to catalog and produce key body odors to one day help medics remotely diagnose injuries and treat soldiers on the battlefield.

Gives a whole new meaning to the word "diag*nose*," doesn't it?

I'm still not convinced. Cyrano Sciences is a company with a one-page Web site, and Artificial Reality Ltd. shows up as a company that owns the domain packline.com. Packline describes itself as a "manufacturer of a wide range of filling & sealing machines for paste products such as yogurt, cream cheese, jam, choco paste, ice cream, etc., and liquid products such as juices, alcoholic and soft drinks, milk, etc.—bag forming and filling machines for food and household articles—complete line for bottles, from blowing bottle machine to filling, capping, and packing equipment." Smells fishy.

Don't get me wrong, I'm still nerd enough to be fascinated by the new tech toys that pop up. I can't wait to get my hands on some of this stuff.

High-Speed Connectivity

Yes, it's going to get faster, and it's going to happen in small increments and huge jumps. In April 1998, GTE announced it would supply ADSL access into the local Santa Barbara area. My own little digital backwater will get higher-speed access from home! GTE says speeds will be "50 times faster than conventional modems."

What's ADSL? Doesn't matter. It's one of dozens of acronymonious technologies that promise decent streaming video at a price that's not just for the rich or the addicted.

There are also compression, prioritization, and reservation systems that all work unless you're looking to invest in some hot new start-up. Which one wins is immaterial. Internet over cable. TV over Internet. Internet over satellite. They're all fighting for breakthroughs, and I have infinite faith in man's ability to conquer the laws of physics as we know them. What matters is that giga-bucks are being spent to get us our bits faster. That will make a huge difference in how we use the Web.

With fast enough speeds (I define "fast enough" as the ability for everybody to be engaged in a live, two-way video conference at the same time while downloading the next version of Windows), the Web changes into a telephone/television/Internet communication thingy. Let's call it the Tele-videonet or TVN.

You want to read the stats on your favorite quarterback as he's making a game-winning play? Click. Want to see what that frock Barbara Walters is wearing costs and how it would look on you? Click. Want to never see another ad for Taco Bell as long as you live? Click.

Interfaces

This is another area where people are spending lots of time and effort to improve. Why? Because what we have now is not, was never, and is unlikely to ever be User Friendly.

How about digital customer service reps?

Digital Employees

This item is from the April 12, 1998 issue of *Edupage.* If you don't know about *Edupage,* you should. It's a summary of news about information technology provided three times a week as a service by Educom, a Washington, D.C.-based consortium of leading colleges and universities seeking to transform education through the use of information technology. To subscribe to *Edupage,* send an E-mail to listproc@educom.unc.edu with the message: subscribe edupage Jim Sterne (if your name is Jim Sterne; otherwise, substitute your own name).

> DIGITAL TALKING HEADS A newly launched employee leasing firm is taking a decidedly virtual approach to filling jobs. Using technology developed at NASA's Jet Propulsion Laboratory, Digital Personnel Inc. offers businesses a stable of virtual employees—photo-realistic, computerized talking heads to use for fielding complaints or taking product orders through the Internet. "We offer ready-to-talk talking heads to companies," says DPI's owner. "I see it as a natural evolutionary next step for the Internet. If you think about how every time you go to look up the Web page of a company, you'd much rather talk with someone than read a bunch of text. It's the difference between reading the telephone book and asking someone what the number is. . . . I can't imagine any company not wanting their Web site to have a human interface, whether it's the IRS or Home Shopping Network." The talking heads can be preprogrammed with canned responses to frequently asked questions, or operate as a facade for an artificial intelligent agent, or even serve as photogenic masks for human customer reps.
>
> *Tampa Bay Business Journal,* April 6, 1998

War Room for Executives

For only $70,000 the SAP Management Cockpit is likely to become the next CEO toy of choice (Figure 14.1).

Mission control: The specially designed room presents key information graphically

Figure 14.1   SAP wants to give your boss's boss's boss a view into the entire corporation.

WALLDORF, Germany—March 30, 1998—SAP AG, the world's leading provider of enterprise application software, has bought the rights to the Management Cockpit, an innovative visual information system that will dramatically help board-level executives make rapid, effective decisions using the vast amounts of corporate data and information available in the SAP R/3 solution and through external data sources. Developed by Prof. Patrick Georges and his company, N.E.T. Research, the Management Cockpit uses information from the SAP Business Information Warehouse in R/3 to display graphical views of corporate data on panels of a corporate "War Room" environment.

A team of neurologists, human-intelligence scientists, and computer engineers specializing in human intelligence, productivity, and neuroscience created the Management Cockpit at N.E.T. Research to help teams of executives and senior managers easily comprehend key company and market metrics and make strategic decisions. The Management Cockpit is a specially designed room resembling a huge airplane cockpit filled with visual displays. Its Flight Deck has a six-screen, high-end PC and a Wall-Display System with 18 backlit panels, supported by software for visually presenting information on the surrounding walls.

The SAP Business Information Warehouse feeds the Management Cockpit with all relevant data, including information from transaction systems and external sources, providing executive teams with up-to-the-minute corporate data in view at all times. The Management Cockpit helps these teams use the powerful R/3 solution in high-level strategy sessions and in daily operations to see immediate interrelationships in cross-functional business data, external market trends, and targeted variances against plan. As a result, executives can create new strategies and quickly make well-informed group decisions.

3-D Is Still Looking for a Home

Every now and again I come across technology that seems a little gratuitous, a little over the top, a little bit like technology for technology's sake. When that happens, I quickly check my pulse. Have I stopped breathing? Have I reached that age when anything new-fangled seems pointless?

MULTIDIMENSIONAL MARKETING

From *CIO Magazine*, March 1998

I've always been a strong detractor when it comes to Chat for business purposes. Nobody types fast enough to hold my attention, and there's little worth reading that's created on the fly during a man-

gled, seven-way conversation. Chat is fine for thirteen-year-old boys who want to have adult conversations with nineteen-year-old girls who turn out to be other thirteen-year-old boys. But for business, it's a bore. No chat please, we're business.

I felt the same way about using virtual reality for marketing until I wandered around Internet World conference in New York just before Christmas. Suddenly there were serious tools for making 3-D worlds, bubble pictures, and zoom-in photos. But I wasn't really convinced until I went to a milk factory in Iceland. First—the Internet World exhibition hall floor.

Virtual Selling Space

Products like VRCom from ExoVision (www.exovision.com) and 3D Webmaster from Superscape (www.superscape.com) are what you might expect from Disney on the Web. Think Tim Berners-Lee in Toontown: blocky graphics, swirling movement, and awkward controls in a reasonably representational environment. There was no trouble recognizing the virtual store or the shelves or the products on display.

I could walk around the city and find the stores and then find the door and walk inside the stores. I could rotate the camera and see what the back looked like. I could look through the viewfinder and click on the components to get lists of features and reams of specifications. But drawings are still drawings: more cartoon than reality. I wanted photo-realism. I found it in the next aisle over.

Say Cheese

I looked over the shoulders of the people eyeing the efforts by eVox (www.evox.com). eVox is a service company using tools like Quick-TimeVR, RealVR, OLiVER, and a host of others to create a 360-degree panoramic view of, for example, the inside of cars on the Microsoft CarPoint site; a virtual tour of the operating rooms at Cedars-Sinai Hospital; and even a CD-ROM that Warner Brothers uses to specifically detail how their licensed characters like Bugs Bunny may and may not be reproduced. What you end up with is a photograph you can turn around in and view from all sides.

They also create images that can be turned and zoomed for closer inspection. Nifty. Now you can get a real close look at that Ferrari you had your eye on. The combination of 360-degree backgrounds and photographic objects you can fly around is powerful.

(Continued)

MULTIDIMENSIONAL MARKETING (Continued)

The fact that they provide a library of royalty-free VR images is even nicer. It starts the little gray cells in a marketer's head working overtime.

But there's one drawback—it's really only 2½-D. If you want to show off the fabulous five-story atrium interior of your new hotel, you're stuck. You can't look up. Not unless you wander over to the next booth.

I was stopped in my tracks when the image in the browser went from the horizon to the zenith and back down the other side. It was hard to keep my balance. I wondered how many pictures had been stitched together to make that spherical image. Turns out the answer is two 35mm, fisheye snaps make a photo-realistic, look-any-which-way-you-want image. All except for a little disk at the bottom where the camera was standing.

But I still wasn't satisfied. I wanted more. So I left the show floor and I went to the keynote speech given by that Pepsi dropout and Apple kickout, John Scully.

Feature Applause

Yes, Scully droned on about how the Internet was making history. Yes, he talked about his latest investments and start-ups and such. But then he brought out a demo that got a reaction the likes of which I hadn't seen since James Gosling showed off bouncing heads in Java (www.bouncing heads) in 1995.

It was a full-motion video. Then it stopped and he zoomed out. It was a video on a TV set in a room with the video still running. Then he zoomed out. It was a TV set in a room of an apartment and we were looking down the hall into the room with the TV. Then he zoomed out. The apartment was on the 40th floor of a building in the middle of a city. Then the city was in a frame on an easel in the middle of a desert. Then he panned left and right.

On the right was another TV set with a video of a fashion show. He clicked on one of the models walking down the runway and up popped information on the articles of clothing she was wearing, including pricing and a purchase form. The audience applauded. Me too.

I've been ready to see a VR picture of the hotel room I'm going to stay in. I've been ready to zoom in on the face of the watch and decide if I like the font they used to show the date. I've been ready for the fully immersive, 3-D environment that will help me learn how to assemble the desk or configure the sound system. Now the Web is ready for me.

But the whole thing seemed sort of empty. It was just me, wandering around in a make-believe world with rendered and photographed images. I was lonely. Then I went to Iceland.

The Emerald City Was Never Like This

The only folks who would establish their headquarters office in a refrigerator in Reykjavik are the kind of people who see things from a different angle. The people at OZ Interactive (www.oz.com) see things from different angles for a living. They make Web-based, 3-D, interactive, multiperson, chat-world software. From a different angle, they could see that the huge old fridge doors that were used to keep the milk cold could also be used for keeping the people warm.

The processing plant had used gravity to power the processing of the milk through the course of pasteurization and bottling. Now the plant is occupied by people who have to create their own gravity. And light. And sound. They create the tools that create the worlds that marketers can use to create the offers that sell goods.

OZ Interactive wants you to experience the World Wide Web a little differently than you're used to. They want you to get involved, personally. With multiuser capabilities and point-to-point audio communication, OZ Virtual is a place where your cartoon does the talking and the walking. OZ Virtual is a 3-D interactive home where the droids and the avatars play.

You can create your own avatar and not only type your thoughts through it, but imbue it with an array of gestures. You can nod, shake your head, jump for joy, or play air guitar if you think that will help you get your point across. OK—so how is this of interest to marketers? What are you selling?

A farmer wants to see a full-on, 3-D rendering of the $100,000 combine he's thinking of buying. He wants to point to the engine compartment and have the door lift away, exposing the workings inside. He wants to see what it's going to take to switch from a 30" row cutter to a 23" row cutter. We could do all that with products on display at Internet World, but the farmer may also want to chat with some of the other farmers who are taking a look at it and get their opinions.

The customer support manager for a PC company wants people to see an animation of how different sound cards and memory can be installed in a system. She wants somebody to be able to raise her hand to ask a question, signaling a human to virtually appear and explain. Your product is not as complicated as all that? The

(Continued)

MULTIDIMENSIONAL MARKETING *(Continued)*

Swedish telecommunications company Ericsson (www.ericsson.com) has decided on the OZ solution for a virtual private trade show.

Ericsson Goes Mobile

The Ericsson World is a fun place to shop. It's a multichambered world with different types of products in each room. Wander in and point to a specific mobile phone and the action begins; a multimedia extravaganza describing your voice communication device of choice. Confused? Lost? No problem, just call on the angel, hovering nearby.

Not all inhabitants in the room need to be humans. Based on a text-analysis artificial intelligence engine, the angel is your guide. "Where are the smaller phones?" "Where are the PCS phones?" "Can I use this GSM phone in the United States?" and other questions turn the angel into a consultant. Direct answers, advice on where to look next (including "Follow me."), and the ability to suggest contacting a human make this droid a true guardian angel.

When it is time to talk to a human, you can actually talk; the conversation is no longer text only. In a virtual room full of avatars, you can hear the buzzing of conversations around you but you can't quite make out what they're saying. You move a little closer to one group. Their voices are soon loud enough to hear, and you can join the discussion. They see you arrive, you hear their comments and wait for your turn to jump in. Virtual conference, here we come.

So will 3-D virtual worlds replace trade shows? Sure! Just as soon as radio puts newspapers out of business, television kills theater, and the Web is the only way people get information. Keep your fingers crossed, but don't hold your breath. In the meantime, marketers have a new arrow in their quiver. Time will tell what these new tools can do to help increase sales.

XML

Here's a neat idea. We have HTML (Hyper-Text Mark-up Language), and we all (sort of) agree on a standard version of it so all browsers can read all pages. That's the theory, anyway. But the browser wars are being fought feature by feature when they're not being fought in the Senate. When the boxing browsers can agree on standard HTML tags they can both read, we can all use them. For a while we couldn't use frames because they showed up differently on Microsoft's Internet Explorer than on Netscape's Navigator. Due to the need for standardization, the number of tags is limited.

Now comes eXtensible Mark-up Language (XML), which allows the developers of each page to decide what sorts of tags they want. When the page is called by a surfer, the definition of that tag is downloaded along with the page.

A tag called <USD> might be defined as a price quoted in U.S. dollars. When the browser sees that tag, it is told to display the numbers with a $ at the front and a decimal point before the last two digits. It might also know to find all the <USD>'s in the right column and add them up. Nifty.

Dentists can define tags for specific teeth or diseases or type of pictures they've taken of their patients' molars. A pharmacist can browse the patient record, and at a click, the prescription can be entered into the system. The <Medication> tag means the same to the dentist, the pharmacist, the hospital, and the insurance company.

The possibility is that XML tags can become the meta-lingua-franca of any given industry. If we all agree that an automobile tire should be tagged with <Cartire>, then it'll be that much easier to assemble a vehicle. If we all agree that <springw>, <springd>, <springt>, and <springm> stand for a spring's weight, diameter, thickness, and material, then people assembling everything from wristwatches to garage door openers and Slinkys can search, find, and order products more easily.

APPLIED TECHNOLOGY

If you combine all of the above, what might you get? Forrester Research says that by the year 2002, 10 percent of U.S. households will have refrigerators that alert you when it's time to buy milk, intelligent sprinklers that turn on when the weather forecast calls for sunny skies, and cars that send you e-mail when their oil needs changing.

We as marketers must keep our eyes open so that we can "skate to where the puck is going to be." We have to start thinking like science fiction writers. Think of all the different technologies described here, and remember that they will quickly be integrated into the software applications we use daily. Think in terms of months.

I was lucky enough to attend a lecture by Arthur C. Clarke, delivered at Foothill College in Los Altos Hills, California, in the late 1960s. That was before the moniker Silicon Valley had been assigned, before Steven Jobs had long hair, and before *Star Wars* was either a movie or a government program. Clarke was asked about his vision for the future of education. He related the following story:

> A young boy at the beach scampers between tide pools. He reaches down into one and pulls out a small shell with tiny claw legs sticking out. Curious, he holds his find near his wristwatch and asks, "What is it?"
>
> The wristwatch analyzes the specimen and replies, "It's a hermit crab. It lives in tide pools all over the world. This is a young one. It will grow to be twice that size and finds protection from predators by living with anemone."
>
> "What happens when it gets too big for its shell?"
>
> "It leaves its shell and finds another."
>
> "Can I take it home?"
>
> "No, it would die. But you can find an empty one and take it home."
>
> The child carefully places the crab back in the water, continues his search, and pockets an empty crab shell. The interaction has been coded as an educational experience and recorded in the school database via satellite.
>
> At the end of the week, a question about turtles will appear on a test to see if the child understands the difference between animals that live in borrowed shells and those that grow their own.

The Interior Designer

If you think like a science fiction writer, it's not hard to imagine the following:

The workstation beeps, announcing an incoming call.

"Hi, Connie, this is Allen. Hope I'm not interrupting."

"Hiya, Allen. Not at all, I'm delighted for the excuse to ignore this billing for a while. What's up?"

On Connie's screen a small video window pops up, showing Allen in his architectural studio. "You know that new house Michael has been talking about on Maui?"

"Off again?"

"On again. Full steam. I've finished the preliminary drawings, and he said he wanted to see it decorated. You wanna take a quick look and see what you think?"

"Sure!" says Connie, clicking on the small Receive button next to Allen's image. "I've been waiting for him to move on this. Oh, Allen, it's beautiful!" She swings around the side of the house to view it from the water. "Two docks? His and hers?" The words Resident and Guest appear and hover over their respective landings. "Ahh. And what about inside? Did he mention anything in particular?"

"You know Michael," says Allen with a grin. "He says 'Just let Connie do it,' and then starts suggesting the living room should be marble, the main fireplace should be slate, and the front hall should be sandstone . . ."

"Sounds like our boy. That was all? Didn't he mention wall treatments, bedspreads, or throw pillows?"

"Nope. Just that he wanted to see what you thought it should have."

"Marble, slate, and sandstone. Let's see . . . floor" she says, holding down the Alt key, "marble, Seravezza, midnight gray."

"That looks nice," says Allen as the floor of the model on his screen fills with color, "and the veins match the rocks along the lagoon. How did you know about this one?"

"I saw it at Peter and Kathy's new office, very nice, by the way. They have some Santa Barbara Stone I can't wait to put someplace, but this one seems to be the right fit here. Now, then, fireplace, Welsh slate, cadet blue."

"That looks more green than blue."

"So does the lagoon. Front hall, floor, Vermont slate, Seashell 4."

"Looks like you're on a roll," Allen laughs, "Have fun with it. I think you'll like the upstairs."

"Oh, I think so, too. I always love your stuff. Oh, but wait a second Allen." Connie hits a couple of keys. The model Allen transferred came complete with dimensions. Connie's database of materials, colors, and textures includes manufacturers. After automatically sending update requests, a spreadsheet appears on both screens showing material quantities needed, suppliers' bids, and lead times required. "Looks like that Welsh slate delivery will kill us. If he's all ready to start, I don't want to be the one holding things up. Let's see." Pressing the Alt key again, Connie adds, "We need cadet blue slate for the fireplace from any vendor with delivery in less than four weeks."

The spreadsheets update with new dealers and delivery dates. The color in the drawing changes to a muddy aquamarine. "No, no, no. Give me some time to try a few more things. Besides, the wall treatment will help."

"Copy me when you send it to Michael, OK?"

"Will do. See you later, Allen."

Android Customer Support

"If you've rebooted and the same error came up *before* you ran the totals, then, well, I'm stumped," says Jeeves, the cartoon-like character in a small video window on Bob's screen. "So, I've logged your problem and have routed it to somebody who can help." Another window appears. "This is

Melissa. She's just taking a quick look at our conversation and will be able to ask a few more intelligent questions than I can."

"It looks," says Melissa, reading intently and pausing to finish, "like the problem might be insufficient memory." She looks into the camera at the customer. "Did you upgrade to version 3.6?"

Sensing the head movement, Jeeves remains quiet to let the customer answer.

"Uhmm, I think that was the first thing we tried. Right, Jeeves?"

"Downloaded first thing, Bob. You're right. Melissa, is there another way to improve the memory without a hardware upgrade?"

"Let's try resizing the cache," she says and sends a small diagnostic tool down the line. Once everybody is happy that the fix works, Melissa adds it to the Jeeves customer service database for future reference.

THE FUTURE OF MARKETING

Technology is no longer what's exciting on the World Wide Web. What's exciting is how the Web really is changing the way we do business.

Intranet

There's an entire shelf of books dedicated to intranets in almost any book store. The power of instant information dissemination is not limited to those outside your company. Internal communication cost savings and time-to-market improvements are so much and so many that the figures are almost unbelievable. The research companies have stopped measuring the return on investment of intranet implementations. How wet is the rain?

It's incumbent on your corporate information systems department to provide the basic networking infrastructure. You shouldn't have to install and maintain your own telephone. You should just decide the best ways to use it. This is the same with an intranet. If your firm is not providing the tools and training necessary to get you up, running, and connected, you have two choices: either raise hell and make it happen or find another place to work where they don't use slide rules and buggy whips anymore.

The gear is too cheap and the value too high for you to let another day go by letting the competition outmaneuver you in this area.

Marketing Department Access

Look inward to begin. Think about how your job would be better, tasks accomplished faster, and programs executed more cheaply if you gave yourself access to information. What if you could post schedules that both you and the product development team could update? What if you could see what was getting out the door in the next few weeks from manufacturing, updated daily? What if you could post a piece of collateral for the legal department to mark up? Think of using the Web as an internal front end to all of your systems, such as order processing, sales forecasting, and cross-brand program planning.

Think in terms of work flow. How do things get done? How does work get approved? How can meeting rooms be scheduled? Browser-based tools will make you better able to support your customers, upper-level management, and the sales department.

Sales Force Access

How much time do you or your staff spend on the phone with salespeople? Salespeople who want release dates, who want special features added, who need the latest pricing sheets or compatibility charts. Salespeople who are just about to walk into a meeting and need it *now*.

Wouldn't it be nice if the answer was, "Take a look at the SalesWeb under Pricing and you'll find what you're looking for."

Collateral It seems the tools created for a sales force are constantly changing. It's not possible to keep enough units on the shelf to satisfy the demand. Yet, when it's time to reproduce them, they're out of date. The physical reproduction of marketing materials will never go away. Just think of all the things you duplicate:

- Company profiles
- One-page flyers
- Data sheets
- Six-page brochures
- Concepts and facilities guides
- Tutorials
- Case studies
- Article reprints

They will always need to be available as leave-behinds, direct mail pieces, or presentation handouts. But the information in most of them will be most valuable to your sales force if they are current.

Internal documents such as the following are also time critical:

- Competitive evaluations
- Qualification guides
- Object-handling guides
- ROI calculations

The ability to get electronic copies on demand gives your sales force an edge.

Presentations A great deal of time goes into creating and distributing presentation materials—overhead foils, 35mm slides, diskettes with electronic presentations. Instead, put those materials on your internal Web and let the field force download and duplicate them when necessary.

We used to arm our sales reps with hundreds of slides so they could tailor the presentation to the prospect. Hours would be spent in hotel rooms rearranging foils for the morning presentation. This sort of activity will never stop. But the activity will involve online decision making, not physical sifting and sorting. Sales presentations delivered through a Web site give the ability to match the presentation to each audience's different interests. The salesperson no longer has to thumb through four dozen transparencies to find the right picture. Instead, he or she can click on the link and continue the presentation.

Proposals Proposal boilerplate should be kept updated and available by the home office. This ensures the right legal wording and makes the job of creating a proposal all the easier for those on the road. The salesperson calls up the appropriate sections, cuts and pastes, and can print out a customized proposal in minutes.

Schedules Everybody in the sales and marketing departments can benefit from seeing product release dates, upcoming trade show rosters, marketing program plans, and meeting schedules.

Access to Products Half of sales training concentrates on the fine arts of cold calling, qualifying, negotiating, and closing. The marketing department, however, is called in to make sure the sales force knows what to say about the product line, and what not to say. Up-to-the-minute, hyperlinked product descriptions will cut down on a large percentage of the phone calls your department gets from salespeople. Detailed specifications can answer the majority of their questions. If you add some back-end processing to your internal Web database, salespeople can use their computers for product configuration and pricing.

Access to Customer Service and Order Processing Before showing up for a closing call to upgrade a customer to a bigger and better machine, sales reps would like to make sure the maintenance crew isn't in there fixing the old one again. They'd also like to see if the deliveries of supplies have been on time. The customer will already know and will have every expectation that the salesperson will know as well.

Access to Each Other Several areas of communication that fall squarely in the realm of the sales department tend to require marketing support anyway. Get them used to the idea of using the Web for opportunity management, sales training, call report forms, forecast forms, and tracking each other's reference lists.

It's Another Kettle of Fish

Building an intranet is not something you do in your spare time. Assign a new task force and read up. I recommend two books by Mellanie Hills: *Intranet as Groupware* and *Intranet Business Strategies* (John Wiley & Sons, 1996).

Extranet

If the Internet has done nothing else, it's brought new life to those who wish to coin new terms. Had you cornered the buzzword market in 1993, you could be comparing portfolios with Bill Gates. The focus of our attention for the moment is the extranet.

The local area network (LAN) is what ties your computer to the ones down the hall. The wide area network (WAN) is what ties your department to the other departments in your company, even though they're located in far-flung cities. The Internet (network of networks) is the glue that ties the networks from different companies together. The intranet is what you get when you create Web services for use inside your company and you don't let anybody else have access to it. Intranets are for internal use only.

Until someone invented the extranet.

The term "extranet" was coined to describe intranets that talk to each other. If you allow a customer to access your intranet to get information, voila! You have an extranet. The extranet concept goes way back. We used to call it EDI, for electronic data interchange. Now it's a lot cheaper, and it's become a competitive weapon. The race will go to the organization that delivers access to information. People have come to expect access to their finances via ATMs, online tax returns, and touch-tone trading. They will come to expect a lot more. Federal Express set the pace, and now the rest of us are catching up.

In this world of distributed, client/server, object-oriented, peer-to-peer computing, the World Wide Web has become the network architecture and the Web browser the Graphical User Interface of choice. Through this medium, the company that opens its electronic doors the widest will walk away with the business. They will provide access to and through the enterprise—not just to customers and prospects, but to employees and vendors as well.

This is the area that will take today's corporations and turn them inside out. Many companies have spent many dollars creating narrow electronic data interchange systems for their special clients. Now it is time to start creating wide interchange systems for all their clients.

In 1995, the passage read:

> The World Wide Web is in its infancy, and it will mutate frequently. But if you look just over the horizon at the competitive world of tomorrow, you'll see it at its logical extreme. You'll see customers demanding instantaneous intelligence about the status of their orders, your average of stock on hand, and your estimated time of delivery. They'll want to see their current balances and have online options about methods of payment. They'll want to review discussions your other customers have had about the good, the bad, and the ugly. Ubiquitous electronic data interchange and a terminal on every desk. The company with the most freely available information wins.
>
> Customers will expect a feedback screen at every turn so they can speak their minds. They will expect prompt replies. The customers will become part of the process and, through their suggestions, help shape the process. Your whole company will be on display, and your customer will be part of the operations committee as well as the product planning council.

Those wonderful old AT&T "You Will" commercials are as dated as those paragraphs. Replace the future tense with present tense, and you begin to see the picture.

Distribution Chain Access

The first to jump on the extranet bandwagon were those selling things through channels. Harley Davidson dealers want to put their finger on a specific part's recall history. They want to do their own data entry for reimbursement on a warranty repair and order parts and accessories online. They can. Part recall histories are online. Warranty claims are paid in 48 hours instead of a month. Engine assembly diagrams are on-screen. Before, dealers tried to connect their various accounting and inventory systems to Harley Davidson headquarters. Now, it's all webbified.

The distribution chain was just the beginning. Letting vendors into your intranet was next.

Supply Chain Access

In the middle of 1998, Chevron decided it was going to buy online, $2.7 billion worth of annual purchases from more than 200 vendors at first to prove the point. Then, it is going after the rest of the almost $10 billion in purchasing. It wants to go online to buy (not shop for, but actually purchase) refinery components, oil field parts, and services. And, being a 500-pound gorilla, its vendors will comply.

Incorporated in 1670, Hudson's Bay Company now has 400 stores across Canada. Three hundred of its vendors are tied into its extranet. They use it every day to see how much of their products were sold the day before and get a handle on manufacturing demand and delivery schedules.

At Microsoft, if you want to buy a chair, it's there. It's there on the intranet along with dozens of other approved-for-purchase chairs from approved-for-business vendors that have already negotiated approved-for-payment prices. Click on the chair you want; your boss gets notified that you want to spend more money. Your boss clicks the approval button, and the chair is ordered. No fuss. No muss. No $175 purchase order process. Now it costs Microsoft $5 to buy a chair. How many chairs do you think it buys? What sort of a dent do you suppose that puts in its overhead column and goes right to the bottom line?

The distribution channel is extranetting, and the supply chain is extranetting. But things start to get really interesting when you let customers inside the firewall.

Customer Access

It's just a matter of peering through the looking glass from the other side. Let's say you sell chairs. What would you give to have your products on the Microsoft intranet?

Zona Research (www.zonaresearch.com) calls the culmination of all of the above "the smooth ripple." It all starts with a click. She orders a chair, the purchase order is approved by a neural net, and the picking/packing slip prints out in the supplier's warehouse while Federal Express is notified there is a package to pick up. It's not science fiction. Your salespeople must be out there cutting deals to show up on customer intranets before the internal electronic catalog is too crowded. Your marketing materials must include intranet-friendly information.

When AT&T wants to make a proposal for a large network installation, it sends all of the proposal documentation on a CD. All singing, all dancing multimedia? No. Show-all, tell-all HTML. An installation project of that size requires the review of dozens of different people with different responsibilities in different offices in different time zones. Make multiple CDs and ship them out? No. Send one, with instructions that it is to be installed on the company intranet for all to see.

The opportunity is tremendous. Give prospective customers all the information any of them could want at gigabit speeds. Then give them some collaboration tools. The art of the deal becomes the automation of the deal when the application helps the prospective customer select options, approve configurations, and arrive at conclusions. Give them spreadsheets for competitive comparison, design a process for balloting, and orchestrate the internal decision-making process. Then make the sale.

Astute marketers are also finding ways to incorporate not just their message but their whole ordering process onto other companies' intranets. If you run a travel company, for example, you can offer great discounts on a client's intranet pages. You can incorporate all of your client's internal business rules in the bargain, and the client would get automated travel policies that ensure coach seating and low-fare scheduling (unless the traveler is a member of the board). Vendors have become software purveyors as the offspring of EDI turns marketing extroverts into "intraverts." And the competition is heating up.

National Semiconductor is all extranet, all the time. In March 1997 it knew the Net was the way to go. By the end of that year, it had customized customer service applications running for different customers. It was able to pass shipment requests of sample chips to the marketing team, so it could keep its finger on the pulse of leading-edge developers.

Phil Gibson, director of interactive marketing, made sure the import of this data was understood. "There's a fairly common pattern in the development of sophisticated electronics. A design engineer orders a sample and hooks it up to a test bed. If it looks like it'll work, he orders a handful for prototyping. If it still looks good, he orders a couple of hundred for a test production run. At this point, our salespeople, and they may be several layers down the distribution channel, are well aware that a large order could pop out of this company the second they decide to go into a test market run. That's when we get real close to the customer so manufacturing can be ready the split second they turn on full-scale production. With the information from our extranet, marketing and sales can track the trends across multiple industries."

Phil Gibson sees to it that design engineers get everything they need. He even offers them CDs with the National Semi Web site on them (Figure 14.2) so they can get to the standard information faster and have links to that which changes all the time.

Then came the sales order process. Leads are tracked and orders placed. "Everything comes in through the extranet," according to Phil. "We don't pay commissions without the sale being approved on the site."

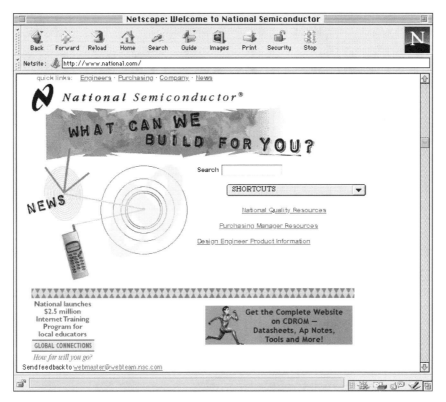

Figure 14.2   National Semiconductor has a site for sore design engineers.

When the design engineers stopped coming up with "must have" features, and when the salespeople were pleased with the reports they were getting in the field on their 3Com Palm Pilots, Phil looked at the next level: the buyers (Figure 14.3).

Buyers have one job and one job only. Get the stuff the engineers want, when they want it, at the best price possible. They don't care about speeds, feeds, sizes, temperature, or form-factors. Price and availability are all they have on their minds.

Price information crosses over multiple organizations. If a buyer has an approved requisition on his or her desk for a large number of parts, he or she wants to be able to comparison shop. The parts are identified by a very specific National Semiconductor part number, but the price and availability might change from distributor to distributor. The solution? Access.

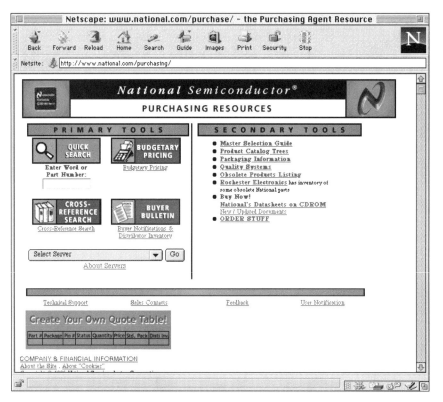

Figure 14.3   National Semi's special area caters to purchasing agents. Smart.

The National Semi Purchasing Web site lets buyers look at the inventory levels of 50 distributors and make the buy. Some distributors have enough stock; others do not. The price may be higher at the distributor in Taiwan, but because the customer factory is in Malaysia, the difference in shipping is significant. The time and money it saves the purchase agent are remarkable.

The ability to provide such service is helping National Semi become the vendor of choice, edging out its paranoid competitors. It did it by finding a way to bring buyers and sellers together. This model isn't limited to giant manufacturing companies. In fact, the concept has spawned a whole new buzzword.

Vortex

A lot of people out there want to buy used cars, and a lot of people out there want to sell used cars. Nothing new. Bringing them together has been the purview of the classified section of the newspaper. That's not worthy of a new buzzword like "vortex."

But what if you take a generic classified ad section, make it about only cars, and add pictures? You send people with cameras out to take the pictures, and you publish them in a weekly used car flyer. Innovative? Yes. New? Not by a long shot. Vortex? It's the right basic principle. Now, apply that principle to the Web.

Asian Sources On-Line (www.asiansources.com) was the 1997 Tenagra Award Winner for Successful Internet Business Model. The press release from Tenagra said in part:

> Asian Sources On-Line is recognized for the 1997 Tenagra Award for Internet Marketing Excellence for their extraordinary success in using the Internet to help bring buyers and suppliers together on a global basis. They have successfully created the world's leading community of importers and exporters using electronic commerce to enhance trade efficiency and profitability. Using Asian Sources On-Line, importers can locate suppliers, make initial inquiries about pricing and availability, and negotiate the price of Asian-made goods on the Internet.
>
> A manufacturer in a remote city in China can call Asian Sources in the morning; the company can take digital photos of their products and gather all the data about them in the afternoon; and Asian Sources On-Line can have this information on an importer's desk in New York or Frankfurt or Sydney the following day.

Every market has the potential. RealBid (www.realbid.com) (Figure 14.4) is another such example.

As reported in the *Wall Street Journal* (September 10, 1997):

> The company's revenue comes from charging a fee to solicit letters of intent or actual bids for properties from a selected group of potential buyers. All responses are due by a fixed deadline to provide an even playing-field for all investors, to get the highest possible bids, and ensure that the listings aren't stale. Within two hours after (Prudential Real Estate Investors) warehouses were listed at the Web site at 8:00 a.m. last Wednesday, for example, Real-Bid contacted over 90 selected investors by e-mail or fax. Investors can sign on to the site to see pictures and descriptions of the property, floor plans, maps of its location, and other information.

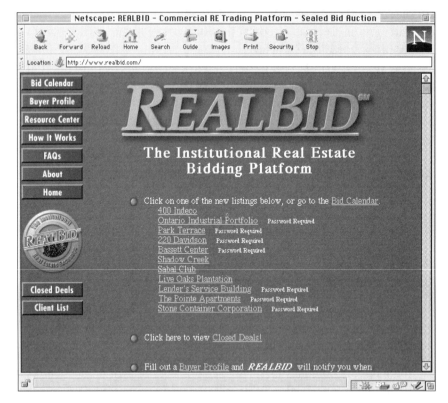

Figure 14.4   RealBid gets a fee for putting buyers and sellers of commercial real estate together.

This is another case of vortexing. It's a matter of aggregating context and drawing a crowd. Think of it as selling on the per-lead basis, but on a grand scale. Be on the lookout for vortexing in your industry. Be on the lookout for the potential of *being* a vortex in your industry.

Most of all, think about the fact that the Internet is bringing a brand new type of competitor to your industry.

Incomprehensible Competition

Competitors. We all have them. There used to only be three kinds; now there's a fourth. It used to be that there were direct competitors, the companies that sell what you sell to the customers you sell to. Then there were the indirect competitors, the companies that sold things that weren't quite competitive, but gave buyers a choice. Do they buy a pick-up truck or a sport utility vehicle? Then there was the third kind, do nothing. It's always an option. Maybe they won't buy a new vehicle at all. Years of experience taught you how to compete with these three. You compare features to features, you compare benefits to benefits, and you compare have to have not.

Now there's a stealth competitor out there. One that you didn't expect, in fact, didn't even notice until you looked to see where your customers were drifting—the Internet.

The *Wall Street Journal* is a source of financial information. It competed against *Investors Business Daily* and *Baron's.* Now it competes against CBS MarketWatch and CNNfn, which used to stick to the television set. It competes against *Fortune* and *Forbes,* which used to stick to the magazine rack. But now, everybody in the financial information business is on the Web. Not really a surprise.

The surprise comes from companies that have never been in the financial information business. The *Wall Street Journal* is looking over its shoulder to see a software company making serious inroads into the territory (Figure 14.5).

It's not just an information source. In Intuit's own words, "At Quicken.com, consumers and businesses find one-stop shopping for insurance and mortgages as well as information on investing, planning, and taxes. Intuit will apply the same relentless customer focus to Quicken.com until it is the most visited personal finance destination on the Web."

Intuit isn't taking on the *Wall Street Journal* alone. It's taking on mortgage brokers, insurance agents, and tax and estate planners.

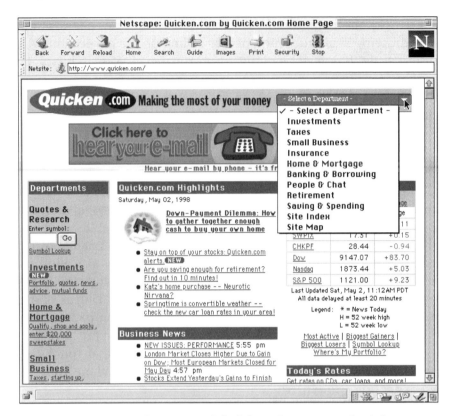

Figure 14.5 **Intuit has turned Quicken from a product to a service.**

If you're in the payroll business you know Intuit has taken away your customers who prefer to do it themselves. But have you been watching the Net? Online services like Virtual Payroll (Figure 14.6) are not showing up in your phone book. But they are showing up online.

Virtual Payroll offers electronic payroll headache reduction:

Direct deposit of paychecks into your employee bank accounts (via ACH)

Electronic tax filing of your federal 941 deposits (via EFTPS)

Download and print employee earnings statements and paystubs

Preparation of all state and federal quarterly and annual payroll tax returns

Download and print your payroll, management, and payroll tax reports

Figure 14.6 Virtual Payroll is a hint of what's to come.

Automatic filing of all quarterly and annual federal and state payroll tax
  returns

Magnetic media filing of employee W-2s

Security features including encryption, password protection, and SSL
  (Secure Sockets Layer) servers

Enter payroll data on line via our secure Web site

If you run a nice little print shop, look out for iPrint (www.iprint.com)
(Figure 14.7). They'll let you customize your order for business cards, Post-
It Notes, invitations, t-shirts, letterhead, rubber stamps, mouse pads,
mugs, envelopes, labels, sweatshirts, aprons, memo pads, announcements,
bumper stickers, and tote bags. Can they really compete with Kinkos and
the mom & pop place down the street? They can when they finish signing
deals with OfficeMax and Sir Speedy.

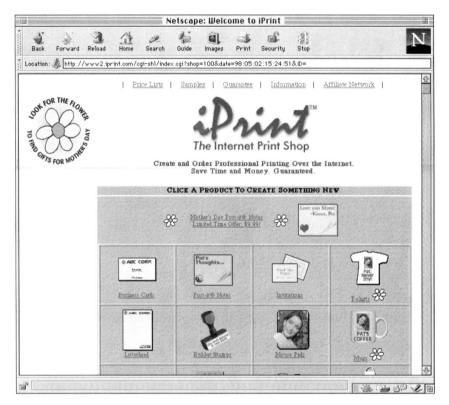

Figure 14.7   iPrint believes virtual is better.

If you can buy it online . . . If you can compare any two products and any prices online . . . doesn't that reduce everything to a commodity?

Commoditization

The value of the middleman used to be a function of distribution of goods. Now it's a distribution of information. When all the makers of a product are online at once, I need some way to filter through all the noise to compare the different offerings. That's where shopping services come in—they filter.

Shopping Services

Compare.net (www.compare.net) is taking the Consumer Reports approach to shopping support. If you're interested in multiple brands of a particular product, you can get the side-by-side comparison (Figure 14.8).

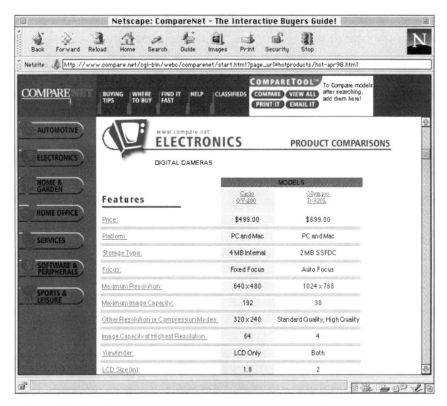

Figure 14.8   Compare.net lets you do some serious comparative shopping.

But one thing the Web does so well is let you compare prices for the object of your acquisitive desire.

The first shopping services to appear were the travel sites. Web front-ends tacked onto a tried-and-true system of airfares and seat availability. We've been used to the idea that the computer can find the lowest price tickets for us. Now it's time for other items to become commodities. In 1996, Andersen Consulting put up the BargainFinder (http://bf.cstar.ac .com/bf) as a proof-of-concept. When put to the test, the site seems to work—somewhat. Of the nine stores it looked in, it couldn't find anything at three of them, two weren't working, two had prices, and two decided they didn't like the idea. They were said to be "blocking out our agents." We can say the concept has been proven.

BargainFinder was first. Later implementations seem to be much better. The Excite search engine-cum-Web-portal has added a Shopping Channel to its site that does a very serious price comparison. After narrowing down the search to a few pages of DVD players, it's easy to see that I can save $5 by buying the Panasonic DVD-A100 from Tek Discount Warehouse for $449.95 instead of from Video Discount Warehouse for $455.00 (Figure 14.9).

Excite doesn't depend on the open servers of strangers. It cuts deals with willing vendors, scans the vendor databases every night, and loads its own database. Going out over the Internet for information is all well and good, but sometimes it's best to have your own local data.

Auctions

One other model that creates commodity markets is the auction house. Onsale (www.onsale.com) is the best known of these. All types of products at all types of prices go on sale every day. These folks are sharp. They know that an auction isn't a chore—it's fun. The button doesn't say "How to bid"

Figure 14.9   Excite Shopping makes price comparisons very easy.

or "How to buy." It says, "How to play." People don't buy things at auction, they win!

This type of site is a true market-price setting endeavor. How much is the public willing to pay for computers, home electronics, and Omaha Steaks?

One of the more interesting recent developments is a site called Priceline (www.priceline.com). (See Figure 14.10.) They were so sure of the interest they would garner, they hired William Shatner to do their radio commercials. They sell airline tickets. No, that's not right. They let you buy airline tickets. And they're not stopping there.

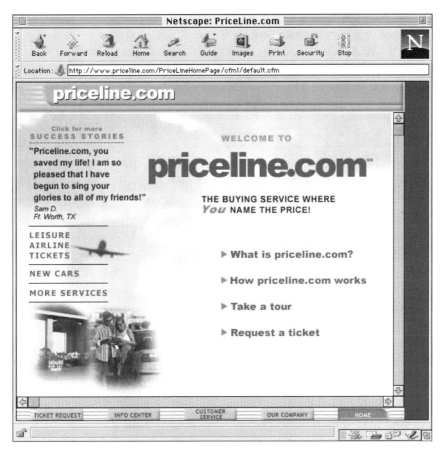

Figure 14.10   Priceline lets you set the price and lets the seller decide whether to sell.

PRICELINE

Priceline is a buying service that lets consumers name their price. They post their request 24 hours a day and guarantee their offer with a major credit card. Priceline then goes about finding a seller who decides whether or not to fill the request.

With Priceline, there is no auction, no bidding, and no back and forth. Consumers simply name their price and let Priceline find a seller.

The first service available through Priceline enables leisure travelers to name their own price for airline tickets. Click on "Leisure Airline Tickets" on our Home Page to find out more information on this exciting service. This summer, you'll be able to name your price for a new car!

Now you can name your own price for airline tickets and let airlines pick the flights where they have empty seats.

Priceline works to try to get you advance purchase or economy fares when you can't get them yourself.

With Priceline, you can name any price you want. However, to maximize your chances of getting a seat at your price, we strongly recommend that you do not request ticket prices below the airlines' lowest advance purchase fares. To increase your chances of getting tickets at your price, Priceline uses its proprietary databases and also searches millions of constantly changing published fares.

Are you ready, willing, and able to let software 'bots roam your site looking for price and availability? If not, your competitors may find a whole new marketplace full of buyers looking for a bargain and naming their own price.

Soon we'll all have our own 'bots scouring the electronic shelves for bargains. Keep in mind just what a 'bot can do with this definition adapted from "Delegating to Software Agents" by Allen Milewski and Steven Lewis that I found in the AT&T Attic (www.att.com/attlabs/archive/agents.html):

Currently, the term "agent" is used to describe an extremely wide range of systems. Nearly all definitions contain some combination of the following traits.

Ability to work asynchronously and autonomously

The trait most generally assumed for intelligent agents is that they can function autonomously, and without intervention from humans.

Ability to change behavior according to accumulated knowledge

The ability to "learn" may be the second most generally assumed trait associated with intelligent agents. An often-proposed use of agents is to anticipate the user's information needs in searching databases by maintaining an "interest profile" based on past search preferences. Since any user's interest changes across time, so must the agent's understanding of it.

Ability to take initiative

A truly intelligent agent must have the ability to perform tasks based on its own goal structure, separate from that of the user. This constitutes an agent acting on its own initiative. The environments that led to this proposal were those in which the agent knows a great deal more than the user about both the subject matter and strategies for using it to solve problems.

Inferential capability

A trait often associated with agents is the ability to make inferences. By this is meant the ability to go beyond the specific, concrete instructions of the user and solve problems using some form of symbolic abstraction. For some definitions, these abstractions are in the form of rule-based inferences, such as those used in expert systems. For other definitions, inferences can be based on probabilistic or case-based reasoning.

Prior knowledge of general goals and preferred methods

This trait can be viewed as an extension of both the "learning" and the "inference" traits. It has to do with the recognition in both human and AI problem-solving literature that solutions to many real-world problems require an understanding of general goals. Many have proposed a "goal-hierarchy" procedure, where solution paths can be altered in midstream.

How on earth will these agents, roaming wildly through the Internet, have any idea what your product's best features and special benefits are? How about a common data standard?

Data Standards

Remember XML? What happens if you take XML one step further? It's not likely that the whole world is suddenly going to agree that part numbers will all be tagged <part>. After all, there are <parts> and there are <components> and there are <subassemblies>. But it is possible that a third party could create a dictionary for a given industry. Then, it wouldn't matter if you used <pieces> as a part number tag; you could register it with the third party. When I send you a document that included parts tagged with <constituent>, you could take a quick gander at the third party's Web-accessible database to translate <constituent> to <part> to <pieces>.

Suddenly everybody communicates.

That's the thinking behind something called Information and Content Exchange (ICE). A surprisingly mixed bag of backers is pushing for ICE, including Adobe, CNET, Firefly Network, JavaSoft, Microsoft, National Semiconductor, Preview Travel, Tribune Media Services, and Vignette.

ICE makes it possible for disparate databases to talk to each other. It means that a manufacturer of chips can publish a database of specifications and pricing that can be picked up by all of its distributors in real time. All of your information can be replicated across the Internet, and you can be sure that the price and description you put up an hour ago will be the price and description seen by everybody on all those other Web sites. This goes beyond sites being able to point to your Web pages. This means a sales application could grab your proper pricing on the fly.

And don't forget the possibility of sharing user profiles between sites. Given a standard like P3P, if you log into my site, I can ask four or five of my cooperative marketing partners for the inside scoop on you and yours and make some quick decisions about your credit rating, what products to recommend, and how much training I should suggest—all automagically.

Brand Is King

When all of your products are scattered about the Web and can be compared in a flash to all of your competitor's products, there's one thing that becomes more important than all of the technology put together: your brand.

> The brand started as a mark of ownership. When it grew up, it became a mark of trust, a mark of consistency. You weren't buying a steer from a stranger passing through. You were buying it from one of the biggest spreads this side of Boline. Healthy cattle. A happy herd. It was sure to be a good animal. You buy a bottle of Heinz 57, and it tastes just like the last one. A Big Mac tastes the same in Portland, Oregon, as it does in Portland, Maine.
>
> We reach for the familiar package because it's what we bought last time, it's what Mom used to buy, or it's what our significant other asked for. Or, maybe we did an in-depth evaluation of price to quality to emotional satisfaction and made a decision. Twenty years ago. The product may have changed, the packaging may have changed, the manufacturer may have changed. But we still gravitate toward the tried and true.

A brand is not a name. A brand is not a positioning statement. It is not a marketing message. It is a promise. Made by a company to its customers and supported by that company.

If not, it would be enough just to change the name of San Francisco's Candlestick Park to 3Com Park. As Jamie Graham put it in *Advertising Age's Creativity* magazine (January/February 1997), "It won't be long before we're vacationing in Pearl Drops (formerly Yellowstone) Park, admiring 2000 Flushes (Niagara) Falls, and the Pontiac Grand Am Canyon."

Back in the good old days (say, 1992), you had to have a good deal of money to be a publisher. You had to have backers who vetted you and had confidence in you. If you wanted to advertise your products on television, you had to pay dearly for the privilege. It used to be that "As seen on TV" meant that you had a large enough company to have a large enough budget to buy ad space that was reserved for the likes of the major players.

Today, anybody with $20 a month can have a Web page up on AOL or GeoCities or any of hundreds of local access providers. Anybody willing to allow ads on their Web site can barter them for free ads on others' sites. Today, everybody is a publisher, and everybody is an advertiser.

As Steve Hayden (part of the Apple "1984" television commercial team) said in an article in *Advertising Age* (November 1996), "In a world of information overload, brands become ever more important. Icons with virtual memory, brands save time. I may have intelligent agents that can go out and assemble pages of reports on every camcorder on the market, but I don't have time to read them. I'll buy Sony."

With so many choices of content, and with such an assortment of sources, people will depend more and more on the feelings of trust they hold for the companies they do business with. If you already have a strong brand, you now have a new place to make it stronger. If you don't, you have a momentary opportunity to get out there on the Net ahead of the competition and establish yourself.

What Makes People Click: Advertising on the Web (Que, 1997)

Customer Control

I've implored you to ask your customers what they want.

In Europe, I am still told that my wild ideas about the Internet will never fly. OK, they say, maybe in America, but over here we are different. People do not want large organizations knowing their wants and desires. People do not want to express their desires outside of the norm in an overt way. Companies are in the business to create and sell goods, not cater to individual customers. We make shoes. They buy them. That's all.

The world has become smaller than that. The customer who gets a taste of being in control of the relationship will not be pleased settling for less. If local companies won't treat their customers well, global companies can. If you don't treat customers well, your competitors can.

Plan on a new type of business that takes into account credit-card readers in keyboards, telephones that can be used to make purchases, educated buyers who know exactly what they want, and people coming to your site for the first time without a clue.

MAKE YOUR MISTAKES TODAY

Once a year I watch a football game. Such is my uncontrollable interest in sports. The game I watch is the Superbowl, and, although I watch intently, I couldn't tell you who won this year, much less who played. I watch because I want to see who advertises. I want to see what they're advertising. I want to know what messages their creative people have created. I want to track who they're targeting and what new techniques they're using to reach that audience.

After four quarters of football, I am suddenly qualified to compete with companies willing to pay $1 million for 30 seconds of TV time. I have seen what they did, and I can mimic them. I can utilize their market research by targeting the same audience. I can imitate their tried and tested computer animations. I can intercept their customers and end-run their entire marketing expenditure.

It's much more difficult for companies that come late to the Internet marketing game. Yes, they can look at their competitors' World Wide Web sites. Yes, they can see the programming tricks used to achieve specific effects. Yes, they can even hire the competition's technicians. But they are not immediately qualified to compete. They cannot instantly acquire the evolutionary internal changes their competition has made since the Web sites went live: new procedures for managing an online, interactive, in-your-face customer.

Pushing your Web site to the edge and a little beyond will help you and your company learn the intricacies of dealing with your public one-on-one. New procedures, new staffing, and new responses to old questions will all be a part of the learning process.

You don't need to throw an overabundance of resources at an Internet presence. Nobody is going to let you. But make sure your best and brightest are at the heart of your experimentation. They will be leading the company into a new way of communicating with customers. They will be finding out what your customers want.

A corporate presence on the Internet can greatly enhance a company's sales and marketing efforts. However, a fair amount of strategy, planning, management support, and tight execution are required. The Internet is growing faster and changing faster than any other communications medium to date. If you wait for things to calm down and get standardized, you will only allow your competitors to get the jump on you.

So, go surf the Web some more. Reassemble a team. Read some more books. Get some more tools. Rewrite your site style guide. Go upstairs and demand a larger budget so you can go make all the mistakes you need in order to be one of the survivors.

Ernie Kovacs was a big part of the beginning of television. He is often remembered for saying that television, as a medium, was neither rare nor well done. The World Wide Web is no longer rare. But parts of it are very well done, and we've only just started. You have a chance to make a difference.

Electronic Frontier Foundation's Overall Privacy Statement

This Overall Privacy Statement verifies that Electronic Frontier Foundation is a member of the TRUSTe program and is in compliance with TRUSTe privacy principles. This statement discloses the privacy practices for the entire Web site.

TRUSTe is an independent, nonprofit initiative whose mission is to build users' trust and confidence in the Internet by promoting the principles of disclosure and informed consent. Because this site wants to demonstrate its commitment to your privacy, it has agreed to disclose its information practices and have its privacy practices reviewed and audited for compliance by TRUSTe. When you visit a Web site displaying the TRUSTe mark, you can expect to be notified of:

- What information this site gathers/tracks about you
- What this site does with the information it gathers/tracks
- With whom this site shares the information it gathers/tracks
- This site's opt-out policy
- This site's policy on correcting and updating personally identifiable information
- This site's policy on deleting or deactivating your name from our database

Questions regarding this statement should be directed to Electronic Frontier Foundation's site coordinator or TRUSTe (www.truste.org) for clarification. To return to the site, please use the "Back" button on your browser.

INFORMATION THIS SITE GATHERS/TRACKS

We collect aggregate information site-wide, including anonymous site stats. We also log domain names and/or IP addresses. On certain pages such as the EFF Membership Form, we give users the option of providing us with names, addresses, phone numbers, fax numbers, e-mail addresses, demographics, preferences, other personal information, and various other kinds of details. This more personal information is not gathered by us without users' knowing and active permission and participation.

USE OF THE INFORMATION THIS SITE GATHERS/TRACKS

We review and discard the information in some cases (e.g., IP address logs for file transfers), while in others we may use the information to tailor our users' Web experience, generate anonymous statistics, or contact users via e-mail or postal mail (e.g., to send newsletters, action alerts, pledge drive promotions, etc.). Personal information that has been volunteered to us may also be combined with data from third parties, such as Congressional district maps, to improve our services to members. No such combining will be done for marketing purposes. If the user permits, we may also share the information with other, similar, nonprofit orgainizations. This option is "off" by default.

SHARING OF THE INFORMATION THIS SITE GATHERS/TRACKS

EFF may share (but to date has not shared) members' contact information, only with permission, to similar nonprofit organizations. Contact and other information about our users might be temporarily "shared" with third parties that fulfill orders, verify credit cards, process orders in online currencies such as First Virtual or DigiCash, etc. These off-site assistants and fulfillment houses will be required to make no further use of such information, nor disclose it to others, just like in-house EFF employees.

OTHER INFORMATION ABOUT YOUR PRIVACY AT THIS SITE

This site is a cofounder of the TRUSTe program (a global initiative for establishing consumer trust and confidence in electronic transactions by protecting online privacy via industry-standard online privacy policy disclosure). EFF's site generally stores no information about its visitors, with the exceptions of basic logging for site statistics (just machine addresses, not personal e-mail addresses), and information provided by users who fill out our online membership, order, guestbook, or contest forms. Under no circumstances does EFF compile "audit trails" of which users are browsing what pages, and under no circumstances will EFF sell, rent, loan, or give personally identifiable user information to marketeers. Here are some genuine examples of what our logs contain. EFF's site does not monitor private communications (e.g., e-mail) at all, much less make any use of such communications. EFF's site does not display or make available users' or members' personal information, such as contact information, even if it is already publicly available.

OPT-OUT POLICY

This site has a page located at mailto:membership@eff.org devoted to their opt-out policy.

If you would like to opt-out of being solicited by this site or third parties, please contact:

Membership Dir., membership@eff.org, (415) 436-9333, 1550 Bryant St., Suite 725, San Francisco, CA 94103, USA.

CORRECT/UPDATE POLICY

This site has a page located at mailto:membership@eff.org devoted to their change and update policy.

If you would like to correct and/or update your personally identifiable information, please contact:

Membership Dir., membership@eff.org, (415) 436-9333, 1550 Bryant St., Suite 725, San Francisco, CA 94103, USA.

DELETE/DEACTIVATE POLICY

This site has a page located at membership@eff.org devoted to their delete and deactivate policy.

If you would like to be deleted or deactivated from this site's database, please contact:

Membership Dir., membership@eff.org, (415) 436-9333, 1550 Bryant St., Suite 725, San Francisco, CA 94103, USA.

URLs You Owe It to Yourself to Check Out

Advertising Law Internet Site   www.webcom.com/~lewrose/home.html
   Just as the name implies. Consider yourself forewarned.

ClickZ   www.clickz.com
   Andy Bourland's Internet marketing publishing empire.

Internet Advertising Resource Guide   www.admedia.org
   A lot of links to places of interest and of value.

Internet-Marketing List Archives   www.i-m.com
   The archives of the best Internet marketing discussion list ever and
   still worth reading through even though it's been closed for a few
   years.

Internet Publicity Resources   www.olympus.net/okeefe/pubnet
   Steve O'Keefe's handy pointers.

The Internet Sleuth Business & Marketing Search Page
   www.isleuth.com/busi-market.html
   Search more than a dozen great marketing resources from one page.

Kim Bayne's Marketing Lists on the Internet   www.wolfBayne.com/lists
   Holds the updated List of Marketing Lists.

Michael Tchong's Iconocast   www.iconocast.com
   Weekly newsletter that's a must for advertisers and just fun for the
   rest of us.

Nua   www.nua.ie/surveys/index.cgi
> More Internet statistics than you can shake a stick at.

Net Marketing (from the producers of *Advertising Age*)   www.netb2b.com
> News, trends, developer directory, and more.

Tenagra's Internet Marketing Resources   http://marketing.tenagra.com
> A variety of pointers to valuable marketing resources.

Wilson Internet Services   www.wilsonweb.com
> Dr. Ralph F. Wilson's amazing compendium of pointers and articles and advice and, yes, more. Especially valuable for the small-business person.

Two lists worth listening to regarding advertising:

The Internet Advertising Discussion List   www.internetadvertising.org
The Online Advertising List   www.o-a.com

This list merely scratches the surface of what's out there. But, as this is the Web, these sites will eventually point the way toward everything you need to see.

Index

Page references in italic type indicate illustrations